This book to be given
to Lee Burns

MYSTERY
OF
THE
AGES

MYSTERY
OF
THE
AGES

*Did you ever ask yourself: "Who am I?
What am I? Why am I?" You are a mystery.
The world about you is a mystery.
Now, you can understand!*

HERBERT W. ARMSTRONG

I want to extend my gratitude to Aaron Dean,
who collaborated in the writing and preparation of this book.
Without him, since my near loss of eyesight, this book
could not have been produced.

Library of Congress Cataloging in Publication Data
Armstrong, Herbert W.
        Mystery of the ages.
        1. Bible—Criticism, interpretation, etc.
        2. Life. I. title.
BS511.2.A63 1985   230'.99   85-12953
ISBN 0-396-08773-6
ISBN 0-396-08808-2 (pbk.)

*I would like to dedicate this book
to the memory of my wife of 50 happy years,
Loma Armstrong.*

AUTHOR'S STATEMENT

Why did I write this book? I have lived a long, active, interest-packed life covering the last eight and a half years of the 19th century and all of the twentieth to the present.

I have lived through the horse and buggy age, the automobile and industrial age, the air age, the nuclear age and now into the space age. I have seen America live through the agrarian age when farmers walked behind their horse-drawn ploughs singing happily, and into the urban age when Midwest American farmers are groaning and fighting for more government subsidies to prevent the extinction of farm life.

I have seen this twentieth century develop into a state of awesome advancement and achievement industrially and technologically. Paradoxically, I have seen alarming escalation of appalling evils, crime and violence and the crucible of nuclear war develop to threaten the very extinction of the human race within the present living generation. These conditions and facts are indeed mysteries that have remained unsolved and now need to be explained.

I have traveled over the four quarters of this globe we call earth. I have rubbed shoulders with the rich and the very poor and those in between. I have visited with captains of industry, emperors, kings, presidents and prime ministers. I have rubbed shoulders with and come to know the totally illiterate and poverty-stricken poor. I have seen this world firsthand at close range as have only the very few.

And through this long and pulsating eventful life I have asked myself many questions that were deep mysteries to me, and remain unanswered and unexplained mysteries to the world as a whole.

When I was five, my father said I was going to be a Philadelphia lawyer when I grew up, because I was always asking so many questions about so many things. I wanted to UNDERSTAND. I craved UNDERSTANDING. King Solomon, the wisest man who ever lived, desired wisdom, and God gave him wisdom above all others. After so many years I realize now that the same God has given me the UNDERSTANDING of life's deepest mysteries that remain an enigma in most minds.

How did all this happen? I was reared in a Protestant church until the age of 18, but I never heard these plaguing questions explained in church. If the Bible reveals the answers, why so many denominations of Christianity and so much disagreement as to what the Bible says?

But who can understand the Bible? I certainly never had understood it. And even if one does, can one believe the Bible? Does it speak with any authority? That question puzzled me and is the mystery to be cleared up in this volume. How I came to understand began at age 34, in the year of 1926. But it only began there. The final crystal-clear reason that impelled me to write this book did not fully reveal itself to my mind until December of 1984. It was a mind-boggling realization—a pivotal truth—that will be made clear in this book.

The beginning of opening my mind to the truth covered in this book began in the summer of 1926.

I asked myself: "Who am I? WHAT am I? WHY am I?" I tried to reason out the answer, but I couldn't. It was a mystery. Then, that very autumn I was confronted with a mind-disturbing challenge on a biblical question and the theory of evolution. This resulted in opening my mind to amazing vistas and depths of knowledge and understanding.

It all started with the question of the theory of evolution and the religious question of Sunday observance.

I knew that the Bible was the world's number one selling

book. Yet to me it had been an enigma. I could never
understand it.

I said, "The Bible says, 'Thou shalt observe Sunday.' " I
was asked how did I know? Had I read that in the Bible?

I answered that I knew because all the churches observe
Sunday and I supposed the source of their teaching was the
Bible.

But my marriage was at stake on the question. I was
forced into an in-depth study and research into the Bible and
also into the theory of evolution, which was at that time
rapidly gaining acceptance in the field of higher education.

My in-depth study into the works of Darwin, Huxley,
Haeckel, et al led me to question the authority of the Bible
and even the existence of God.

These intellectual thinkers had become aware of the
increasing knowledge about the universe. They could not
square this expanding knowledge with the religious teaching of their time. My researches into the thinking of the
founders of the evolutionary theory recalled to mind what I
then read in the eighth chapter of the Psalms—how King
David, a monarch of an ancient nation, looked at the stars
in the sky, noted the expansion of the vast universe and
began to think. He wondered in his mind, what was he?
What was man—in the vast expansion of the endless
universe? I found that this ancient king had never received
the full answer to the questions that plagued his mind. But
I was later to discover, in my same research, how the final
answer was revealed to the apostle Paul and explained in
the second chapter of the book of Hebrews. I was
determined to find absolute proof of the existence of God
and of the authority of the Bible, or to reject both. Most
people, I realized, accept or reject a belief on careless
assumption due to whatever they have heard, been taught,
or assumed without proof. I wanted to understand. And I
wanted to be sure on positive proof, not on careless
assumption or wishful thinking.

After many months of virtually night-and-day intensive
study, the answers were revealed to me with proof that was
positive and absolute.

No longer was the existence of God taken carelessly for

granted because I had always heard it or been taught it. I found absolute and positive proof of the existence of the Supreme Creator God and also of the absolute authority of the Holy Bible as the Word of God—the revealed message and knowledge of God for mankind.

I found the Bible to be a coded book, with answers to the paramount mysteries confronting all humanity.

The revelation of these mysteries was lost, even to the Church of God, although the revelation of them has been preserved in the writings of the Bible. Why, then, has the world not clearly understood? Because the Bible was a coded book, not intended to be understood until our day in this latter half of the twentieth century. I learned, in this night-and-day study, why it is the most misunderstood book, even though it is the world's best-seller. The full explanation or truth of any one subject is seldom made complete and clear in any one passage. Other portions, factors, or phases of the subject are usually contained in one or several other passages in other parts of the Bible either in the Old or New Testament. A true and full understanding of this subject is profitable only when these perhaps several other passages, scattered throughout the Bible, are put together.

Vistas of knowledge and understanding that have remained the chief mysteries of life to most people were opened to my astonished eyes and mind. But it is recorded in that book that in these very days in which our generation lives, the great mystery would be cleared. And indeed it was to my astonished mind.

I learned that the Bible is like a jigsaw puzzle— thousands of pieces that need putting together—and the pieces will fit together in only one way. Then the picture becomes crystal clear to the one willing to believe what God our Creator says.

This present book merely puts the many pieces of the great puzzle together so they can be clearly understood.

As you read and reread this book, compare constantly with your own Bible. See these truths with your own eyes in your own Bible. And open your mind to God's leading you into his TRUTH as you do. It will make a lot of sense as nothing ever did before.

Time may prove this to be the most important book written in almost 1,900 years. Not because of literary excellence or flowery language of scholarship that it has purposely avoided, but because of its plainness of speech in clarifying the most important knowledge ever revealed from the supreme source of understanding of that which has mystified all humans since man first appeared on earth.

This world's humanity has been blinded to who, what and why man is—how man appeared on earth. Man has been mystified by his inability to solve his problems, or find answers to the perplexing questions of mankind and the world he inhabits.

All these mysteries were long ago revealed by the one supreme authority of all knowledge, but in a coded message not allowed to be revealed and decoded until our time.

The Church was infiltrated during the first century with another gospel. Many false teachings and false churches under the name of "traditional Christianity" arose. As God reveals in Revelation 12:9, the whole world has been deceived. These basic truths have been kept a mystery. Even sincere and well-meaning men among the clergy have received their teaching from other men as handed down traditionally in these churches. They have assumed these false teachings to be the true teachings of the Bible. Instead of putting the various pieces of the jigsaw puzzle properly and sensibly together, it has become the practice and custom to read an already-believed false teaching into each particular scripture, taken out of its context. In other words to interpret the scriptures to say what they have already been taught and come to believe. The Bible needs no interpretation because it interprets itself. This becomes clear when one sees the various scriptures of each subject properly put together, as the Bible itself says, "here a little, and there a little" (Isa. 28:10). Even the world of a professed traditional Christianity has been deceived.

I have often said it is much more difficult to unlearn an erroneous supposed truth than it is to learn a new truth. Even in these past 58 years I had not fully and clearly realized the significance of the fact revealed in Genesis 3:22-24—that, in fact, God had closed the Holy Spirit and eternal life to mankind in general until the removal of Satan at the Second

Coming of Jesus Christ. Traditional Christian teaching had always assumed there is a contest between God and Satan —that God has been trying desperately to "get the world saved," but in this great controversy Satan has been winning. In other words, God had sent Jesus Christ at his First Coming to try to win this ongoing war against Satan. Traditional Christianity has taught that "whosoever will may come" and be "saved" through Jesus.

For some years I had come to partially realize the error of this assumption, but the full truth on this point had not come crystal clear to me until very recently. This truth is indeed mind-boggling. It clears what had been clouded in mystery.

It is hoped that this book, written since God's time for it has come, will open many eyes to the truth of these long-hidden mysteries.

And now, in my 93rd year, I have been led to write this book before this event-packed life ends, to share with as many as care to know, the answers that the great supreme mind of God reveals in his Word—if one is only willing to understand that Word.

Table of Contents

Table of Contents

If the truth about God is mystery number one revealed in the Bible, assuredly the truth about angels and evil spirits is second in order. Is the existence of spirit beings fact or a myth? Is there, after all, a devil? Did God create a devil? If there are holy angels, what is their purpose and function? The Bible clearly states that this world is actually ruled by unseen principalities of evil spirits. Do evil spirits affect and influence humans and even governments today? Do evil spirits affect even your own life? This question seems enveloped in total mystery.

Certainly third in order is the mystery of your own life—of humanity as a whole. What and why is humanity? Is man an immortal soul? Do the dead know what the living are doing? Is man a flesh and blood being with an immortal soul within? Is there meaning and purpose to human life? Did we evolve through unintelligent material forces without meaning or purpose? Why are humans beset with seemingly unsolvable problems?

Fourth in line of the not-understood mysteries is the civilization that has developed in man's world. How did it develop? Why do we find a world of awesome advancement and progress, yet paradoxically with appalling and mounting evils? Why cannot the minds that develop spacecraft, computers and marvels of science, technology and industry solve the problems that demonstrate human helplessness?

Next, in the development of human society on earth, is the mystery of the Jew and the ancient nation of Israel. Are the Jews the ancient nation of Israel? Why did God raise up one special nation? Why are they God's "chosen people"? Are they God's favorites? Does God discriminate against other nations? Is God a respecter of persons? What is Israel's purpose in the divine order of things?

Come now to the mystery of the Church. Why should there be the institution of the Church in the world? Is there some purpose for it, not understood even by the religion of traditional Christianity? Is the Church one Christ-originated Church or does it consist of many differing sects and denominations? Is the Church well organized on a definite pattern originated by Christ? Is there government and authority in the Church? Is it a large universal Church of many millions of members or a small and persecuted Church? How could one recognize the true Church today?

Finally, why the mystery of the kingdom of God? Jesus' gospel message was "the kingdom of God." Is the kingdom of God something within each person? Is it something that may be set up in men's hearts? Is it the institution of the church? Or is it something else altogether? Why this mystery of the very gospel of Jesus Christ?

These are the SEVEN GREAT MYSTERIES that concern the very lives of every human being on earth. The PLAIN TRUTH of all these mysteries is revealed in the Bible, but none of the churches or theologians seem to have comprehended them.

WHY? The Bible is the basic mystery of all.

If one begins reading the Bible continuously from beginning to end, one becomes bewildered. The Bible simply cannot be read like any other book. It is a mystery because it is a coded book. It is like a jigsaw puzzle, with perhaps thousands of various pieces of different forms and shapes that can be fitted together in only one precise pattern. The truths of the Bible are revealed here a little, there a little, scattered from beginning to end, and revealed only through the Holy Spirit within those surrendered and yielded to God, willing to have confessed error and wrongdoing, and yielding to BELIEVE Christ the Word of God. Jesus was the Word in Person. The Bible is the same Word in print.

No one can have the Holy Spirit, which alone can open the human mind to understanding of this Word of God, without a complete repentance and an implicit belief in Christ as well as believing what he says. Repentance can only follow admission of being wrong—of wrongdoing and wrong believing. The most difficult thing for any human seems to be to admit being wrong—to confess error of belief and conviction—to unlearn false knowledge as well as to learn true knowledge.

Is it any wonder, then, that the Bible is the book that nobody knows or understands?—or certainly almost nobody.

God deliberately coded his book so that it would not be understood until our modern time. Why was this purposely done? Even that is a mystery. The pages that follow will explain.

In the 12th chapter of Daniel we read even that devout man of God could not understand that which was given to him to write as part of the Bible. He said he heard, but understood not. The revealing angel said, "Go thy way, Daniel: for the words are closed up and sealed till the time of the end" (Authorized Version).

Today we have reached that time. God has opened to understanding his Word to those he has chosen, who have yielded and surrendered to him and to his blessed sacred Word. In the 12th chapter of Daniel, it says at this time of the end the "wise" would understand, but "none of the wicked shall understand." Who, then, are the "wise" who may understand the Bible?

"The fear of the Lord is the beginning of wisdom" (Ps. 111:10) and "a good understanding have all they that do his commandments" (same verse). Yet traditional Christianity has generally denied God's commandments—says they are done away, nailed to the cross. The clergy and theologians of organized "Christianity," therefore, cannot and do not understand the Holy Bible.

How, then, can we, in this book, understand and reveal to the reader these boggling mysteries? That question will be answered in the Introduction to follow.

HOW THE SEVEN MYSTERIES WERE REVEALED

The world's number one concern today is the question of human survival! Science and technology have produced the weapons of mass destruction that could blast *all human life* off this earth!

So many nations now possess nuclear weapons that one madman could ignite the nuclear World War III that could erase all human life from this planet.

Yet the truth of God, if known and acted on, could have saved humanity from this threat and all its evils!

Stop a moment.

THINK on this.

You live in a world seemingly far advanced in science, technology, higher education and diffusion of knowledge. People think it's a world of GREAT PROGRESS. We send men to cavort about on the moon and return them safely back to earth. Unmanned spacecraft land on Mars and send back to earth close-up photographs of the Martian surface. Other unmanned spacecraft fly close to Jupiter and send back astonishing pictures of Jupiter and the rings of Saturn. Surgeons transplant human hearts and other organs.

It's a magic, entrancing push-button world where work is done largely by machines. It's the glamour dreamworld of the three "Ls"—leisure, luxury and license.

But paradoxically, it's also a world of IGNORANCE! Even

the educated *know not* how to solve their problems and the world's evils. They *know not* the way of PEACE or the TRUE VALUES of life!

About one half of the world's population is still illiterate, in the grip of abject poverty, living in filth and squalor. The grim reapers of starvation and disease take human lives by the millions.

It's an unhappy, restless world in frustration, staring a hopeless future in the face. It's a world ridden with escalating crime and violence, immorality, injustice (even in its courts of law), dishonesty, corruption in government and business, and continual wars, pointing now to the *final* nuclear World War III.

WHY this paradox of "PROGRESS" amid DEGENERATION?

God's Truth Would Have Solved!

True religion—God's truth empowered with the love of God imparted by the Holy Spirit—would have pointed the way, and led to happiness, abundance and eternal salvation.

When you see what's wrong with the world's religions, you'll have pinpointed the *cause* of all world evils!

What *is* religion? It is defined as the worship of, and service to, God or the supernatural. It is man's relation to his Creator. Some religions have perverted that definition. They worship not the God who created them, but gods which *they* have created. Religion involves one's conduct, one's principles, one's way of life and one's concept of the hereafter.

The real CAUSES of all this world's religious confusion—and all its evils—are revealed in SEVEN BASIC MYSTERIES that decry this babylon of religious confusion and the resulting world chaos!

But now God's time has come! He now sends a voice to cry out with amplified world-covering power to reveal the *way out* of this senseless madness, into the world of PEACE and righteousness that soon *shall* grip the earth!

In the book of Isaiah is a "NOW" prophecy: "The voice of him that crieth in the wilderness, Prepare ye the way of the Lord. . . . lift up thy voice with strength; lift it up, be not afraid; say . . . Behold, the Lord God will come with strong

hand, and his arm shall rule for him: behold, his reward is
with him, and his work before him" (Isa. 40:3, 9-10).

That voice now cries out!

The prophet Malachi confirmed this: "Behold, I will
send my messenger, and he shall prepare the way before me:
and the Lord, whom ye seek, shall suddenly come to his
temple, even the messenger of the covenant, whom ye delight
in: behold, he shall come, saith the Lord of hosts" (Mal.
3:1).

The Elijah to Come

Both of these prophecies have a dual application. First, they
refer to John the Baptist, who prepared the way before Jesus'
human ministry more than 1,900 years ago. BUT, as a
prototype, or forerunner, these prophecies foretell one to
prepare the way before Christ's Second Coming as the King of
kings and Lord of lords to RULE over ALL NATIONS!

Malachi's prophecy, like Isaiah's, if you will read on past
the first verse, refers to a human messenger preparing the way
before Christ's now imminent Second Coming, this time in
supreme POWER AND GLORY as Ruler over all nations!

Understand the duality principle here. These prophecies
refer to a type and its fulfillment.

John the Baptist was a voice crying out in the *physical*
wilderness of the Jordan River area, preparing for the human
physical Jesus' First Coming to a *material* temple at
Jerusalem, to a *physical* Judah. But that was a prototype, or
forerunner of a voice "lifted up" (greatly amplified by modern
printing, radio and TV), crying out in the midst of today's
spiritual wilderness of religious confusion, announcing the
imminency of Christ's Second Coming as the spiritually
GLORIFIED Christ, to his spiritual temple (the Church resurrected to spirit immortality) (Eph. 2:21-22).

Jesus came, over 1,900 years ago, to announce the FUTURE
kingdom of God. He's coming this time to ESTABLISH that
kingdom. That end-time last warning message is now going
out worldwide in amplified power.

It's going before kings, emperors, presidents, prime
ministers of nations—and to their peoples, on all continents
and all nations of the earth!

How in this age of religious confusion could one come to know these seven basic mysteries of the ages that decry this world-gripping conglomeration of beliefs?

Why, in general, are people in Thailand Buddhist; those in Italy, France and Spain Catholic; those in the Arab world Islamic? Primarily, of course, because they and those around them grew up being taught, and automatically accepting, those faiths. To expect one of them to discover the TRUTH (hidden from them and also contrary to the teachings of childhood and adulthood that engulfed them) would seem to be expecting the impossible.

Why do most people believe the things they believe? Few, indeed, ever stop to ask themselves in retrospect how they came to accept the beliefs that have found lodgment in their minds.

The Source of TRUTH

You probably have seen pictures of the statue *The Thinker*. A man sitting alone, leaning forward, elbows on his knees, his hand supporting his head. There, supposedly, he sits in deep thought, hour after hour, day after day—just thinking!

Supposedly that statue depicts the manner in which some of the religions of the world came into being.

But *The Thinker* had nothing to think *from!* No foundation for his thinking. No facts on which to base his conjectures.

The human mind is not equipped to manufacture truth with no basis for that truth!

However, few, it seems, really *think!*

Most people accept carelessly what they are taught from childhood. And, coming into maturity, they accept that which they have repeatedly heard, read or been taught. They continue to go along, usually without question, with their peers. Most people do not realize it, but they have carelessly *assumed* what they believe without question or proof. Yet they will defend vigorously and emotionally their convictions. It has become human nature for people to flow with the stream—to go along with the crowd—to believe and perform like their peers around them.

Further, most people stubbornly refuse to believe what

they are unwilling to believe. There's an old saying, "He who is convinced against his will is of the same opinion still."

I was no different. Of myself, and of my own volition, I would never have discovered these GREAT TRUTHS.

But then, the prophet Moses never would have discovered the truths he wrote—the first five books of the Bible. It required a miraculous act of GOD, in the incident of the burning bush, to open his mind and to reveal to him the things of GOD. Moses did not seek God. God called and drafted Moses. Even on being confronted by the very voice of God, Moses protested. He stuttered! He felt he could not qualify for the task. God said he would have Moses' brother Aaron be his spokesman and brought Moses to acquiescence. God's command was irresistible. Moses yielded.

The apostle Paul, centuries later, never would have come to know or reveal for us God's TRUTHS of his own will. He was "breathing out threatenings and slaughter against the disciples of the Lord" (Acts 9:1). But the living Jesus struck him down blind, brought him to his senses and instructed him both in knowledge and in what Christ determined he should do. Christ in Person revealed to him many of the TRUTHS you will read here.

How, then, did I come to understand the precious knowledge of the TRUTH? Certainly not on my own, or because I sought it or because of any virtues of my own. But Jesus Christ struck me down in a manner quite different from the apostle Paul's experience, yet nonetheless painfully and effectively.

Such basic TRUTHS are *revealed*, not thought out in any human mind. They come from God, not man! And in all biblically recorded cases the initiative was God's!

Jeremiah protested that he was too young. But God said: "Do not say, 'I am only a youth'; for to all to whom I send you you shall go, and whatever I command you you shall speak" (Jer. 1:7, Revised Standard Version). Isaiah protested that he was a man of unclean lips, but God caused him to accept the appointed mission. Jonah tried to run away on a ship but God compelled him to deliver his commanded message. Peter and Andrew wanted to be fishermen but Jesus called on them to forsake all and to follow him.

Similarly, I wanted to be an advertising man, but God brought me by circumstances not to my choosing to the mission he had in store for me.

I repeat, at this point, this is the crux of the whole matter: the initiative is God's. His purpose shall stand. The world is full of religions that originated in the imagination, reasoning and speculating of certain humans. But they had no true basis to reason from. The TRUTH is REVEALED from GOD!

But, does not everybody have access to biblical truth? Yes, people *suppose* the *churches* teach what is revealed in the Bible.

So I give you, now, a brief synopsis of the experience by which Jesus Christ struck me down, so to speak, and revealed ASTOUNDING TRUTHS! Biblical truths *not* believed or taught by the churches.

The Awakening—Spark of Ambition Ignited

I was born of ordinary but stable and upright parents, with an ancestry in the Quaker faith. I have my genealogy all the way back to Edward the First of England and a line extending back to King David of ancient Israel. I have been astonished to discover this genealogy and the fact that I am, on one side of my family, actually of "the house of David." My forebears emigrated from England to Pennsylvania with William Penn, a hundred years before the United States became a nation.

I had been reared from earliest childhood in the Quaker faith, but religious interest in those formative years was passive.

At age 18 I virtually dropped all interest in religion, and ceased attending church. I had, at 18, put myself through an intensive self-analysis, coupled with a survey of the occupations and professions to determine where I belonged—to avoid being the proverbial square peg in the round hole.

Even at that age I had observed that most people were simply victims of circumstance. Few had ever planned intelligently their future lives. Many or most had stumbled into whatever job they found open. They did not choose where, in what part of the country or the world, they should live. They had been buffeted about by circumstance. Those who went to college chose whatever course or profession that appealed to them at the time.

But when I was yet only 16, a summer-vacation employer had, by praise for work well done and general encouragement, aroused the burning fire of ambition within me. Ambition is not only the desire for accomplishment, it includes the will and the drive to *pay the price!*

This self-analysis at age 18 led me into the advertising profession and a business life. I studied diligently, "burning the midnight oil," instead of seeking youthful pleasures.

I became unusually successful. I worked hard, had a reputation as a "hustler." I studied diligently, worked toward self-improvement. All this, of course, developed great self-confidence, which was later to be replaced by a different kind of confidence—FAITH in Christ.

I selected the jobs where I would learn, and "sold myself to my employers," choosing fields that threw me into contact with successful men.

In 1915 I established my own business as a publishers' representative in Chicago, Illinois. I managed to represent the nine leading bank journals of the United States—journals read by chief officers of banks. I did business with the presidents of many of the nation's largest industrial corporations in the Middle West. I attended state and national bankers' conventions, got to know many of the leading bankers of South LaSalle Street, Chicago, and Wall Street, New York. I was making an income, by age 28, equivalent to approximately $375,000 per year measured by today's dollar value.

It was at this height of my early business success that God began dealing with me. I had been recently married.

The Unrecognized Call

In a matter of days after our marriage, while living in Chicago, my wife had a dream so vivid and impressive it overwhelmed and shook her tremendously. It was so realistic it seemed more like a vision. For two or three days afterward everything else seemed unreal—as if in a daze—and only this extraordinary dream seemed real.

In her dream she and I were crossing the wide intersection, only a block or two from our apartment, where Broadway diagonally crosses Sheridan Road. Suddenly there appeared an awesome sight in the sky above. It was a dazzling spectacle—the sky filled with a gigantic solid mass of brilliant stars, shaped like a huge banner. The stars began to quiver and separate, finally vanishing. In her dream, she called my attention to the vanishing stars, when another huge grouping of flashing stars appeared, then quivering, separating and vanishing like the first.

As she and I, in her dream, looked upward at the vanishing stars, three large white birds suddenly appeared in the sky between us and the vanishing stars. These great white birds flew directly toward us. As they descended nearer, she perceived that they were angels.

"Then," my wife wrote a day or two after the dream, in a letter to my mother that I have just run across among old family pictures, "it dawned on me that Christ was coming, and I was so happy I was just crying for joy. Then suddenly I thought of Herbert and was rather worried."

She knew I had evidenced very little religious interest, although we had attended a corner church two or three times.

Then it seemed in her dream that "Christ descended from among them and stood directly in front of us. At first I was a little doubtful and afraid of how he would receive us, because I remembered we had neglected our Bible study and had our minds too much on things apart from his interests. But as we went up to him, he put his arms around both of us, and we were so happy! I thought people all over the world had seen him come. As far as we could see, people were just swarming into the streets at this broad intersection. Some were glad and some were afraid.

"Then it seemed he had changed into an angel. I was terribly disappointed at first, until he told me Christ was really coming in a very short time."

At that time, we had been going quite regularly to motion picture theaters. She asked the angel if this were wrong. He replied Christ had important work for us to do, preparing for his coming—there would be no time for "movies." (Those were the days of the "silent" pictures.) Then the angel and the whole spectacle seemed to vanish, and she awakened, shaken and wondering!

In the morning, she told me of her dream. I was embarrassed. I didn't want to think about it, yet I was afraid to totally dismiss it. I thought of a logical way to evade it myself, and still solve it.

"Why don't you tell it to the minister of the church up on the corner," I suggested, "and ask *him* whether it means anything."

With that, I managed to put it out of my mind.

Let me say here that in about 99,999 times out of 100,000, when people think GOD is speaking to them in a dream or vision in this day and age, it is pure imagination, or some form of self-hypnotism or self-deception. But if this was a vision from God, like Jonah, I tried to run away. But subsequent to this, in God's due time, God dealt with me in no uncertain terms, even as he had dealt with Moses, Isaiah, Jeremiah, Jonah, Andrew, Peter and the apostle Paul.

Business Disintegrates

Then came the devastating flash depression of 1920. It was not long-lived, but disastrous for the year. My big advertising accounts were in the farm tractor and implement and other manufacturing fields, rather than the metropolitan banks. All my big-commission clients, including such corporations as Goodyear Tire & Rubber, J.I. Case, Moline Plow, John Deere and Company, Emmerson-Brantingham and Dalton Adding Machine, went into receivers' hands. One nationally known corporation president of my acquaintance committed suicide. Through no fault of my own, my business was swept out from under my feet by forces beyond my control.

Out of Portland, Oregon, where I had moved with my family, I established an advertising service for laundry owners. The laundry industry was 11th in the country in dollar volume of business, yet the most backward. I teamed with an efficiency expert, in my judgment top in the nation in his field. I took on only clients who allowed us to put their businesses on a new efficiency basis—both in the quality of laundering service and in business methods, which I supervised. I had to be able to make promises in the advertising that my clients would fulfill.

But in 1926 a national advertising agency based in the East sold the Laundry Owner's National Association a bill of goods—to put big-space advertising in the national women's magazines. The association had power to obligate every member to a commitment for this magazine advertising equal to approximately 85 percent of the justifiable advertising expenditure each local laundry could make. I knew nothing of this until it was a closed deal. I had been doubling and trebling the business volume of each of my clients. My business was growing. Again a highly successful business was swept out from under my feet through causes over which I had no control.

But there was a reason—God was taking away my advertising business.

Disturbing Dual Challenges

Then, in the fall of 1926, at age 34, it seemed that the roof had caved in and I was crushed! I was assailed by very disturbing dual challenges.

My wife, after nine years of happy marriage, began keeping the seventh-day Sabbath instead of Sunday!

I was aghast! I was angry. To me that was religious fanaticism! What would business contacts think? But she claimed to have found this teaching in the Bible.

All the arguments came instantly to mind. They were of no avail.

"But the Bible says," I protested, "Thou shalt observe SUNDAY!"

"Can you show that to me in the Bible?" she asked.

"Well, no," I replied. "I don't know much about the Bible. My interests and studies have been in the area of business. But all these churches can't be wrong—they take their beliefs from the Bible, and they all observe Sunday."

"If," she smiled sincerely—but to me exasperatingly— "you can show me where the Bible commands Sunday observance, I'll go back to it."

There was no dodging the challenge. My marriage depended on it!

Coincidentally, a sister-in-law, newly married and fresh out of college, hurled at me a second humiliating challenge.

"Herbert Armstrong," she accused contemptuously, "you are just plain *ignorant!* Everybody who has any education *knows* human life has come by evolution."

I was proud. I had not neglected study and education. I thought I knew the facts about evolution, and I didn't believe in it. But now I had to admit I had never pursued a thorough, in-depth research of the particular question.

Following on the heels of my wife's "fanaticism," this challenge was humiliating. This double jolt to my pride hit me immediately after the second time my business had been destroyed. The effect was devastating. It was utterly frustrating. Nevertheless I was determined to prove both my wife and sister-in-law wrong.

The dual challenge drove me into a determined almost night-and-day research. That intensive study continued for six months before I found the proved answer. Yet the study has never ceased to this day.

Both challenges focused on a common starting point— the book of Genesis in the Bible and the subject of origins—although that was only the beginning.

These challenges came at a period in life when I had ample time on my hands. I plunged with intense concentration into the study.

Researching the Bible and Darwin

I did not begin the research in Genesis. First I delved thoroughly into the works of Darwin, Lyell, Haeckel, Huxley, Spencer, Vogt, Chamberlin and More, and even into the earlier works of Lamarck and his theory of "use and disuse," which preceded Darwin's "survival of the fittest" hypothesis.

Immediately those writings appeared convincing. (They necessarily are, to have won virtual universal acceptance in the world of higher education.) I readily understood how the field of education had been gripped in the clutch of the evolutionary concept.

Evolution is the agnostic's or atheist's attempted explanation of the presence of a creation without the preexistence of an intelligent Creator.

This initial stage of my research rudely shook my faith in the existence of God. It brought me to realization that I had *assumed* the reality of God, because from childhood I had heard, and therefore assumed, it. For a while my head was swimming. Was all I had ever believed mere myth and error, after all? Now I was determined to know the TRUTH! My mind was being cleaned out from ideas and beliefs previously taken for granted.

Of all the writings on evolution, Dr. P.E. More alone had culled out many discrepancies in the theory. Yet he, too, went along with the doctrine overall.

But now I had, first of all, to prove or disprove the existence of God. It was no casual or superficial study. I continued in this research as if my life depended upon it—as, in actual fact, it did, as well as my marriage. I also studied books on the other side of the question.

Suffice it to say here that I did find irrefutable PROOF of the existence of God the Creator—and I found proof positive of the fallacy of the evolutionary theory. The overwhelming array of college brainwashed minds to the contrary notwithstanding. I had the satisfaction of winning the admission of one Ph.D. thoroughly steeped in evolutionary thought—who had spent many years in graduate work at the University of Chicago and at Columbia—that I had definitely chopped down the trunk of the evolutionary tree. Like Dr. More, though, she had been so thoroughly brainwashed in evolution she had to continue in what she had acknowledged was PROOF of its falsity.

Also I had the enjoyment of being able to cause my sister-in-law to "eat those words" branding me as "ignorant." All of which was mere vanity on my part, which I had not yet eradicated.

I had proved the reality of THE GREAT MAJESTIC GOD! But my wife's challenge was still tormenting my mind. Already, in the evolutionary research, I had studied Genesis.

I knew each of the world's religions had its own sacred writings. Once God's reality was proved, I had expected to continue in the pursuit of comparative religions to see if any such sacred writings proved authoritative. Through which of these—if any—did GOD speak to mankind?

Since I had to research the Sabbath question anyway, and already I had delved into Genesis, I decided to continue my study in the Bible.

A Doctrine at a Time

I came across, early, the passage in Romans 6:23: "The wages of sin is death." I stopped, amazed. "Wages" is what one is paid for what one has done. Here I was staring at a statement diametrically opposite to my Sunday school teaching (prior to age 18).

"Why," I exclaimed, "how can that be? I was taught in church that the wages of sin is EVERLASTING LIFE in an eternally burning hell."

Another shock came on reading the last part of the same verse: "but the gift of God is eternal life through Jesus Christ our Lord."

"But," I questioned in disillusionment, "I thought I already had eternal life—I am, or I have—an immortal soul. Why should I need it as a gift?"

I researched the word *soul* by means of a Bible concordance. Twice I found the expression, "The soul that sinneth, it shall die" (Ezek. 18:4 and 18:20).

Then I remembered I had read in Genesis 2 how God said to the first humans, who were souls, "But of the tree of the knowledge of good and evil, thou shalt not eat of it: for in the day that thou eatest thereof thou shalt *surely die*."

In Genesis 2:7 I read how God formed man of the dust of the ground and breathed into his nostrils the breath of life, and man (dust—matter) "became a living soul." This stated plainly that a soul is physical—formed from matter. I found that the English word *soul* is translated from the Hebrew *nephesh* and that in Genesis 1 fowl, fish and animals—all three—were *nephesh*, as Moses was inspired to write.

Next, I happened to read where Jesus said, "And no man hath ascended up to heaven, but he that came down from heaven, even the Son of man" (John 3:13). I researched the heaven and hell teaching further. I saw where the inspired Peter, on the day he received the Holy Spirit, said, "For David is not ascended into the heavens" (Acts 2:34).

In this in-depth study of the Bible, I had the use of all the biblical helps—concordances, Greek-English and Hebrew-English lexicons, commentaries, Bible dictionaries and religious encyclopedias. The latter three of these, I found, were the works of scholarly but carnal minds. In historical facts and matters of a material and physical nature, they give help in research, but in God's revelation of spiritual knowledge I found them of little help.

I also used, in questionable passages, the Hebrew Old Testament and the Greek New Testament, with the lexicons. And I used every translation or version then published—especially the Moffatt, Ferrar Fenton, Smith-Goodspeed, American Revised and the Williams New Testament.

My Experience Unique

My research was totally different from that of students in a seminary. They absorb what they are taught in the doctrines of their denomination. Education has become a matter of memory training. The child, and the adult student as well, is expected to accept and memorize whatever is taught.

For example, in an elementary grade one of my grandsons was once asked by the teacher, "Who discovered America?"

"The Indians," promptly answered the grandson. The teacher was astonished.

"No, Larry, don't you know that Columbus discovered America?"

"No, Ma'am, the Indians were already here to greet Columbus when he finally arrived."

The lad was given a zero for his answer and severely instructed to always remember that the book says Columbus discovered America!

A pupil, or a student in high school or university, is graded on memorizing and believing what he is taught by the textbook, the teacher, instructor or professor.

In the first dummy copy of the magazine *The Plain Truth* that I put together in 1927—seven years before the magazine was actually published—I had an artist draw a picture of a schoolroom, with children sitting at the desks, each with a funnel stuck into his or her head. The teacher was pouring out of a pitcher ready-made propaganda into each child's head.

A student enrolled at a Methodist seminary receives Methodist doctrine and teaching into his head. A Catholic student studying in a Catholic seminary is taught Roman Catholic teachings. A student in a Presbyterian seminary is given Presbyterian doctrines. A student in Germany studying history is instructed in one version of World Wars I and II, but a history student in the United States is taught a somewhat different version.

But I had been called specially by the living GOD. I was trying to prove the very opposite of what I found clearly and unmistakably to be what the Bible SAYS! I was taught by Christ what I did not want to believe but what he showed me was TRUE!

Jesus Christ is the *personal* Word of God. He, in person, taught the original 12 apostles and the apostle Paul. The Bible is the SAME Word of God IN PRINT today. Thus it was the same Jesus Christ who taught both the original apostles, beginning A.D. 27, and 1,900 years later, beginning 1927, myself.

And let me add here that my study of God's revelation of truth has never ceased. Later Christ used me in founding three liberal arts colleges—including one in England. Through constant study, teaching and collaboration with spirit-minded faculty members in theological courses, my mind has remained OPEN. And knowledge of God's revealed truth has increased.

But in my initial six months' intensive in-depth study I was undergoing a process of UNlearning—discovering that church teachings had been the diametric opposite of Bible TRUTH!

"Eating Crow"

This is not the place for a lengthy, detailed account of my intensive search in the Bible, and of my conversion. I had been bent on proving to *my* satisfaction that "all these churches can't be wrong, for their teachings came from the

Bible!" The essential point here is the simple fact that I did find irrefutable PROOF of the divine inspiration and supreme AUTHORITY of the Holy Bible (as originally written) as the revealed Word of God. Even all the so-called contradictions evaporated upon unbiased study.

The most difficult thing for any human mind is to admit being wrong. It was not more easy for me than for others. But God had brought me, through circumstances, to the point where he had made me willing.

To my utter dismay and chagrin, I was forced to "eat crow" in regard to my wife's supposed "fanaticism." It was not what I *wanted* to believe *then*. But by that time I had taken a severe beating. I had to accept PROVED truth, contrary to what I had wanted to believe!

It was humiliating to have to admit my wife had been right and I had been wrong in the most serious argument that ever came between us.

Disillusionment

But to my utter disappointed astonishment, I found that many of the popular church teachings and practices were *not* based on the Bible. They had originated, as research in history had revealed, in paganism. Numerous Bible prophecies foretold it. The amazing, unbelievable TRUTH is that the SOURCE of these popular beliefs and practices of professing Christianity was, quite largely, paganism and human reasoning and custom, *NOT the Bible!*

I had first doubted, then searched for evidence, and found PROOF that God exists—that the Holy Bible is, literally, his divinely inspired revelation and instruction to mankind. I had learned that one's God is what a person OBEYS. The word *Lord* means MASTER—*one* you OBEY! Most people, I had discovered, are obeying *false* gods, rebelling against the one true CREATOR who is the supreme RULER of the universe.

The argument was over a point of OBEDIENCE to GOD.

The opening of my eyes to the TRUTH brought me to the crossroads of my life. To accept it meant to throw in my lot with a class of humble and unpretentious people I had come to look upon as inferior. It meant being cut off from the high and the mighty and the wealthy of this world, to which I had aspired. It meant the final crushing of VANITY. It meant a total *change of life!*

Life and Death Struggle

It meant real REPENTANCE, for now I saw that I had been breaking God's law. I had been rebelling against God in many more ways than just breaking the Sabbath command. It meant turning around and going THE WAY OF GOD—the WAY of his BIBLE—living according to every word in the Bible, instead of according to the ways of society or the desires of the flesh and of vanity.

It was a matter of which WAY I would travel for the remainder of my life. I had certainly reached the CROSS-ROADS!

But I had been beaten down. God had brought that about—though I didn't realize it then. Repeated business reverses, failure after failure, had destroyed self-confidence. I was broken in spirit. The SELF in me didn't want to die. It wanted to try to get up from ignominious defeat and try once again to tread the broad and popular WAY of vanity and of this world.

I had been part of this world. I did not realize, then, that this was not God's world but Satan's. I came to realize that accepting God's truth meant being called out of this world—forsaking this world and its ways, and even to a great extent my friends and associates in this world. Giving up this world, its ways, interests, pleasures, was like dying. And I didn't want to die. I think one of the greatest tests that everyone whom God has called faces, is giving up this world and being part of it. But now I knew that this world's way was WRONG! I knew its ultimate penalty was DEATH. But I didn't want to die *now!* It was truly a battle for LIFE—a life and death struggle. In the end, I lost that battle, as I had been losing all worldly battles in recent years.

In final desperation, I threw myself on his mercy. If he could use my life, I would give it to *him*—not in a physical suicide, but as a *living* sacrifice, to use as he willed. It was worth nothing to me any longer. I considered that I was only a worthless piece of human junk not worthy to be cast on the junk pile.

Jesus Christ had bought and paid for my life by his death. It really *belonged* to him, and now I told him he could have it!

From then on, this defeated no-good life of mine was GOD's. I didn't see how it could be worth anything to him. But it was his to use as his instrument, if he thought he could use it.

JOY in Defeat

This surrender to God—this REPENTANCE—this GIVING UP of the world, of friends and associates, and of everything—was the most bitter pill I ever swallowed. Yet it was the *only* medicine in all my life that ever brought a healing!

For I actually began to realize that I was finding joy beyond words to describe in this total defeat. I had actually found JOY in the study of the Bible—in the discovery of new TRUTHS, heretofore hidden from my consciousness. And in surrendering to GOD in complete repentance, I found unspeakable JOY in accepting JESUS CHRIST as personal Savior and my present High Priest.

I began to see everything in a new and different light. *Why* should it have been a difficult and painful experience to surrender to my Maker and my God? *Why* was it painful to surrender to *obey* God's right ways? WHY? Now, I came to a new outlook on life.

Somehow I began to realize a NEW fellowship and friendship had come into my life. I began to be conscious of a contact and fellowship with Christ, and with God the Father.

When I read and studied the Bible, God was talking to *me,* and now I loved to listen! I began to pray, and knew that in prayer I was talking with God. I was not yet very well acquainted with God. But one gets to be *better* acquainted with another by constant contact and continuous conversation.

So I continued the study of the Bible. I began to write, in article form, the things I was learning. I did not then suppose these articles would ever be published. I wrote them for my own satisfaction. It was one way to learn more by the study.

And I can say now, with the apostle Paul, "that the

gospel which [is] preached of me is not after man. For I neither received it of man, neither was I taught it, but by the revelation of Jesus Christ. . . . But when it pleased God . . . to reveal his Son in me . . . immediately I conferred not with flesh and blood: neither went I [to a theological seminary, but I was taught by Jesus Christ, the Word of God (in writing)]" (Gal. 1:11-12, 15-17).

That is why I have said the experience I was painfully subjected to in this original intensive study was unique in human life and conduct in our time. I know of no world religious leader who arrived at his teachings in such a manner. This world's religious teachings did not come from GOD! Only God is infallibly correct!

I was brought, by the spring of 1927, to a complete MIND-SWEEPING! My mind was being *swept clean* of previous assumptions and beliefs—I had been brought through a painful experience.

Twice profitable businesses had collapsed, leaving me frustrated.

Then I was brought to acknowledge that whatever religious beliefs I had held were contrary to the truth of God. Not only what I had believed, but also what the churches believed!

I had taken a beating! I had been brought to realize my own nothingness and inadequacy. I had been CONQUERED by the great majestic GOD—brought to a real *repentance*—and also brought to a NEW ROCK-BASED SOLID FAITH in Jesus Christ and in God's Word. I had been brought to a complete surrender to God and to HIS WORD.

I was baptized, and the infilling of God's Holy Spirit opened my mind to the JOY UNSPEAKABLE of knowing God and Jesus Christ—of knowing TRUTH—and the warmth of God's divine LOVE!

What I once hated I now loved. I found the greatest and most absorbing joy of my life in *continuing* to dig out those gold nuggets of TRUTH from God's Word. Now came a new enthusiasm in Bible study.

And I was led through the years from conversion to understand God's revelation of these seven biblical mysteries that have baffled the minds of humanity and to find that one and only true Church of God, founded by Jesus Christ on the day of Pentecost, A.D. 31.

Evolutionists, educators, scientists, religionists have striven in vain to solve the mystery of the ages —the origin of matter, the universe, and of man—the mystery of humanity—of awesome human accomplishment paradoxically paralleling human evils—of great minds accomplishing the unbelievable while unable to solve human problems.

I now reveal an astounding, rational, common sense breakthrough to the reader, of the SEVEN MAJOR MYSTERIES that have bewildered all humanity.

WHO AND WHAT
IS GOD?

I was returning to my hotel in New Delhi some years ago from a private conference with the late Mrs. Indira Gandhi, Prime Minister of India. Ever since arriving in India I had noticed cows and oxen wandering through the streets. I had never seen such animals straying loosely through city streets in any other country.

"Don't these cattle stray quite a distance from home?" I asked of the car driver.

"Oh yes," he answered.

"But when," I asked, "they wander all over the streets so far away, how do their owners find them, to drive them back home for the night?"

The car driver smiled. "The owners don't. But the cattle and oxen know their owners and where they live. They find their own way home in the evening."

Immediately I thought of the scripture in the first chapter of Isaiah, which I had never understood so perfectly before this living explanation.

"Hear, O heavens, and give ear, O earth: for the Lord hath spoken, I have nourished and brought up children, and they have rebelled against me. The ox knoweth his owner, and the ass his master's crib: but Israel doth not know, my people doth not consider. Ah sinful nation, a people laden with iniquity, a seed of evildoers, children that are corrupters: they have forsaken the Lord ... they are gone away backward" (Isa. 1:2-4).

And this was spoken of ancient Israel, a nation to which God had revealed himself by many evidences and miracles. How much less do other nations know about God—about who and what God is!

Nevertheless, other nations are human beings just like the nation Israel. It is important at the very outset of this chapter that you notice God calls these humans his own children. Many people say, "God just doesn't seem real to me." God is a great mystery to them. Their own human fathers don't seem like a mystery. They seem real.

Why Does God Seem Unreal?

In this chapter I hope we will help make God as real to you as your own human father. God does reveal himself to us in the Bible, if we will just understand it, so that he will seem real to us.

Of the peoples of the Roman Empire, God inspired the apostle Paul to write:

"For the wrath of God is revealed from heaven against all ungodliness and wickedness of men who by their wickedness *suppress the truth.* For what can be known about God is plain to them, because God has shown it to them. Ever since the creation of the world his invisible nature, namely, his eternal power and deity [spiritual], has been clearly perceived in the things that have been made [physical]. So they are without excuse; for although they knew [about] God they did not honor him as God or give thanks to him, but they became futile in their thinking and their senseless minds were darkened. Claiming to be wise, they became fools" (Rom. 1:18-22, Revised Standard Version).

The billions now living on earth not only are ignorant of the most important knowledge—who and what God is—they seem *not to want to know!* They are willingly in ignorance of this most important knowledge and relationship possible in human life!

Astonishing—but TRUE!

And why have humans been *willingly* ignorant of man's

most important relationship? One explanation, only, is possible! All nations have been *deceived* (Rev. 12:9). And the *fact* of this universal deception makes certain the fact of a super DECEIVER! More of this, later.

God UNREAL to the Ancients

The first created man Adam, taking to himself from the forbidden tree the knowledge of good and evil, was at the same time rejecting God as Creator. It is certain that God had revealed somewhat of himself, a certain knowledge to Adam.

Nevertheless Adam had cut himself off from God his Creator. Undoubtedly, some of the knowledge that God had imparted to Adam was successfully imparted from father to son for many generations. Jesus had called Abel, Adam's second son, "righteous Abel." He did the right thing in offering a lamb in sacrifice. Later, Enoch "walked with God." God spoke to Noah and gave him instructions for the building of the ark.

After the Flood certain historic accounts imply that Shem, one of Noah's three sons, had some knowledge of the true God. But undoubtedly, as generation succeeded generation of humanity, knowledge of God had become greatly distorted.

Nimrod, as recorded in chapter four of this book, made a virtual god of himself. Through the succeeding generations and centuries knowledge of the true God faded almost completely. The ancient pagan nations made many different idols out of clay, wood, stone and other materials. Many examples of pagan idol gods have been dug up by archaeologists and may be seen in museums today. As the apostle Paul said, they worshipped the creation rather than the Creator (Rom. 1:25).

First Century A.D. Concept

Coming to the New Testament, we catch a glimpse of the ignorance of any knowledge about God. The scholarly of the world in the first century were the Athenian intellectuals. Some of them encountered the apostle Paul in Athens.

"Then certain philosophers of the Epicureans, and of the Stoicks, encountered him. And some said, What will this babbler say? other some, He seemeth to be a setter forth of strange gods: because he preached unto them Jesus, and the resurrection. And they took him, and brought him unto Areopagus [atop Mars Hill], saying, May we know what this new doctrine, whereof thou speakest, is? . . .

"Then Paul stood in the midst of Mars' hill, and said, Ye men of Athens, I perceive that in all things ye are too superstitious. For as I passed by, and beheld your devotions [objects of worship—Revised Standard Version], I found an altar with this inscription, To THE UNKNOWN GOD. Whom therefore ye ignorantly worship, him declare I unto you. God that made the world and all things therein, seeing that he is Lord of heaven and earth . . . he giveth to all life, and breath, and all things; and hath made of one blood all nations of men for to dwell on . . . the earth . . . for in him we live, and move, and have our being . . ." (Acts 17:18-19, 22-26, 28).

And now what of the scholarly of our Western world *today?* One would think, the most highly educated ought to know WHO and WHAT God is! Suppose you ask at random 100 university deans, "Do you believe in God?" Perhaps three or four would answer, "Oh, I believe in the existence of God—as a 'first cause.' " But they cannot tell you WHO or WHAT God is! They cannot tell you what God is like! God is not real to them. In other words, he is a mystery. Perhaps another six or eight of the hundred will admit they are agnostics—they do not know "for sure" whether God exists.

I have said that education has become a matter of memory instillation. From elementary grades to higher graduate levels of study, our educational systems inject ready-made concepts, ideologies and a mixture of facts and fables into the unsuspecting minds of children, youths and young adults. Students in our school systems are graded according to how well they accept, memorize and can recite or write in tests what has been taught—whether true or false.

Modern education has given universal acceptance to the fable of evolution. Evolution is the agnostic's or atheist's attempt to explain the existence of a creation without the preexistence of the Creator. It removes God from the picture. It blinds itself to the mystery by attempting to remove God altogether.

Material Creation Seems Real

The creation is material, visible, and therefore seems real. The system of modern education has become entirely materialistic. The modern scientific concept denies the invisible and the spiritual as having existence. Yet all our seemingly unsolvable problems and the evils in this world are spiritual in nature.

I quoted above from the first chapter of the book of Romans. The 28th verse says, ". . . they did not like to retain God in their knowledge." Little or nothing is taught about God, but even in the elementary grades the basic concept— the APPROACH to knowledge—is evolution.

Is it any wonder, then, that the scholarly do not know WHO or WHAT God is? They believe what they have been taught.

As I write I recently returned from my second four-day visit in Beijing (Peking), as the first religious leader from the world of Christianity to be invited by the government to speak before large groups at the Chinese capital. I have met in private conference with the vice chairman of the Standing Committee of the National People's Congress, Tan Zhen-lin, and now, on this second visit, with Deng Xiaoping, the unquestioned leader of China.

In speaking with China's leader, I was speaking to the top official now molding the minds and beliefs of over ONE BILLION people—almost a fourth of all the people on earth. China, in population, is the world's largest nation. In very ancient times the religion in China was ancestor worship. Then came Confucianism, rivaled by Taoism. Later Buddhism was introduced from India, then Christianity. Today the nation is communist—atheist.

I found China's leaders to be a very cordial, friendly and courteous people—but knowing WHO and WHAT God is most certainly is not what they are now concerned about. I did not try to tell them WHO and WHAT God is, but I did tell two large and important audiences of leaders what God is very soon going to do—and I announced this forthcoming book, which I am writing now.

India is the second largest nation. What have they known about WHO and WHAT God is? NOTHING!

Russia is third largest in population. They did have Russian Orthodox Christianity, and now atheism.

I am not condemning or judging these people—and I presume they are as well-meaning as any people. God is not judging them NOW—as I shall explain later. Neither is he condemning them. He loves them and will call them all to eternal salvation in his own time. But they DO NOT know WHO or WHAT God is.

In ancient Egypt they worshiped the gods Isis and Osiris. The Greeks and Romans anciently had mythological gods such as Jupiter, Hermes, Dionysus, Apollo, Diana and many others. But they did not know, and their peoples do not know today, WHO and WHAT God is. But *WHY?*

Why Willingly Ignorant?

Already, in the quotation from the first chapter of Romans, I have given you a reason—they were *willingly* ignorant of the things of the true GOD. But *WHY?* Why *willingly* ignorant? In Romans 8:7 it is stated plainly that the natural mind of humans is hostile against God. This does not necessarily mean that all unconverted human minds are actively, intentionally, maliciously hostile. Most humans are passively hostile against God. They simply do not normally think about God. If God is mentioned they become embarrassed and often try to change the subject. They probably do not realize, in their own minds, that they have a hostile attitude toward God. Yet that is the very reason, psychologically, why they want to avoid the subject. In other words, the average person has an unrealized passive hostility against God. Without realizing it actively, they want God to "keep his nose out of their business"— except at a time when they are in deep trouble and they cry out for God's help.

Spiritual things—invisible things—are a mystery to them. They do not understand those things, real though they are, because they cannot see them. They remain a deep mystery so they deny their existence.

There was a cause for this willing ignorance. And the Bible clearly tells us that cause, which is dual: 1) what occurred prehistorically, and 2) what God himself instituted following the original sin of Adam. All this (to be explained in the next two chapters), and the CAUSE of all the escalating evils of today's world, are clearly revealed by God Almighty in his Word the Holy Bible. This will be made plain as we progress.

But first, what does the Bible reveal about WHO and WHAT is God? It is *only* in this inspired book that God reveals himself. But mankind in general has never believed God—that is, *what God says!* God spoke face to face, personally, to Adam and Eve, the first created humans. Then he allowed Satan to approach them. Satan got to Adam through his wife. Our original parents believed Satan when he said, "Ye shall *not* surely die," after God had said, "Thou shalt surely die" upon stealing the forbidden fruit.

When Jesus Christ spoke on earth 4,000 years later, only 120 people believed what he said (Acts 1:15), though he preached his message from God to multiple thousands.

No wonder, then, not one of these religions, sects and denominations, except the small and persecuted Church founded by Jesus Christ (A.D. 31), starting with that 120, believes God, which means these others do not believe what God says in his Word. God's Word plainly reveals who and what God is! But there is a reason for their ignorance. This will be made clear as we proceed.

Just WHO and WHAT, then, is God? How does he reveal himself? Already I have quoted the apostle Paul saying to the Athenian intellectuals that God is the Creator, who designed, formed, shaped and created MAN.

The prophet Isaiah quotes God himself, saying: "To whom then will ye liken me, or shall I be equal? . . . Lift up your eyes on high, and behold who hath created these things, that bringeth out their host by number: he calleth them all by names by the greatness of his might, for that he is strong in power; not one faileth" (Isa. 40:25-26).

Read this in the James Moffatt translation in modern English:

" 'To whom will you compare me, then, and equal me?' asks the Majestic One. Lift high your eyes, look up; who made these stars? he who marshals them in order, summoning each one by name. For fear of him, so mighty and so strong, not one fails to appear."

Further, God himself says to the skeptics: "Now, the Eternal cries, bring your case forward, now, Jacob's King cries, state your proofs. Let us hear what happened in the past, that we may ponder it, or show me what is yet to be, that we may watch how it turns out; yes, let us hear what is coming, that we may be sure you are gods; come, do something or other that we may marvel at the sight!—why," taunts God to the doubter, "you are things of naught, you can do nothing at all!" (Isa. 41:21-24, Moffatt). These scriptures reveal God's power but not what God is, in a manner to make him real to the reader. Other scriptures must do that.

God, Creator of Universe

God is Creator of ALL—of everything in the vast universe—the stars, the galaxies in endless space, this earth, man and everything in the earth.

That is WHAT God is—what he *does*. He CREATES! He designs, forms and shapes. He gives LIFE! He is the great GIVER. And his law—his *way of life*—is the way of GIVING, not GETTING, which is the way of this world.

But what is God *like*? WHO is God? There have been many conceptions. Some believe God is merely the *good* or good intentions, *within* each human—merely some part of each human individual. Some have imagined God was some kind of idol composed of gold or silver, or carved out of wood, stone or other material. The Israelites thought, while Moses was communing with God on Mount Sinai, that God was, or looked like, a golden calf.

Many think God is a single individual supreme Personage. Some thought he was a spirit.

But the generally accepted teaching of traditional Christianity is that God is a Trinity—God in three Persons:

Father, Son and Holy Spirit, which they call a "Ghost." The word *trinity* is not found in the Bible, nor does the Bible teach this doctrine. But more about that later.

God in Prehistory

Now let's go back to the very beginning, in prehistory.

If you were asked where in the Bible to find the very earliest description of God in point of the time of his existence, you probably would say, "Why, in the very first verse in the Bible, Genesis 1:1, of course." Right?

Wrong!

In time-order the earliest revelation of WHO and WHAT God is is found in the New Testament: John 1:1.

"In the beginning was the Word, and the Word was with God, and the Word was God. The same was in the beginning with God. All things were made by him; and without him was not any thing made that was made. In him was life; and the life was the light of men" (John 1:1-4).

"The Word" in this passage is translated from the Greek *logos*, which means "spokesman," "word" or "revelatory thought." It is the name there used for an individual Personage. But who or what is this Logos? Notice the explanation in verse 14:

"And the Word was made flesh, and dwelt among us, (and we beheld his glory, the glory as of the only begotten of the Father,) full of grace and truth."

When he was born as Jesus Christ, he was flesh and blood, materialistic and could be seen, touched and felt. But what was he? As God—as the Logos? That is answered in John 4:24, "God is a Spirit," and spirit is invisible. We know what was his form and shape as the human Jesus. But of what form and shape was he as the Word? We will explain that later.

The Word, then, is a Personage who was made flesh—begotten by God, who through this later begettal became his Father. Yet at that prehistoric time of the first verse of John 1, the Word was not (yet) the Son of God. He divested himself of his glory as a Spirit divinity to be begotten as a human person. He was made God's Son, through being begotten or sired by GOD and born of the virgin Mary.

So here we find revealed originally *two Personages*. One is God. And with God in that prehistoric time was another Personage who also was God—one who later was begotten and born as Jesus Christ. But these two Personages were spirit, which is invisible to human eyes unless supernaturally manifested. Yet at the time described in verse one Jesus was *not* the Son of God and God was not his Father.

Who Was Melchisedec?

We find regarding the beginning of his existence, something further described in Hebrews chapter 7. Speaking of Melchisedec, who was king of Jerusalem in the days of Abraham, it says also that he was the Priest of God Most High. This Melchisedec had existed from eternity—"without father, without mother, without descent, having neither beginning of days, nor end of life; but made like unto the Son of God; *abideth a priest continually*" (Heb. 7:3).

Since Melchisedec was "*like* unto the Son of God," and abides as High Priest forever continually, and Jesus Christ is now High Priest, Melchisedec and Jesus Christ are one and the same Person.

Therefore Christ was "without father, without mother, without descent [in Abraham's time], having neither beginning of days, nor end of life." God also had existed *eternally* with the Word. Jesus, when he was "the Word," was an immortal being who had existed ALWAYS—there never was a time when he did not exist—without beginning of days. He was, then, "like" the Son of God—but he was not yet the Son of God. He also was God, along *with* God.

These passages show that the Word, in the beginning—before ANYTHING had been created—was with God, and he, also, was God. Now how could that be?

There might be a man named John. And John might be with the man named Smith, and John might also be Smith because John is the son of Smith, and Smith is the family name. Yet they are two separate persons.

The only point of difference in that analogy is that the Word, at the time of John 1:1, was not, yet, the Son of God. But he was *with* God, and he also was God.

They were not yet Father and Son—*but they were* the GOD KINGDOM!

That family is composed, now, of God the Father, and Jesus Christ his Son, and many begotten humans who already, NOW, are begotten SONS OF GOD (Rom. 8:14, 16; I John 3:2), forming the Church of God.

That FAMILY aspect—the GOD FAMILY—is vitally important, and this will be thoroughly explained later.

But now, where are we?

Long before anything else existed, there did exist two Supreme Beings, immortal, who ALWAYS had existed. Your mind can't quite conceive that "always," but neither can it quite conceive of *what is* electricity! Yet you know electricity exists and is real!

How Christ Was Creator

So back to our question, "WHO and WHAT is God?" Before *anything* else came into existence there was God and the Word, composed of spirit, not of matter, but nevertheless very real. Two Persons—not three. And, verse 3 of John 1, all things (the universe) were made by the Word.

Now understand this, by adding Ephesians 3:9: ". . . God, who created all things by Jesus Christ."

Let me explain. In the first week in January, 1914, I was sent by a national magazine to Detroit, Michigan, to interview Henry Ford to obtain material for an article on his sensational new $5-a-day wage policy. I saw Henry Ford in the administration building, wearing a business suit with white collar and necktie. Then I looked across the breezeway into the giant factory (then the Highland Park factory) and I saw perhaps thousands of men in overalls, working at machines powered with electrical energy. Mr. Ford was called the *maker* of the Ford car. But he made the cars *by* these workmen, who used the power of electricity and machines.

In the same manner, God the Father is Creator. But he "created all things by Jesus Christ." Jesus is the Word. It is written, "He spake, and it was done" (Ps. 33:9). God tells Christ what to do (John 8:28-29). Jesus then speaks, as the workman, and the Holy Spirit is the POWER that responds and does what Jesus commands.

Thus, as we read further, in Colossians 1, beginning verse 12, "Giving thanks unto the Father, which hath ... translated us into the kingdom of his dear Son ... who is the image of the invisible God [same appearance, form and shape and character] ... for by him were all things created, that are in heaven, and that are in earth, visible and invisible, whether they be thrones, or dominions, or principalities, or powers: all things were created by him, and for him: and he is before all things, and by him all things consist" (verses 12-13, 15-17).

Therefore God's Word reveals that God and the Word—two supreme Personages—coexisted ALWAYS—and before ANYTHING had been created—including this earth and the entire universe.

In the quotation above, Christ is in the image—form and shape—of God. Perhaps it will make God more real to you when you realize he is in the same form and shape as a human being. More proof of this will be given later.

There was a time, therefore, when those two Personages coexisted and NOTHING ELSE did.

No third Person is mentioned—no "Ghost." Is God, then, limited to only two Persons? The false Trinity teaching does limit God to three Persons. But God is not limited. As God repeatedly reveals, his purpose is to reproduce himself into what well may become billions of God persons. It is the false Trinity teaching that limits God, denies God's purpose and has palpably deceived the whole Christian world. Both God and the Word themselves are SPIRIT, and project their Spirit. Let me illustrate. By your eyesight you can see something across the room, or see to the sun or even to stars that are many times the size of our sun, only much farther distant. But through your eyesight you cannot act on those objects. In like manner, God can project his spirit to any place regardless of distance, but through his Spirit God is able to act on such objects or to change it as he wills. Thus, God is omnipresent.

How long must they have thought, and planned, and designed, before even beginning to create anything whatsoever!

But matter—this earth, the stars, nebulae, galaxies—was

not the first thing they created. *They created angels before the creation of matter.*

God speaks of the creation of the earth in the 38th chapter of Job. He says that, at the creation of the earth, all the angels shouted for joy (verse 7). Therefore all the angels already were in existence when the earth was first created.

In Genesis 1:1 it speaks of God creating the earth and the heavens. In the Authorized Version the word *heaven*—singular—is used. But the original Hebrew as Moses wrote, and as other translations render it, is in the plural—*heavens*—implying that the whole material universe was created simultaneously with the earth. This is plainly stated in Genesis 2:4: "These are the generations [beginnings] of the heavens [plural] and of the earth when they were created, in the day that the Lord God made the earth and the heavens."

However, the word *day* in this context is not necessarily a twenty-four-hour day, but a general period of time. That might have been multiple thousands or millions of years ago. Angels were placed on earth before the creation of man. Since angels are immortal spirit beings, they might have dwelt here thousands or millions of years before the creation of man. How many God does not reveal. The earth, at first, was the abode of angels. But, Jude 6, "And the angels which kept not their first estate, but left their own habitation [the earth]. . . ."

What Is God's Appearance?

Now more detail on WHO and WHAT God *is*.

God is Spirit (John 4:24, Revised Standard Version). Why is God not real to so many people? Because God and the Word were composed of SPIRIT, not matter, not flesh and blood, like humans. God is *invisible* to human eyes (Col. 1:15). He does not seem real. To seem real, the mind naturally wants to visualize a definite form and shape. But even though God is composed of spirit and not of visible matter, God nevertheless does have definite form and shape.

What is God's form and shape?

In Genesis 1:26, "God said, Let us make man in our

image, after our likeness." We know the form and shape of man. That is the image, likeness, form and shape of God.

In various parts of the Bible, it is revealed that God has a face, eyes, a nose, mouth and ears. He has hair on his head. It is revealed God has arms and legs. And God has hands and fingers. No animal, fowl, bird, fish, insect or any other kind of life we know of has hands like human hands. Even if any other living being of which we know had a mind to think with, without hands and fingers he could not design and make things as a man does.

God has feet and toes and a body. God has a mind. Animals have brains, but no mind power like man's.

If you know what a man looks like, you know what is the form and shape of GOD, for he made man in his image, after his very likeness!

One of Jesus' disciples asked him what God the Father looks like. Jesus replied: "Have I been so long time with you, and yet hast thou not known me, Philip? he that hath seen me hath seen the Father ..." (John 14:9). Jesus looked like the Father. Jesus was, actually, "God with us" (Matt. 1:23). Jesus was the begotten and born Son of God.

And what was Jesus' appearance? It was that of a human man, for he also was the Son of man. He looked so much like other Jewish men of his day that his enemies bribed Judas to point him out and identify who, in a crowd at night, was Jesus.

So now we know God has the same form and shape as a man. We also know he is composed of spirit, not of matter as is man. Spirit is invisible to human eyes, unless manifested by some special process.

And *if* so manifested we would see both God the Father and Christ now glorified in heaven with faces, though formed and shaped like human faces, as bright as the sun full strength! Their eyes flames of fire, feet like burnished brass and hair white as snow (Rev. 1:14-16).

God's Nature and Character

Most important of all however is what is God's nature—his CHARACTER—like? One cannot know *what* God is unless he knows what his CHARACTER is!

THE CHARACTER of both God the Father and Christ the

Son is that of spiritual holiness, righteousness and absolute perfection.

That character might be summed up in the one word LOVE, defined as an outflowing, loving concern. It is the way of giving, serving, helping, sharing, not the "GET" way.

It is the way devoid of coveting, lust and greed, vanity and selfishness, competition, strife, violence and destruction, envy and jealousy, resentment and bitterness.

God's inherent nature is the way of PEACE, of JUSTICE, MERCY, HAPPINESS and JOY radiating outward toward those he has created!

The Word and God LIVED. What did they do? They created. How did they live—what was their "life-style"? They lived the way of their perfect character—the way of outflowing LOVE. When Jesus was baptized, God the Father said, "You are my be*LOVED* Son." God LOVED the Word. And the Word LOVED God—obeyed him completely.

Two can't walk together except they be agreed. They were in total agreement and cooperation. Also two can't walk together in continuous peace except one be the head, or leader, in control. God was leader.

Their way of life produced perfect peace, cooperation, happiness, accomplishment. This WAY of life became a LAW. Law is a code of conduct, or relationship, between two or more. One might call the rules of a sports contest the "law" of the game. The presence of law requires a penalty for infraction. There can be no law without a penalty for its violation.

God—Author of Government

The very fact of law presupposes GOVERNMENT. Government is the administration and enforcement of law by one in authority. This necessitates authoritative leadership—one in command.

When the only conscious Life-Beings existed, God was leader—in authoritative command. Thus, even when the only conscious Life-Beings were God and the Word, there was GOVERNMENT, with God in supreme command. The government of God is of necessity government from the top down. It cannot be "government by the consent of the governed." Its laws originate and are handed down from God—never legislated by the people—never dictated by the governed how the government over them shall rule them. Since they created other conscious, thinking life-beings, this very fact of necessity put the GOVERNMENT of God over all creation, with God supreme Ruler.

Our human civilization has assumed the prerogative of lawmaking. Human governments, whether city, county, state or national, have lawmaking bodies—city councils, state legislatures, national congress, Parliament, Reichstag, Diet or Knesset. But 6,000 years of human experience have demonstrated the utter incapability of humans to decide right from wrong, or to formulate laws for human conduct and relationships.

Human lawmaking bodies have made so many laws that the average policeman in a city could not possibly keep in his mind a fraction of the laws whose violations he is supposed to act upon. Some may remember a comic strip in American newspapers, "There ought to be a law." The comic strip was poking fun at the very idea that human lawmakers have made so many laws, and yet fail to cover every possible infraction.

God's law is spiritual and can be summed up in one simple but all-inclusive word—love. His law for the guidance of human conduct is subdivided into the two great commandments, love toward God and love toward neighbor. These, in turn, are subdivided into the 10 Commandments. Jesus magnified this law by showing how its principle expands to cover virtually every possible human infraction. The third chapter of II Corinthians shows that God's law is to be applied in principle. It is summed up in one single word, love. Nevertheless, it is so perfect that, by applying its principle, it is a complete law. There is only one perfect lawmaker, and that is God.

Bear in mind the government of God is based on the LAW of God, which is the way of life of outflowing LOVE, cooperation, concern for the good of the governed. And this law of God produces peace, happiness, cooperation through obedience.

God Is a Family

Now once again to Genesis 1:1: "In the beginning God. . . ." This originally was written by Moses as God inspired him. Moses wrote in Hebrew. The Hebrew word translated "God" is *Elohim*—a noun or name, plural in form, but normally singular in grammatical usage. It is the same sort of word as *family, church, group*—one family consisting of two or more members—one church composed of many members—one group of several persons.

It is referring to precisely the same Persons, making up or composing the one God, as we found in John 1:1—the Word and God—and each of those TWO Persons is GOD.

IN OTHER WORDS, GOD IS NOW A FAMILY of Persons, composed so far of only the TWO—God the Father and Christ the Son. But IF the Holy Spirit of God dwells in someone, and he is being led by God's Spirit, then (Rom. 8:14) he is a begotten son of God. But, at the time of Christ's return to earth in supreme power and glory to set up the KINGDOM OF GOD, restoring the GOVERNMENT OF GOD abolished by Lucifer, then all being filled and led by God's Spirit shall become BORN sons of God. The GOD FAMILY will then RULE ALL NATIONS with the GOVERNMENT OF GOD RESTORED!

The Trinity doctrine *limits* God to a supposed three Persons. It DESTROYS the very gospel of Jesus Christ! His gospel is the good news of the now soon-coming KINGDOM OF GOD—the only hope of this world and its mixed-up mankind!

The Trinity doctrine, by contrast, is the doctrine of the great false religion called in Revelation 17:5: "Mystery, Babylon the great, the mother of harlots and abominations of the earth."

By that doctrine, along with others, Satan has DECEIVED all traditional Christianity.

The Trinity Doctrine

The generally accepted teaching of traditional Christianity is that God is a Trinity—God in three Persons—Father, Son and Holy Spirit (which is often called a "Ghost").

How did this Trinity doctrine enter traditional Christianity?

It most emphatically did not come from the Bible. I have quoted Revelation 12:9 saying that all nations have been deceived by Satan the devil. How, then, did the wily Satan introduce this doctrine into "Christianity"?

The history of this question is interesting. It seems incredible that a being like Satan not only could have deceived the whole world, but also "Christianity"—the very religion bearing Christ's name and supposed to be his true religion. Yet, paradoxically, Satan did!

He did it through his great false church, started A.D. 33 by Simon the Sorcerer, described in the 8th chapter of the book of Acts as the leader of the Babylonian mystery religion in Samaria. It is recorded in II Kings 17:23-24 that Shalmaneser, king of Assyria, who had invaded and conquered the northern kingdom—the kingdom of Israel—moved the people out of their land of Samaria, north of Jerusalem, and moved into that land people of the Babylonish mystery religion from the provinces of Babylon. They were, of course, gentiles. They inhabited this area of northern Palestine in the time of Christ. The Jews of Judea in Christ's time would have nothing to do with them, calling them contemptuously "dogs." They still adhered to this pagan Babylonish mystery religion in the first century.

In A.D. 33, two years after Jesus Christ from heaven founded the Church of God on that day of Pentecost, the deacon Philip, who later became an evangelist, went down to Samaria and preached Christ's gospel. This Simon the Sorcerer came with the crowd to hear him.

Simon had bewitched the people of that country, and they followed him as their leader in the Babylonian mystery religion "from the least to the greatest, saying, This man is the great power of God" (Acts 8:10).

When the people believed Philip, preaching the kingdom of God, they were baptized, and this Simon managed to be baptized with them.

Then Simon came to the apostles Peter and John, offering money as a bribe, asking them to give him the power to lay hands on people and have them receive the Holy Spirit. Peter rebuked him strongly. But Simon proclaimed himself a Christian apostle, nevertheless, and called the pagan Babylonian mystery religion "Christianity." He accepted the doctrine of "grace" for the forgiveness of sin (which the pagan religions had never had), but turned grace into license to disobey God (Jude 4). He aspired to turn his pagan religion, under the name "Christianity," into a universal religion, to gain thereby the political rule of the world.

Simon, the "Pater" (Peter) of his counterfeit religion, did not accomplish this in his lifetime. But succeeding leaders, with the headquarters moved to Rome, did, later, gain political control over the Roman Empire and its medieval successor, called "The Holy Roman Empire." This empire is in process of again being resurrected in Europe now!

Counterfeit Gospel

By the sixth decade of the first century, much of the Middle East had turned from the true gospel to a counterfeit (Gal. 1:6-7). As late as the 90s A.D. the apostle John was still living. He wrote the book of Revelation on the Isle of Patmos.

A little later the church started by Simon in A.D. 33 was trying to turn the true Christian Passover (Christ had changed its form from that of sacrificial lambs to unleavened bread and wine) into Babylonian ceremony, now called, in English, "Easter"—named after the goddess Astarte or Ishtar (pronounced "Easter" in some Semitic dialects).

After the death of the apostle John, a disciple of his, Polycarp, waged a controversy over the Passover-Easter question with the bishop of Rome, by then leader of the church started by Simon.

Still later, another disciple of Christ's true Christianity, Polycrates, waged a still hotter controversy over the same Passover-Easter question with another bishop of Rome. This theological battle was called the Quartodeciman Controversy. Polycrates contended, as Jesus and the original apostles taught, that the Passover should be observed in the new Christian form introduced by Jesus and by the apostle Paul (I Cor. 11), using unleavened bread and wine instead of sacrificing a lamb, on the eve of the 14th Nisan (first month in the sacred calendar, occurring in the spring). But the Rome church insisted that it be observed on a Sunday.

About the same time another controversy was raging, between a Dr. Arius, of Alexandria, a Christian leader who died A.D. 336, and other bishops, over calling God a Trinity. Dr. Arius stoutly opposed the Trinity doctrine, but introduced errors of his own.

In A.D. 325, the Emperor Constantine called the Nicene Council to settle these controversies. Constantine was not then yet a "Christian," but as political ruler he assumed control. The Council approved both the Easter-Sunday doctrine and the Trinity. Constantine, then civil ruler, made it a LAW. But he was not able to make it TRUTH!

Satan has deceived the entire world in regard to the very nature of WHO and WHAT God is—as well as of Christ and the Holy Spirit. Also of the GOVERNMENT OF GOD, based on the spiritual LAW OF GOD. And further, of WHAT and WHY man is, what salvation is, how it is received, what is the true gospel, what and why the church is and what of the future!

What Is God Like?

The word *trinity* is not used anywhere in the Bible. I am going to make completely clear, as we proceed, God has not limited himself to a "Trinity." The surprising truth, once understood, is the most wonderful revelation the human mind could receive or contain!

The very first idea or teaching about God being a Trinity began in the latter half of the second century—a hundred years after most of the New Testament had been written. The counterfeit Christianity spawned by Simon the Sorcerer was promoting it vigorously along with the pagan Easter. But the true Church of God vigorously resisted it. The controversy became so violent it threatened the peace of the world. The then-pagan Emperor Constantine called this Nicene Council to settle it. The Roman Emperor's supporters greatly outnumbered the persecuted true Church of God.

You will find a prophecy of these two churches in the book of Revelation. In the 12th chapter is the prophecy of the true Church of God, greatly persecuted. Jesus called it "the *little* flock."

In the 17th chapter you will find the prophecy of the counterfeit church—a very great church, named by God "Mystery, Babylon the great, the mother of harlots" (verse 5). She lined up with and sat astride the political governments. The whole world will gasp in WONDER (verse 8) when this religio-political medieval "Holy Roman Empire" is brought back to life! It is now in the preliminary stages of forming, starting from the Common Market!

False Scripture Added

There is only one small passage in the Authorized Version of the Bible that is generally used by Trinity adherents to support the Trinity doctrine. This passage is found in I John 5:7-8, and is bracketed in the following quotation: "For there are three that bear record [in heaven, the Father, the Word, and the Holy Ghost: and these three are one. And there are three that bear witness in earth], the Spirit, and the water, and the blood: and these three agree in one." The bracketed words were added by editors to the Latin Vulgate translation probably in the early fourth century. They do not appear in *any* of the older Greek manuscripts nor in other modern English translations. They were added to the Latin Vulgate during the heat of the controversy between Rome and Dr. Arius and God's people.

Bible commentaries explain that these words were never written in the apostle John's manuscript or any existing early copies of it. The apostle John in his three epistles and the Revelation speaks of "the Father and ... Son" (I John 1:3), but never of "the Father and the Word," except in this uninspired part of I John 5:7-8.

There was a real reason why the archdeceiver Satan wanted that spurious verse added in the Latin Vulgate from which it crept into the Authorized Version. The Trinity doctrine completely does away with the gospel of Jesus Christ. His gospel is the MESSAGE he brought mankind from God the Father, the good news of the coming KINGDOM OF GOD! That is the ONE thing above all Satan wants to defeat. This will become plain as we proceed.

One world-famous evangelist said: "When I first began to study the Bible years ago, the doctrine of the Trinity was one of the most complex problems I had to encounter. I have never fully resolved it, for it contains an aspect of mystery. Though I do not totally understand it to this day, I accept it as a revelation of God.... To explain and illustrate the Trinity is one of the most difficult assignments to a Christian."

Much is also made of the fact that in a number of places in modern translations the masculine pronoun *he* is carelessly used in connection with the Holy Spirit. But not always—sometimes the Holy Spirit is referred to as *it* in these very same translations. For example, in the passage describing the first coming of the Holy Spirit for the founding of the Church of God on that memorable day of Pentecost.

Holy Spirit Poured Out

The Holy Spirit came from heaven, audibly, sounding like a mighty wind, "and *it* [the Holy Spirit] filled all the house where they were sitting." Next, the Holy Spirit *appeared*— WAS VISIBLY SEEN—manifested—"And there appeared unto them cloven tongues like as of fire, and *it* [the Holy Spirit in the form of divided tongues] sat upon each of them" (Acts 2:2-3). In verse 18, Peter is quoting from the prophet Joel: "I will *pour out* . . . of my Spirit. . . ." The Holy Spirit, like water or a fluid, can be "POURED OUT." Can you pour out a person from one into another—as from God into those assembled there? John 7:37-39: "In the last day, that great day of the feast, Jesus stood and cried, saying, If any man thirst, let him come unto me, and drink. He that believeth on me, as the scripture hath said, out of his belly shall flow rivers of living water. (But this spake he of the Spirit, which they that believe on him should receive: for the Holy [Spirit] was not yet given; because that Jesus was not yet glorified.)"

Again in Acts 10:45, ". . . on the Gentiles also was *poured out* the gift of the Holy [Spirit]."

Summary

Finally, in briefest summary: God is a FAMILY composed at present of the TWO Persons of John 1:1-4, but with many thousands, already *begotten* by God's Spirit, in God's true Church, soon to be born into that divine family at Christ's return to earth. Jesus Christ, by his resurrection, was BORN a divine Son of God (Rom. 1:4)—the *first* so born into the God family (Rom. 8:29).

Both God and Christ are composed of spirit, formed and

shaped as a human person, but with eyes like flames of fire and faces bright as the sun full strength!

God is Creator of all that exists. Both God and the Word (who became Christ) have existed eternally and before all else. From them emanates the Spirit of God, by which God is omnipresent and omniscient. God the Father is the divine Father of the God family, into which truly converted Christians shall be born.

MYSTERY OF ANGELS AND EVIL SPIRITS

COULD ANYTHING be more mysterious than the question of the unseen spirit world? Angelic beings have always been a mystery to people on the earth. Do angels actually exist? Is there, in fact, a Satan the devil? Is Satan a literal, immortal being? Did God create a devil?

Some religions worship gods they believe to be evil spirits. Some of the great cathedrals of the Christian religion are embellished on their exterior with gargoyles, ugly and grotesque carved faces, which are supposed to frighten evil spirits away.

All the evils and troubles in the world are caused by minds clashing with minds. But what is the real cause of clashing of minds? Is there any connection between contentious attitudes and the unseen spirit world? It is a mystery to almost everybody, but the Bible reveals a very real but invisible world—another dimension, as some choose to call it—existing along with our own, absolutely indiscernible to our five senses. It is the spirit world.

In the first chapter of Hebrews, we read of angels serving as God's secret messengers, sent forth to minister to those God has called to salvation and eternal life.

In Ephesians 6 it is stated that our contentions and strivings are in fact not with other human people, but against "principalities, against powers, against the rulers of the darkness of this world, against spiritual wickedness [evil spirits] in high places."

How can this be? Why is the world filled with such clashings and contentions between human minds?

In Ephesians 2:2, humans have been walking "according to the course of this world, according to the prince of the power of the air [Satan], the spirit that now worketh in the children of disobedience." People simply do not realize that there is an invisible spirit power injecting into their minds these hostile attitudes.

Even to professing Christians, these scriptures have been a mystery. Why?

This invisible spirit world (Col. 1:15-16) is very real but because it is invisible it has been a mystery. The fact that holy angels and evil spirits are invisible does not negate their existence. In truth the invisible spirit world is more real than the material and the visible. In fact, most people do not know what electricity is but are well aware of its reality. The Bible explains: "If our gospel be hid, it is hid to them that are lost: in whom the god of this world [Satan] hath blinded the minds of them which believe not" (II Cor. 4:3-4). Satan is the god of this world.

The time of UNDERSTANDING has come.

The Supreme Invisible Power

It was made clear in chapter one that God from eternity has been a family, originally composed of two members, God and the Word who almost 2,000 years ago became Jesus Christ. God is invisible—the supreme all powerful Spirit Being. We saw that God lives. He acts! What does he do? He is the creating family. Perhaps few realize, the very first thing God created was not the earth, suns, other planets—the universe. Before all these he created the angelic beings—a spirit world of myriads of angelic beings.

The Great God through the Word first designed and created these SPIRIT BEINGS—angels, each individually created—millions or perhaps even billions of them! Angels are actual personal spirit beings, each having a mind of greater capacity and ability than human minds, capable of attitudes, purposes and intentions. It is stated that even Jesus as a human was made "a little lower than the angels" (Heb. 2:7). They are composed wholly of spirit. They were given self-containing life—life inherent—immortality. They have no blood circulating in veins and do not need the breath of air to sustain life, but have self-containing inherent life.

Angels are, because created by God, called sons of God (Job 1:6), but they were not begotten and born sons of God.

Why the Creation of Angels?

Why were invisible spirit-composed angels created before all else? Why were they created even prior to the creation of physical matter and the physical universe? Why were they created at all?

Jesus Christ said, "I work and my Father works" (John 5:17). In John 1:1-5 it is revealed that God and the Word (the God family) live. In the preceding chapter we noted how they lived—in mutual love, total agreement and perfect harmony. But if they lived, what did they do? They created. One might say that by profession they were in the creating business. To aid them in the work of creating, governing and managing what was to be created, they first of all created other spirit beings on a lower plane than the God family. Angels were created to be ministers, agents, helpers in God's creation. They were created as servants of the living God.

From eternity God was supreme, which to our human minds means God sat on the throne of all that existed or was to exist. In the 25th chapter of Exodus, we find an earthly description of the very throne of God in heaven, in the description of the ark built by Moses under God's instruction. On either side of God's throne was a super archangel, a cherub, whose wings stretched out covering the very throne of God. This signifies that these superior angels were involved in the very administration of the government of God over all of God's creation. They were aides, ministers, servants, assisting God.

We read about angels in the first chapter of Hebrews. This chapter first speaks of Jesus. "He, ... stamped with God's own character, sustains the universe with his word of power ... and thus he is superior to the angels, as he has inherited a Name superior to theirs. For to what angel did God ever say, 'Thou art my son, to-day have I become thy father'? Or again, 'I will be a father to him, and he shall be a son to me'? And further, when introducing the First-born into the world, he says, 'Let all God's angels worship him.' While he says of angels, 'Who turns his angels into winds [spirits], his servants into flames of fire,' he says of the Son, 'God is thy throne for ever and ever, thy royal sceptre is the sceptre of equity: thou hast loved justice and hated lawlessness, therefore God, thy God, has consecrated thee with the oil of rejoicing beyond thy comrades'—and, 'Thou didst found the earth at the beginning. . . .'

"To what angel did he ever say, 'Sit at my right hand, till I make your enemies a foot-stool for your feet'? Are not all angels merely spirits in the divine service, commissioned for the benefit of those who are to inherit salvation?" (verses 3-10, 13-14, Moffatt translation).

Humans are created a little lower than angels, though we have the awesome potential of becoming far greater. This fact is expressed in the second chapter of Hebrews and will be treated in chapter seven of this work.

And in chapter three we will show humans may be actually begotten as sons of God, as yet unborn.

It will come as news to most readers that angels were created before the earth and the physical universe were brought into existence. Job 38:1-7 shows the angels shouted for joy when God first created the earth. It is stated in both Genesis 1 and 2 that the earth was created at the same time as the entire physical universe.

Angels are invisible, immortal spirit beings with power and knowledge superior to humans (II Pet. 2:11). They have seen all the activities of mankind on the earth and therefore know more about the human mind, psychology, sociology, science and all the arts than any living man.

Angels serve a great function in carrying out God's purpose for humanity. They are his invisible agents often ministering in ways few understand to us poor humans who are heirs of salvation.

Personal Experiences

My wife and I have both experienced this in personal incidents.

When our elder daughter was a baby, Mrs. Armstrong was sleeping with the child beside her on the inside of the bed against a bedroom wall. She heard a voice calling out, "Move Beverly." She thought it was a dream and without waking continued in sleep. She then heard the same voice again, a little louder.

She half awakened, saw nothing, again thought it was a dream, turned over and was once again going to sleep, when the voice a third time was heard, this time loud and emphatic: "MOVE BEVERLY." Bewildered, she moved the child to the other side of her, and a second or two later, a heavy framed picture that hung on the wall immediately over where the child had been lying crashed down on the bed. It might have crushed the child's head or severely injured her. The only explanation was that God sent an angel to save Beverly's life.

In the early days of my ministry, about 1934, I was driving a car one very stormy night in a downpour of rain on a highway south of Eugene, Oregon. I was driving about 40 miles an hour on a very winding road. As I approached a sharp curve in the road, the steering wheel of my car suddenly turned sharply to the left, as if wrenched out of my hand by some invisible force. Directly ahead of me was a wrecked truck.

I just missed it, passing on its left. It was dark, and a wrecked car was standing just ahead of me. The steering wheel of the car was suddenly wrenched out of my hands, and the car turned sharply toward the right. My car passed between the northbound car and the southbound truck back onto the right lane, with not more than a single inch to spare between the wrecked car and truck. I had never experienced anything like it. The steering wheel of my car was turned by some force out of my control and against my hand holding it straight forward.

A previous time, late in 1927, within the first year of my conversion, I encountered a similar experience.

Experience of the Crooked Spine

After my wife and I had made some little progress in gaining biblical understanding on the subject of healing, Aimee Semple McPherson came to Portland.

She held an evangelistic campaign in the Portland Auditorium. My wife and I attended once, and then I went alone another time. We were "checking up" on many religious teachings and groups. Unable to gain entrance, because of packed attendance, I was told by an usher that I might be able to slip in at the rear stage door if I would hurry around. Walking, or running, around the block to the rear, I came upon a sorry spectacle.

A woman and child were trying to get a terribly crippled elderly man out of a car near the stage entrance. I went over to help them. The man had a badly twisted spine—whether from arthritis, or deformity from birth, or other disease I do not now remember. He was utterly helpless and a pitiful sight to look upon.

We managed to get him to the stage door. Actually, I should never have been admitted, had I not been helping to carry this cripple in. He had come to be healed by the famous lady evangelist.

We were unable to gain contact with Mrs. McPherson before the service. And we were equally unable, after the service. I helped get the disappointed cripple back into their car.

"If you really want to be healed," I said before they drove off, "I would be glad to come to your home and pray for you. Mrs. McPherson has no power within herself to heal anybody. I have none. Only GOD can heal. But I do know what he has promised to do, and I believe God will hear me just as willingly as he will Mrs. McPherson—if only you will BELIEVE in what GOD has promised, and put your faith in HIM and not in the person who prays for you."

They gave me their address, just south of Foster Road. The next day I borrowed my brother Russell's car and drove out.

I had learned, in studying the Bible on the subject of healing, that there are two conditions that God imposes: 1) we must *keep his commandments* and do those things that are pleasing in his sight (I John 3:22); and 2) we must really BELIEVE (Matt. 9:29).

Of course I realized that many people might not have come into the understanding about keeping all of God's

Commandments—he does look on the *heart*. It is the *spirit, and willingness* to obey. And therefore some who really BELIEVE are healed, even though they are not strictly "commandment keepers." But once the *knowledge of the truth* comes, they must OBEY. In this case I felt sure that God wanted me to open the minds of these people about his Commandments, and that SIN *is* the transgression of God's LAW.

Consequently, I first read the two scriptures quoted above, and then explained what I had been six months learning about God's law—and particularly about God's Sabbath. I wanted to know whether this cripple and his wife had a spirit of WILLINGNESS to obey God.

They did not: I found they were "Pentecostal." They attended church for the "good time" they had there. They talked a good deal about the "good time" they enjoyed at church. They scoffed and sneered about having to obey God. I told them that, since they were unwilling to obey God and comply with God's written conditions for healing, I could not pray for him.

Was This an Angel?

This case had weighed heavily on my mind. I had been touched with deep compassion for this poor fellow. Yet his mind was not impaired, and I knew that God does not compromise with SIN.

Some weeks later I had borrowed my brother's car again, and happened to be driving out Foster Road. Actually at the time my mind was filled with another mission, and this deformed cripple was not on my mind at all. I was deep in thought about another matter.

Coming to the intersection of the street on which the cripple lived, however, I was reminded of him. Instantly the thought came as to whether I ought to pay them one more call—but at the same instant reason ruled it out. They had made light of, and actually ridiculed the idea of surrendering to *obey* God. Immediately I put them out of mind, and again was deep in thought about the present mission I was on.

Then a strange thing happened.

At the next intersection, the steering wheel of the car

automatically turned to the right. I felt the wheel turning. I resisted it. It kept turning right. Instantly I applied all my strength to counteract it, and keep steering straight ahead. My strength was of no avail. Some unseen force was turning that steering wheel *against* all my strength. The car had turned to the right into the street one block east of the home of the cripple.

I was frightened. Never before had I experienced anything like this. I stopped the car by the curb. I didn't know what to make of it.

It was too late to back into traffic-heavy Foster Road.

"Well," I thought, "I'll drive to the end of this block and turn left, and then back onto Foster Road."

But, a long block south on this street, it turned right *only*. There was no street turning east. In getting back onto Foster Road I was now compelled to drive past the home of the cripple.

"Could it possibly be that an angel *forced* the steering wheel to turn me in here?" I wondered, somewhat shaken by the experience. I decided I had better stop in at the cripple's home a moment, to be sure.

I found him stricken with blood poisoning. The red line was nearing his heart.

I told them what had happened.

"I know, now," I said, "that God sent an angel to turn me in here. I believe that God wants me to pray for you—that he will heal you of this blood poisoning to show you his power, and then give you one more chance to repent and be willing to obey him. And if you will do that, then he will straighten out your twisted spine and heal you completely.

"So now, if you want me to do so, I will pray for you and ask God to heal you of this blood poisoning. But I will *not* ask God to heal your spine unless and until you repent and show willingness to obey whatever you yourself see God commands."

They were now desperate. He probably had about 12 hours to live. They were not joking and jesting lightly about the "good times" at "Pentecostal meetin'." They wanted me to pray.

I was not an ordained minister, so I did not anoint with

oil. I had never yet in my life prayed aloud before others. I explained this to them, and said I would simply lay hands on the man and pray silently, as I did not want any self-consciousness of praying aloud for the first time to interfere with real earnestness and faith. I did have absolute faith he would be healed of the blood poisoning.

He was.

I returned the next day. The blood poisoning had left him immediately when I prayed. But, to my very great sorrow and disappointment, they were once again filled with levity, and sarcasm about God's law. Again they were jestingly talking about having a "good time" at "Pentecostal" meetings.

There was no more I could do. It was one of the great disappointments of my life. I never saw or heard from any of them again.

God's Invisible Agents

God has had angels specifically assigned to supervise and protect his Church throughout all of its history (Rev. 1:4, 16, 20; 2:1, 8, 12, 18; 3:1, 7, 14). He has angels who continually walk through the earth to observe and report back to him the overall conditions on earth (Rev. 5:6; Zech. 4:10; II Chron. 16:9).

And God has angels specifically assigned to look after his begotten human children (Acts 12:15; Matt. 18:10). God promises: "For he shall give his angels charge over thee, to keep thee in all thy ways" (Ps. 91:11).

Twelve of God's angels will be the gatekeepers in the new city of Jerusalem (Rev. 21:12), one for each tribe of Israel. These 12 may be assisting the archangel Michael now.

Angels are messengers. They appeared to Abraham, Lot, Hagar, Moses, Manoah, Gideon, Elijah and many of the prophets and apostles.

When these angels manifest themselves to human beings, they generally do so in the form of men.

The Bible mentions three angels of high rank: Lucifer (Isa. 14:12), now Satan the devil; Gabriel, who appeared to Daniel on two occasions (Dan. 8:16; 9:21), to Zacharias, the father of John the Baptist (Luke 1:19), and later Mary, the mother of Jesus (Luke 1:26); and third, Michael, called one of the *chief princes* (Dan. 10:13), and whom Jude identifies as an *archangel* (Jude 9). Michael is the archangel specifically assigned to protect and minister to the 12 tribes of Israel (Dan. 12:1; 10:2-13, 21) and to the true Church of God today (Rev. 12:7).

The Supreme Creative Accomplishment

God assigns angels responsibilities, but God created within them MINDS—WITH POWER TO THINK, TO REASON, TO MAKE CHOICES AND DECISIONS!

But there was one super-important quality that even God's creative powers could not create instantly by fiat—the same perfect, holy, righteous CHARACTER inherent in both God and the Word!

This kind of character must be DEVELOPED, by the CHOICE and the INTENT of the one in whom it comes to exist.

So mark well this super-vital truism—that perfect, holy and righteous *character* is the supreme feat of accomplishment possible for Almighty God the Creator—it is also the means to his ultimate supreme PURPOSE! His final objective!

But HOW?

I repeat, such perfect character must be *developed*. It requires the free choice and decision of the separate entity in whom it is to be created. But, further, even then it must be instilled by and from the Holy God who, only, has such righteous character to endow.

But what do we mean by righteous character?

Perfect, holy and righteous character is the ability in such separate entity to come to discern the true and right way from the false, to make voluntarily a full and unconditional surrender to God and his perfect way—to yield to be *conquered* by God—to determine even against temptation or self-desire, to *live* and to *do* the right. And even then such holy character is the gift of God. It comes by yielding to God to instill HIS LAW (God's right way of life) within the entity who so decides and wills.

Actually, this perfect character comes only from God, as instilled within the entity of his creation, upon voluntary acquiescence, even after severe trial and test.

I have devoted a few paragraphs to this point because it is the supreme pinnacle means in God's overall PURPOSE!

Now as to the prehistoric angels: God 1) created them with minds capable of thinking, reasoning, making choices and decisions with self-will; and 2) revealed plainly to them HIS TRUE AND RIGHTEOUS WAY. But God of necessity allowed them free moral agency in accepting God's right way, or turning to contrary ways of their own devising.

What was God's ULTIMATE OBJECTIVE for the angels? Beyond question it is that which, now, because of angelic rebellion, has become the transcendent potential of humans!

As the testing ground, and opportunity for positive and active creative accomplishment, God created—brought into existence—the entire vast material universe.

First of all, God had created angels. After that, and for angels and for humans who were to be created later, God formed and brought into existence the earth and the entire universe.

God now created not only matter, but with and in it energy and such laws as man has discovered in the fields of physics and chemistry. God formed matter to be present in both the organic and the inorganic states.

And so we come now to that which is revealed in Genesis 1:1: "In the beginning [of the physical universe] God created the heavens and the earth." These are material and physical.

As previously stated, in the Authorized Version will be found the word *heaven* in the singular. But this originally was written by Moses in Hebrew. And in the Hebrew the word is in the plural—*heavens*—thus including not only our earth, but the entire material UNIVERSE.

It is therefore indicated that *at that time*—after the creation of angels—the entire universe was brought into existence at the same time as the creation of our earth. I find strong indication of this in other biblical internal evidence, and also it is definitely stated in Genesis 2:4.

The Perfect Creation

The original Hebrew words (the words written by Moses) imply a perfect creation. God reveals himself as Creator of perfection, light and beauty. Every reference in the Bible describes the condition of any completed phase of God's creation as "very good"—perfect.

This first verse of the Bible actually speaks of the original PHYSICAL creation in its entirety—the universe—*including* the earth, perhaps millions of years ago—as a perfect creation, beautiful and perfect as far as its creation was a finished, completed work. God is a perfectionist!

In Job 38:4, 7, God is speaking specifically of the creation of this earth. He said all the angels (created "sons of God") shouted for joy at the creation of the earth. This reveals that angels were created *before the creation of the earth*—and probably before the *material* universe. The suns, planets and astral bodies are material substance. Angels are individually created spirit beings, composed solely of spirit.

It will come as a surprise to many to learn that angels inhabited this earth BEFORE the creation of man. This passage from Job implies it.

Angels on Earth Sinned

Other passages place angels on earth prior to man.

Notice II Peter 2:4-6. First in time order "angels that sinned." Next in time sequence, the antediluvian world beginning with Adam, carrying through to the Flood. After that, Sodom and Gomorrah.

This book of books, containing the revealed knowledge of the Creator God, tells us that God created angels as composed of spirit. But can you imagine angels becoming *sinning* angels? Angels were created with power of thought, of decision and of choice, else they have no individuality of character. Since *sin* is the transgression of God's law, these angels rebelled against God's law, the basis of God's government.

But how and when did the angels sin?

Notice carefully what is revealed in II Peter 2:4-5: "For if God spared not the angels that sinned, but cast them down to hell, and delivered them into chains of darkness, to be reserved unto judgment; and spared not the old world, but saved Noah the eighth person, a preacher of righteousness, bringing in the flood upon the world of the ungodly." The words "cast . . . down to hell" in the above verse is an English expression translated from the Greek *tartaroo*, from *tartaros*, found in no other Bible passage. *Tartaros* means a place or condition of restraint.

These verses show that universal sin brings universal destruction to the physical earth. The antediluvian sin, culminating with the Flood, was worldwide, universal sin. Notice: ". . . the earth *was filled* with violence . . . for *all flesh* had corrupted his way upon the earth . . . for the *earth is filled* with violence . . ." (Gen. 6:11-13). "But Noah found grace in the eyes of the Lord. . . . Noah was a just man and perfect in his generations, and Noah walked with God" (verses 8-9). All flesh had sinned—over the whole earth. But *only Noah* "walked with God." So, the Flood destroyed *the whole earth*—all but Noah and his family.

The homosexual and other sins of Sodom and Gomorrah spread over the territory of those two cities. And physical destruction came to their entire area. The sin of the angels was worldwide; the destruction of the physical was worldwide. (And there is reason to believe, as will be explained in chapter seven, universe wide.)

The verses quoted above place the sinning of the angels *prior* to the antediluvian sins that started with Adam, *prior* to the creation of man. And *that* should be a surprise revealing of one phase of the mystery! Angels inhabited this earth *before* the creation of man.

It is revealed in Isaiah 14 and Ezekiel 28, that God placed the archangel Lucifer, a cherub, on a throne on the earth. He was placed there as a ruler over the entire earth. God intended him to rule the earth by administering the government of God over the earth. And the government of God was administered on earth until the rebellion of the sinning angels.

How long these angels inhabited the earth before the creation of man is not revealed. It might have been millions—or even billions—of years. More on that later. But these angels sinned. Sin is the transgression of God's law (I John 3:4). And God's law is the basis of God's government. So we know these angels, apparently a third of all the angels (Rev. 12:4), sinned—rebelled against the government of God. And sin carries penalties. The penalty for the sin of the angels is not *death*, as it is for man. Angels are immortal spirit beings and cannot die. These spirit beings had *been given dominion* over the PHYSICAL EARTH as a possession and an abode.

The universal, worldwide sin of the angels resulted in the physical destruction of the face of the earth.

God Rules His Creation

God is Creator. God is also Ruler over his creation. He preserves what he creates by his government. What God creates, he has created for a purpose—to be used, improved, developed, preserved and maintained. And this use is regulated by God's government. When the angels rebelled against God's government, the development and improvement of the earth—"putting the icing on the cake"—ceased. The preservation and development of the physical earth and all its original beauty and glory ceased—and physical destruction to the surface of the earth resulted!

By this angelic sin, Lucifer became Satan the devil and his angels became demons.

God is Creator, Preserver and Ruler.

Satan is destroyer!

So, now we read in Jude 6-7: "And the angels which kept not their first estate, but left their own habitation, he hath reserved in everlasting chains under darkness unto the judgment of the great day. Even as Sodom and Gomorrha, and the cities about them in like manner, giving themselves over to fornication, and going after strange flesh, are set forth for an example, suffering the vengeance of eternal fire."

Now back to Genesis 1:1-2. Verse 1, as stated above, implies a perfect creation. God is the author of life, of beauty, of perfection. Satan has brought only darkness, ugliness, imperfection, violence. Verse 1 shows the creation of a perfect, if unfinished earth, glorious and beautiful. Verse 2 reveals the result of the sin of the angels.

"And the earth was [became] without form, and void." The words "without form, and void" are translated from the Hebrew *tohu* and *bohu*. A better translation is "waste and empty" or "chaotic, in confusion and in a state of decay." The word *was* is elsewhere in Genesis also translated *became*, as in Genesis 19:26. In other words, the earth, originally created perfect and beautiful, had now become chaotic, waste and empty, like our moon, except earth's surface was covered with water.

David was inspired to reveal how God renewed the face of the earth: "Thou sendest forth thy spirit, they are created: and thou renewest the face of the earth" (Ps. 104:30).

A Surprising Truth

Now another surprise for most readers. Here is another bit of the missing dimension in knowledge, actually revealed in the Bible, but unrecognized by religion, by science and by higher education.

From verse 2 of Genesis 1 on, the remainder of this first chapter of the Bible is *not* describing the original creation of the earth. But it *is* describing a renewing of the face of the earth, after it had become waste and empty as a result of the sin of the angels.

What is described from verse 2 on, in the supposed creation chapter of the Bible, did occur, according to the Bible, approximately 6,000 years ago. But that could have been millions or trillions of years after the actual creation of the earth described in verse 1!

I will comment later on the length of time it might have taken before all earth's angels turned to rebellion.

The earth *had become* waste and empty. God did not create it waste and empty, or in a state of decay. God is not the author of confusion (I Cor. 14:33). This same Hebrew word—*tohu*—meaning waste and empty, was inspired in Isaiah 45:18, where it is translated "in vain." Using the original Hebrew word, as originally inspired, it reads: "For thus saith the Lord that created the heavens; God himself that formed the earth and made it; he hath established it, he created it not in vain [tohu], he formed it to be inhabited."

Continue now with the remainder of verse 2 of Genesis 1 (the earth had become chaotic, waste and empty): "And darkness was upon the face of the deep [the ocean or fluid surface of the earth]. And the Spirit of God moved upon the face of the waters. And God said, Let there be light: and there was light. And God saw the light, that it was good: and God divided the light from the darkness" (verses 2-4).

Satan is the author of darkness. The rebellion of the

angels had caused the darkness. God is the author of light and truth. Light displays and enhances beauty, and also exposes evil. Darkness hides both.

The verses that follow in this first chapter of the Bible describe the renewing of the face of the earth, yielding beautiful lawns, trees, shrubs, flowers, vegetation—then the creation of fish and fowl, animal life, and finally man.

The Great Lucifer

But first, before coming to man, we need to fill in the prehistory portion.

How did this sin of the angels come to take place? How did it start?

Remember, God the Creator *preserves,* improves and enhances what he creates by his government. What he creates is created to be used. This earth was to be inhabited and used by angels, originally.

When God placed angels—apparently a third of all (Rev. 12:4)—on the newly created, perfect, beautiful and glorious earth, he set over them, on a throne, to administer the government of God, an archangel—the great cherub Lucifer. There were only two other beings of this extremely high rank of cherub, Michael and Gabriel.

So far as is revealed, these are the supreme pinnacle of spirit-composed beings within God's power to create. This Lucifer was a super being of awesome, majestic beauty, dazzling brightness, supreme knowledge, wisdom and power—perfect as God created him! (Ezek. 28:15). But remember, there is one thing God cannot create automatically and instantly by fiat, and that is perfect righteous character. So God of necessity created in him the power of choice and decision, or he could not have been a being of individuality and character.

At this juncture a truth must be explained almost never understood. God creates in a principle of duality. I have compared it to a woman baking a cake. When she takes the cake out of the oven, it is not yet a finished production until she puts the icing on the cake. When God created the earth and other planets this system of duality was involved.

What had been created was perfect as far as it existed up

to that point. But it was not yet a finished or completed creation. God intended the angels to add their own workmanship to the earth's surface. He intended them to work over the surface of the earth, to improve it, to embellish it, beautify it—in other words "put the icing on the cake."

The same principle of duality applies to the creation of the angels. Perfect righteous character cannot be automatically created by fiat. The angels themselves, of necessity, were required to have their part in the development of character, and their creation could not be actually finished until this character had been perfected.

Lucifer, Later Satan

I want you to grasp fully the supreme magnificence of this zenith of God's created beings. Two different biblical passages tell us of his original created state.

First, notice what is revealed in Isaiah 14. (This famous chapter begins with the time, shortly ahead of us now, when the Eternal God shall have intervened in this world's affairs. The people of Israel—not necessarily or exclusively the Israelis or Judah—shall have been taken as captive slaves, and God shall intervene and bring them back to the original promised homeland.) "And it shall come to pass in the day that the Lord shall give thee rest from thy sorrow, and from thy fear, and from the hard bondage wherein thou wast made to serve, that thou shalt take up this proverb against the king of Babylon, and say, How hath the oppressor ceased! the golden city ceased! The Lord hath broken the staff of the wicked, and the sceptre of the rulers. He who smote the people in wrath . . . he that ruled the nations in anger, is persecuted, and none hindereth" (verses 3-6).

This is NOT speaking of the king of ancient Babylon, Nebuchadnezzar. The time is yet ahead of us—but shortly ahead. It is speaking of the modern successor of that ancient Nebuchadnezzar. It is speaking of the one who will be RULER of the soon-coming resurrected "Holy Roman Empire"—a sort of soon-coming "United States of Europe"—a union of 10 nations to rise up out of or following the Common Market of today (Rev. 17). Britain will NOT be in that empire soon to come.

This united Europe will conquer the House of Israel—*if* you know who Israel is today, and I do *not* mean Judah, known as the Israelis today. All that involves a number of other prophecies, which there is not room here to explain. (This is explained in our free book *The United States and Britain in Prophecy*.)

But this "king of Babylon" shall at the time of this prophecy have been utterly defeated by the intervention of the living Christ in his power and glory. Continue on:

"The whole earth is at rest, and is quiet: they break forth into singing. Yea, the fir trees rejoice . . . and the cedars of Lebanon, saying, Since thou art laid down, no feller is come up against us" (verses 7-8).

(I want to interpose an interesting bit of information right here. The cedars of Lebanon, biblically famous, are almost totally cut down. Only one small clump of these trees remains, high in the mountains. I have seen and photographed them. However, perhaps the finest specimen of the cedars of Lebanon surviving on earth is on what was previously our Ambassador College campus in England. We prized it highly. It is interesting to see that this prophecy, written some 500 years B.C., should record the fact that these beautiful and stately trees would become so largely felled.)

This passage in Isaiah 14 speaks of the doom of this coming human king at the hands of the glorified, all-powerful Christ. It refers to him as Satan's chief political ruler and military destroyer, to be totally deceived by Satan in the years very shortly ahead of us.

Satan's Earthly Throne

Then, coming to verse 12, this human earthly type of Satan the devil suddenly transposes to Satan himself—the former archangel, Lucifer:

"How art thou fallen from heaven, O Lucifer, son of the morning! how art thou cut down to the ground, which didst weaken the nations!" A better translation here is: "How art thou, who didst weaken the nations, cut down to the ground." The RSV translates it: "How you are cut down to the ground, you who laid the nations low!" This the former Lucifer did through the human political-military leader in his power—spoken of in the first 11 verses.

The name Lucifer means "Shining star of the dawn," or "Bringer of light," as God first created him. Now continue: "For thou hast said in thine heart, I will ascend into heaven, I will exalt my throne above the stars [angels] of God."

Notice, Lucifer had a throne; he was a ruler. His throne was on earth, for he was going to ascend into heaven. Continue: "I will sit also upon the mount of the congregation [God's heavenly throne], in the sides of the north: I will ascend above the heights of the clouds; I will be like the most High" (verses 13-14). Actually, it is plain that Lucifer had nothing less in mind than knocking the Creator God off his throne and becoming supreme God himself.

Apparently he planned to put himself in place of God, over the universe!

But finally, as the context returns again to the human type: "Yet thou shalt be brought down to hell [Heb. *sheol*], to the sides of the pit" (verse 15).

From that point, the thought returns to the human king. Lucifer was the supreme masterpiece of God's creative power, as an individually created being, threatening, as a Frankenstein monster, to destroy his own maker—and assume all his powers to rule the whole universe.

Literally this prophecy is speaking of a war in heaven to occur in our present time described in Revelation 12:7-9: "And there was war in heaven: Michael and his angels fought against the dragon; and the dragon fought and his angels, and prevailed not; neither was their place found any more in heaven. And the great dragon was cast out, that old serpent, called the Devil, and Satan, which deceiveth the whole world: he was cast out into the earth, and his angels were cast out with him." And also Daniel 12:1-2: "And at that time shall Michael stand up, the great prince which standeth for the children of thy people: and there shall be a time of trouble, such as never was since there was a nation even to that same time: and at that time thy people shall be delivered, every one that shall be found written in the book. And many of them that sleep in the dust of the earth shall awake, some to everlasting life, and some to shame and everlasting contempt."

Satan's rebel rule was NOT a government based upon the principle of love—of giving, of outgoing concern for the good of others, but based on SELF-CENTEREDNESS, on vanity, lust and greed, on envy, jealousy, the spirit of competition, hatred, violence and destruction, on darkness and error, instead of light and truth, on ugliness instead of beauty.

Notice here, once again, the principle of duality. Isaiah 14:12-14 applies to a time prior to the creation of the first human, Adam. But in Revelation 12:7 and in Daniel 12:1 Satan at the end of the 6,000 years allotted to his rule on earth's throne, tries once again to seize God's throne in heaven.

Lucifer a Created Being

Look now at the other biblical passage describing this supreme angelic creation of God, in Ezekiel 28.

Actually, the entire concept in Ezekiel 26 speaks of the ancient great commercial city of Tyre. It was the commercial metropolis of the ancient world, even as Babylon was the political capital. Tyre was the New York, the London, the Tokyo, or the Paris of the ancient world. The ancient Tyre, port of the world's shippers and merchants, gloried *herself* in her beauty, even as Paris in our time.

Chapter 27 carries on with comparisons to passages in the 18th chapter of the book of Revelation referring to a politico-religious leader to come (verses 9-19).

But coming to chapter 28, the theme comes more completely to the time just now ahead of us, the same time depicted in Isaiah 14. Ezekiel 28 speaks of the prince of Tyre, an earthly ruler, of whom the ancient king of Tyre was a type. God says to the prophet Ezekiel: "Son of man, say unto the prince of Tyrus [actually referring to a powerful religious leader to arise SOON, in our time], Thus saith the Lord God; Because thine heart is lifted up, and thou hast said, I am a God, I sit in the seat of God, in the midst of the seas; yet thou art a man, and not God, though thou set thine heart as the heart of God: Behold, thou art wiser than Daniel; there is no secret that they can hide from thee: with thy wisdom and with thine understanding thou hast gotten thee riches, and hast gotten gold and silver into thy treasures [or "treasuries"—

RSV] ... and thine heart is lifted up because of thy riches: therefore thus saith the Lord God; Because thou hast set thine heart as the heart of God; behold, therefore I will bring strangers upon thee, the terrible of the nations ... they shall bring thee down to the pit, and thou shalt die the deaths of them that are slain in the midst of the seas" (Ezek. 28:2-8). (Compare with II Thessalonians 2:3-4, speaking of "that man of sin ... who opposeth and exalteth himself above all that is called God ... so that he *as* God sitteth in the temple of God, shewing himself that he is God.")

What a Super Being!

But at this point, as in Isaiah 14, the lesser human antitype lifts to a greater spirit being. Instead of the prince of Tyre—a human man—it now speaks of the KING of Tyre. This is the same Lucifer.

Ezekiel the prophet continues:

"Moreover the word of the Lord came unto me, saying, Son of man, take up a lamentation upon the KING of Tyrus, and say unto him, Thus saith the Lord God; Thou sealest up the sum, full of wisdom, and perfect in beauty" (verses 11-12).

Please read that again! God would never say anything like that of a human man. This superb spirit being filled up the sum total of wisdom, perfection and beauty. He was the supreme pinnacle, the masterpiece, of God's creation, as an individually created being, the greatest one in the almighty power of God to create! The tragic thing is that he rebelled against his Maker!

"Thou hast been in Eden the garden of God" (verse 13). He had inhabited this earth. His throne was here. "Every precious stone was thy covering ... the workmanship of thy tabrets and of thy pipes was prepared in thee in the day that thou wast created" (verse 13). He was a *created being*—not born human. He was a spirit being—*not* human flesh. Great genius and skill in music was created in him. Now that he has become perverted in all thinking, acting and being, he is the real author of modern perverted music and the modern rock beat—of discordant moans, squawks, shrieks, wails—physically and emotionally excitable beats—unhappy, discouraged moods. Think of all the supreme talent, ability and potential in a being created with such capacities. And all perverted! All gone sour—all dissipated, turned to hatred, destruction, hopelessness!

Yet, take courage. The awesome human potential, if we care enough about it to *resist* Satan's wiles and evils and discouragements and to persevere in *God's way*, is infinitely superior and higher than Lucifer's—even as created, *before* he turned to rebellion and iniquity!

But continuing the particular revelation of this crucially important missing dimension in knowledge: "Thou art the anointed cherub that covereth; and I have set thee so," says God of this Lucifer. This takes us back to the 25th chapter of Exodus, where God gave Moses the pattern for the ark of the covenant. The description begins with verse 10, and verses 18-20 show, in the material pattern, the two cherubs who were stationed at each end of the very throne of God in heaven—the throne of the government of God over the entire universe. The wings of the two cherubs covered the throne of God.

Trained at Universe Headquarters

This Lucifer, then, had been stationed at the very throne of God. He was trained and experienced in the administration of the government of God. God chose such a being, well-experienced and trained, to be the king ruling the government of God over the angels who inhabited the whole earth.

Continue: ". . . thou wast upon the holy mountain of God; thou hast walked up and down in the midst of the stones of fire." This is not talking about any human being. But continue: "Thou wast perfect in thy *ways* from the day that thou wast created, till iniquity [lawlessness] was found in thee" (Ezek. 28:15). He had complete knowledge, understanding and wisdom. But he also was given full powers of reasoning, thinking, making decisions, making his choice. And, with all this foreknowledge—even of results and consequences—this superb being, the highest that even God could create by fiat, turned to rebellion against his Maker— against the way that produces every good. He turned to lawlessness. He had been trained in the administration of perfect law and order. As long as Lucifer continued in this perfect way, there was happiness and joy unspeakable over the whole earth. There was glorious peace—beautiful harmony, perfect love, cooperation. The government of God produced a wonderfully happy state—as long as Lucifer was loyal in the conduct of God's government.

What Caused the Angels' Sin?

What caused the angels on earth to sin, to turn to lawlessness? Certainly the ordinary angels did not persuade this great superbeing to turn traitor. No, it was in him that iniquity was found. But, after how long? We don't know. God does not reveal that! It could have been any number of years from one or less to millions times millions.

And then, even after Lucifer himself made the decision to rebel and try to invade God's heaven to take over the universe, it is not revealed how long it took him to persuade all of the angels under him to turn traitor and follow him.

I know well the method he used. He uses the same method still today in leading deceived humans into disloyalty, rebellion, and self-centered opposition against God's government. First, he turns one or two to envy, jealousy and resentment over an imagined injustice—then into disloyalty. Then he uses that one or two, like a rotten apple in a crate, to stir up resentment, feelings of self-pity, disloyalty and rebellion in others next to them. And, as each rotten apple rots those next to it until the whole crate is rotten, so Satan proceeds.

If, in the government of God on earth today, the "rotten apples" are not thrown out early enough, they would destroy the whole government. But, once thrown out of the crate, they cannot do any more damage to those in the crate.

But *think* how long it must have taken the soured and embittered Lucifer to turn millions of holy angels into resentment, bitterness, disloyalty, and finally open and vicious rebellion. It could have taken hundreds, thousands or millions of years. This was all before the first human was created.

All this happened after the original creation of the earth,

described in verse 1 of Genesis 1. Verse 2 of this creation chapter describes a condition *resulting* from this sin of the angels. The events described in verse 2, therefore, may have occurred millions of years *after* the original creation of the earth.

The earth, therefore, may have been created millions of years ago. But continue this passage in Ezekiel 28: "By the multitude of thy merchandise they have filled the midst of thee with violence, and thou hast sinned: therefore I will cast thee as profane out of the mountain of God: and I will destroy [remove] thee, O covering cherub, from the midst of the stones of fire. Thine heart was lifted up because of thy beauty, thou hast corrupted thy wisdom by reason of thy brightness: I will cast thee to the ground . . ." (verses 16-17). At this point the context returns to the soon-to-appear, human, religious-political ruler—of whom the prince of ancient Tyre was a forerunner.

Earlier in this chapter, I showed you how physical destruction, ugliness and darkness had covered the *face* of the earth, as the result of the sin of Lucifer (who is now the devil) and these "angels that sinned" (now demons), and how in six days God had renewed the face of the earth (Gen. 1:2-25).

Why the Creation of MAN?

But why did God create man on the earth (Gen. 1:26)?

Look at this situation as God does. God has given us humans minds, like the mind of God, only inferior and limited. God made us in his image, after his likeness (form and shape), only composed of matter instead of spirit. But God says, "Let this mind be in you, which was also in Christ Jesus" (Phil. 2:5). We can, to some degree, think even as God thinks. How must God have looked at the situation, as he started renewing the face of the earth—after the colossal debacle of the angels!

He had created a beautiful, perfect creation in the earth. He populated it with holy angels—probably millions of them. He put over them, as king, on an earthly throne, the archangel—the cherub Lucifer. Lucifer was the supreme masterpiece of God's creative power as a single separately created spirit being. He was the most perfect in beauty, power, mind, knowledge, intellect, wisdom, within the almighty power of God to create. God can create nothing higher or more perfect, by instantaneous fiat.

Yet this great being, knowledgeable, trained and experienced at God's own throne in heaven over the universe and the administration of the government of God, had rejected that government, corrupted his way, rebelled against administering or even obeying it. He had led all his angels astray and into the sin of rebellion.

Now consider further. Apparently the entire universe had been created also at the time of the earth's creation. There is no evidence either in God's revealed Word, nor in science, that any of the planets in endless outer space had been inhabited with any form of life. But God does nothing in vain. He always has a purpose.

Apparently all such planets in the entire universe NOW are waste and empty—decayed (*tohu* and *bohu*)—like the earth was, as described in Genesis 1:2. But God did not create them in such conditions of decay—like our moon. Decay is *not* an original created condition—it is a condition *resulting from a process* of deterioration. Evidently if the now fallen angels had maintained the earth in its original beautiful condition, improved it, carried out God's instructions, and obeyed his government, they would have been offered the awesome potential of populating and carrying out a tremendous creative program throughout the entire universe. When they turned traitor on earth, their sin must have also brought simultaneously physical destruction to the other planets throughout the universe, which were potentially and conditionally put in subjection to them.

Earth to Become Universe Headquarters

It will be explained in chapter seven of this work that God's purpose is to make this earth, ultimately, the headquarters of the entire universe.

Remember, this earth, originally, was intended to be the abode of a third of all the angels. The angels, beholding the earth at its creation, found it so beautiful and perfect they shouted spontaneously for JOY (Job 38:4-7). It was to provide a glorious opportunity for them. They were to work it, produce from it, and preserve and increase its beauty.

And at this point, it is well to understand the nature of God's original creation: It is like the unfinished furniture available in some stores. This furniture is "in the raw"—it is finished all but for the final varnish, polish or paint. Some can save money by doing this *finishing* themselves—provided they have the skill to do so. This furniture may be of fine and superb quality—yet lacking the final beautifying *completion.*

So it is with God's creation. It is *perfect,* but subject to a beautifying finish that God intended angels to accomplish. The original "unfinished" creation was produced by God *alone.* But he intended angels, prehistorically, and MAN, now, to utilize creative power—to finish this part in God's creation—of adding the final beautifying and utilitarian phases of what shall be the FINAL COMPLETED CREATION!

And whether or not it had been revealed to the angels, it was a supreme TRIAL AND TEST. It was to be the PROVING GROUND of obedience to GOD'S GOVERNMENT and their fitness to develop into final finished creation the millions of other planets in the vast universe. For what is revealed in God's Word indicates that God had created the entire PHYSICAL universe at the same time he created the earth. The seventh word in Genesis 1:1 should be translated "heavens." This word includes the vast universe, not just this earth's atmosphere.

Radioactive elements and the law of radioactivity prove that there was a time when MATTER did not exist. GOD is a spirit. God is composed of spirit. God was before ALL ELSE—the CREATOR of all. Angels were created prior to the earth. What God reveals strongly implies that matter had never existed before the original creation of the earth—that the entire *physical* universe was brought into being at that time.

God's Purpose for Angels

So the angel potential was to take over the entire universe—to improve and finish the billions of physical planets surrounding the uncountable stars, many of which are SUNS. The sun in our solar system is merely an average-size sun. Some that we see as stars are actually many, many times larger than our sun. Our solar system, vast beyond the imagination of most minds, is only a *part* of our galaxy, and there are many galaxies! In other words, the physical UNIVERSE that the mighty God created is *vast beyond imagination!* How GREAT is the GREAT GOD!

He intended angels to have a vital part in the final creation of the endless universe!

(But God may not have then fully revealed this awesome potential to the angels, for one third of them set out to take it from him by force, without first qualifying.)

For this far-reaching purpose, God established his GOVERNMENT on earth over them. The administration of the GOVERNMENT OF GOD over this globe was delegated to the super archangel—the great cherub Lucifer.

Bear in mind that even the holy angels and archangels—including this super cherub Lucifer—of necessity were endowed with ability to think, to reason, to form attitudes, and to make choices and decisions.

As explained previously, God started this Lucifer out with everything going for him. He sealed up the sum of wisdom, beauty and perfection. He was PERFECT in all his ways from the instant he was created UNTIL INIQUITY—rebellion, lawlessness—was found in him (Ezek. 28:15).

He had been trained and was thoroughly experienced in administration of the GOVERNMENT OF GOD at the very throne of the endless UNIVERSE! He was one of the two cherubs whose wings covered the throne of God the MOST high (Ezek. 28:14; Ex. 25:20).

How Sin Entered

He was created gloriously beautiful—*perfect* in beauty, but he allowed vanity to seize him. Then he turned to erroneous reasoning. God's law—the basis of God's government—is the way of LOVE—outgoing concern for the good and welfare of others, love toward God in obedience, humility and worship—the way of giving, sharing, helping, cooperating. He reasoned that competition would be better than cooperation. It would be an incentive to excel, to try harder, to accomplish. There would be more pleasure in serving SELF and more enjoyment.

He turned *against* God's law of LOVE. He became jealous of God, envious, and resentful against God. He allowed lust and greed to fill him, and he became bitter. This inspired a spirit of *violence!* He deliberately became his Maker's adversary and enemy. That was *his* choice, not God's—yet allowed by God!

God changed the adversary's NAME to what he became, SATAN the DEVIL—Satan means adversary, competitor, enemy.

Satan directed his supernatural powers henceforth to EVIL. He became bitter not only against God, but against God's law. He used his subtle wiles of deception to lead the angels under him into disloyalty, rebellion and revolt against the Creator and finally into a WAR of aggression and violence to attempt to depose God and seize the throne of the UNIVERSE.

As long as Lucifer remained loyal and administered the GOVERNMENT OF GOD faithfully, this earth was filled with wonderful and perfect PEACE. The angels were vigorously HAPPY to the extent of JOY! The law of God's government is THE WAY OF LIFE that CAUSES and produces peace, happiness, prosperity and well-being. Sin is the WAY OF LIFE that has *caused* all existing EVILS.

The penalty of sin by the angels was *not* death—for God had made them immortal spirit beings who cannot die. What God gave them was THIS EARTH as their abode and opportunity to qualify to possess and beautify the entire UNIVERSE.

Their penalty (they are still awaiting final judgment up to now) was disqualification—forfeiture of their grand opportunity, perversion of mind, and *a colossal earthwide CATA-CLYSM* of destruction wreaked upon this earth.

As a result, the earth came to the condition briefly described in Genesis 1:2. Lucifer was created a perfect bringer of LIGHT. Now he became author of DARKNESS, error, confusion and evil.

So the rebellion of the angels that sinned (II Pet. 2:4-6; Jude 6-7; Isa. 14:12-15; Ezek. 28:12-17) brought this extreme cataclysm to the earth.

How must God have looked at this situation after the colossal debacle of Lucifer and the angels that sinned?

LUCIFER was created the most perfect in beauty, mentality, knowledge, power, intellect and wisdom within the almighty power of God to create in a being, with power to think, reason, make choices and decisions on his own. God knew that no higher, more perfect being could be created as an initial creation.

Origin of Demons

Yet this superior being, trained and experienced at the very throne of the GOVERNMENT OF GOD over the universe, had resorted to wrong reasoning and made a diabolical perverted decision. He worked on the angels under him until he turned their minds to rebellion also. This, incidentally, might have taken Lucifer millions of years. In all probability he had to begin perverting the minds of his angels one at a time, at first. He had to cause them to feel dissatisfied, wronged by God, and inject into them resentment and bitterness.

When Lucifer allowed thoughts of vanity, jealousy, envy, lust and greed, then resentment and rebellion, to enter and occupy his mind, SOMETHING HAPPENED TO HIS MIND! *His mind became perverted, distorted, twisted!* His thinking became warped. God gave him and the angels control over their own minds. They can never straighten them out—never again think rationally, honestly, rightly.

I have had a number of personal experiences with demons through a few demon-possessed people. I have cast out demons through the name of Christ and power of the Holy Spirit. Some demons are silly, like spoiled children. Some are crafty, sharp, shrewd, subtile. Some are belligerent, some are sassy, some are sullen and morose. But *all* are perverted, warped, twisted.

Do Satan and his demons affect and even influence humans and even governments today? Do evil spirits affect even your own life? These questions will be answered in chapter four of this book.

As God surveyed this cataclysmic tragedy, he must have realized that since the highest, most perfect being within his almighty power to create, had turned to rebellion, it left God himself as the only being who *would not* and *cannot* sin.

And God is the Father of the divine God family or kingdom.

Notice John 1:1-5. The Word who was "made flesh" (verse 14) has existed always—from eternity—with the Father. God the Father has created all things—the entire universe—by him who became Jesus Christ (Eph. 3:9; Col. 1:16-17).

When Jesus was on earth, he prayed to God, his Father in heaven. The Father spoke of Jesus as "my beloved son, in whom I am well pleased." Jesus lived on earth as a human, tempted in all points as we are, yet without sin.

The fourth word in the English Bible is "God" (Gen. 1:1). And the original Hebrew word is *Elohim,* a noun plural in form, like the English word *family, church* or *group.* The divine family is God. There is one God—the one family, consisting of more than one Person.

God saw that no being less than God, in the God family, could be *certainly* relied on never to sin—to be like God—who cannot sin. To fulfill his purpose for the entire vast universe, God saw that nothing less than himself (as the God family) could be absolutely relied upon to carry out that supreme purpose in the entire universe.

Why Humans Succeed Fallen Angels

God then purposed *to reproduce himself,* through humans, made in his image and likeness, but made first from material flesh and blood, subject to death if there is sin unrepented of—yet with the possibility of being born into the divine family begotten by God the Father. God saw how this could be done through Christ, who gave himself for that purpose.

And that is why God put man on the earth! That is what caused God to do this most colossal, tremendous thing ever undertaken by the supreme, almighty God—to reproduce himself! The following chapter will make this undeniably clear. One last important comment before ending this chapter.

God's supreme overall purpose is to create, even to the extent of reproducing himself, and also that God must reign supreme over all his creation. Apparently God has chosen this earth to become his universe headquarters, and the seat of even the supreme throne of God. (See I Corinthians 15:24.) But Satan had overthrown the government of God on the earth. Now God purposed to restore his government over the earth through man, created in the image of God and finally to become part of the God family. We should heed Paul's admonition not to be ignorant of Satan's existence, or of his devices, nor let him get an advantage of us (II Cor. 2:11). Our supremely important purpose will be made clear in following chapters.

Good News

You have heard the saying about "good news and bad news." The latter part of this chapter has given you the bad news. The good news is God's purpose through mankind and the fact that the two thirds of the angels who are holy and righteous outnumber the demons and remain as God's invisible agents to minister to and help in the righteous character development of the myriad of humans who shall yet become the sons and heirs of the Supreme God and members of the great God family.

THE MYSTERY OF MAN

IT SEEMS incredible indeed! Higher education teaches technical courses in human physiology, anatomy, anthropology and psychology. The universities take man apart and study him minutely inch by inch. They study every facet and phase of man. They take the human brain apart and study it, yet the human mind remains a total mystery to even the most advanced psychologists. They do not know WHAT man is or WHY he came to be! That is the great Mystery Number 3 that has never been understood by humanity.

Is he merely the highest animal species, descended by resident forces, with no intelligent planning or designing, by the process of evolution? Why does man have the thinking and reasoning ability and possess all the human fund of knowledge that is impossible for animals to have? Is he an immortal soul? Is he human flesh and blood with an immortal soul within him? Just what IS a human person, after all?

And WHY?

Why is mankind here on the earth? Did we simply *happen*? Or was there DESIGN and PURPOSE?

We say there is a CAUSE for every effect. The effect, here, is man. Man is *here*. How—WHY did he come to be here? Was he *put* here, or did he just *happen* by blind, senseless, unintelligent processes of evolution?

We ought to *want* to know!

This is a mystery that has baffled higher education.

Higher education during the twentieth century has come, with virtual unanimity, to accept the evolutionary theory. It no longer even considers the possibility of a designed and planned creation by a God of supreme mind, perfect intelligence, and limitless power. But the evolutionary theory cannot in any degree explain a paradoxical world of awesome accomplishment that is at the same time utterly helpless to solve its problems of mounting and continually escalating evils. It can give no purpose for human existence. Higher education contemptuously ignores, without any consideration whatsoever, the biblical truths revealing man's presence on the earth and the causes of the present state of civilization. Education in the civilized world today has become entirely materialistic. Education has become a combination of the agnosticism of evolution, the politics and economics of Karl Marx and the morals and social patterns of Sigmund Freud. Higher education remains in utter ignorance of the mystery of mankind and of human civilization.

But higher education does not know. And it doesn't *want* to know! When we invade the questions of WHAT and WHY, the intellectuals—the custodians of KNOWLEDGE—shy away or stand up and fight. Of the questions WHAT and WHY is man, they are willingly ignorant!

So, education shuts its mind, and its mouth in tight silence. Science doesn't know. Religion does not reveal, for it also doesn't know!

Yes, incredible—but TRUE!

God Enters the Picture

WHY this willful ignorance? Because GOD is involved. Satan is hostile against God. Satan sits on the throne of this earth and has blinded the minds of the intellectuals as well as all other levels of society. Consider, for a moment, the most highly trained mind with several letters of advanced degrees following his name. He is highly trained in certain specific areas in which he has extensive, complicated and intricate knowledge. But ask him about some area of knowledge outside his specialized field and he is as much in ignorance as those who are lacking in the more advanced labyrinths of education.

The primary divisions of this world's civilization—government, religion, education and science, technology, industry—all shy away from GOD. They want GOD to keep his nose out of their affairs! The mention of God embarrasses them.

This ignorance cannot be explained except by the invisible and unaware influence of the supernatural evil power of Satan the devil and the unseen demoniacal spirit beings. When we read in Revelation 12:9 that all the world has been deceived by Satan, it does not exclude those of advanced intellect. Jesus Christ thanked God that the real truths are hidden from the wise and prudent and revealed to those who are babes in materialistic knowledge.

In the first chapter of this book we have covered the questions of WHO and WHAT is GOD. And we find God is quite REAL. God is more than one single person—God is a family—God is the supreme divine family—he is the Creator of all that is, and he has an ultimate PURPOSE—the creation of perfect, holy, righteous and spiritual CHARACTER, in MAN made immortal, to become part of that God family.

So the presence of MAN on the earth must have a definite relation to the PURPOSE of GOD the Creator.

With these basically important questions and statements we must ask, *WHY* all the evils in today's sick and chaotic world? This world now faces, with no solution, its number one problem—the question of HUMAN SURVIVAL! Can human life on earth survive even through the short remainder of this twentieth century? Can humanity survive both the population explosion and the nuclear power his mind has produced that can annihilate that entire population?

Consider now what has been covered about God's PURPOSE for the angels that sinned on earth. For that angelic rebellion leads directly to God's PURPOSE for MAN—to our question of WHAT and WHY is MAN?

Earth's Face in Devastation

Instead of improving, beautifying, completing earth's creation, the sinning angels brought it to desolation and ruin.

Come now to Genesis 1:1-2: "In the beginning God created the heavens [RSV] and the earth. And the earth was without form, and void; and darkness was upon the face of the deep. . . ."

The original Hebrew for "without form, and void" is *tohu* and *bohu*—meaning "waste, desolate, deteriorated." The word *was* is also translated "became." Thus possibly after millions of years, all had come to be oceanic surface—and light had been by angelic lawlessness turned into darkness.

Let me here interject a biblical principle within the immediate context. There is this instruction in Isaiah: "Whom shall he teach knowledge? and whom shall he make to understand doctrine? . . . precept must be upon precept, precept upon precept; line upon line, line upon line; here a little, and there a little" (Isa. 28:9-10). But most who try to apply this principle in biblical understanding take each "little" verse out of its context, to "interpret" their own ideas into it.

The Holy Bible is unique among all books ever written. The very fact that its truths are revealed here a little, there a little means it is a coded book, not to be understood until our present time of the end as explained elsewhere in this volume. Those who have tried to read the Bible directly and continuously from the beginning have been bewildered. Many have simply thrown up their hands and said, as I myself did once, "I just can't understand the Bible." That is why Bruce Barton said the Bible is the book nobody knows. As I have explained elsewhere the Bible is like a jigsaw puzzle. Until the various pieces of a jigsaw puzzle are put properly together, the true picture does not emerge.

Much, directly concerned with what is in Genesis 1, is filled in by other passages of Scripture in other parts of the Bible.

So now, let's UNDERSTAND the background. Genesis 1:1: God created the heavens and the earth. We have already seen, in chapter two, that the heavens (or the universe) and the earth were created after the angels. Earth's angels had not completed the creation of the earth by improvement, development and beautification. Rather, they had brought it to desolation and ruin. The GOVERNMENT OF GOD had been nullified on earth.

And now, of all living beings in the universe, ONLY GOD

could be certainly relied upon never to depart from the way of his law. No higher, more perfect being could be created than the cherub, Lucifer, who rebelled. Character cannot be automatically created by fiat. Godly spiritual character is the habitual action and conduct of the person or created entity to come to a knowledge of the true ways of God, and to exercise the will to follow those ways even against opposition, temptation or self-desire to the contrary. Character must be developed with the assent, will and action of the separately created entity. It is imparted by God and must be willingly received by that entity. So God now determined, or had predetermined, to accomplish the SUPREME creative feat—by *reproducing himself!* That was to be accomplished through MAN! God knew this must be brought about through MATTER.

Man in God's Image

To prepare the earth for the creation of man, God renewed the face of the earth. This is explained in Psalm 104:30: "Thou sendest forth thy spirit, they are created: and thou renewest the face of the earth."

Now back to Genesis 1:2: The earth had come to be in a state of ruin. ". . . And the Spirit of God moved upon the face of the waters."

The first thing God did was turn darkness back into LIGHT as originally made. God said, "Let there be light: and there was light" (Gen. 1:3).

So in six days God RENEWED THE FACE OF THE EARTH (this renewing was not its original creation, but restoring it to the condition of its original creation) preparing it for the creation of MAN!

God separated the dry land from the oceans. He created then the plant life on the land, then the sea life in the water, the animal life. In the Hebrew in which Moses wrote, the vertebrates are called *nephesh* in verses 20, 21, 24. The translators correctly rendered *nephesh* in these three verses into the English words "living creatures." Yet in Genesis 2:7, speaking of man, the same word *nephesh* was translated "soul" because the translators falsely thought that only humans are souls. The word *nephesh* literally means "life of animals," referring to physical life and not spirit.

Once again the earth was a perfect, but as yet unfinished, creation—lacking the finishing touches.

As was written earlier, God creates in dual stages. This might be compared to baking a cake. First the basic cake comes from the oven. But it is not complete until the second stage is added—the icing on the cake. This beautifies, enriches and completes the cake.

God placed Lucifer and his angels on the earth. But he intended them to complete the creation by putting on, as it were, the finishing touches to beautify, improve and enrich the earth. But the angels sinned, resulting in bringing chaos, confusion and darkness to this planet.

Now God renewed the face of the earth for MAN, made to become in the character image of God and also in the likeness or form and shape of God. And God intended man to complete the finishing touches by improving and beautifying the earth—putting, as it were, the icing on the cake, to have man's part in the final creation of the earth. Instead, man has ruined, polluted, defiled, deteriorated almost every portion of the earth his hands have touched or acted upon.

The Purpose of Man on Earth

WHY did the Creator God put MAN on the earth? For God's ultimate supreme purpose of reproducing himself—of recreating himself, as it were, by the supreme objective of creating the righteous divine character ultimately in millions unnumbered begotten and born children who shall become God beings, members of the God family.

Man was to *improve* the physical earth as God gave it to him, *finishing* its creation (which sinning angels had deliberately refused to do) and, in so doing, to RESTORE the GOVERNMENT OF GOD, with God's WAY of life; and further, in this very process FINISHING THE CREATION OF *MAN* by the development of God's holy, righteous CHARACTER, with man's own assent.

Once this perfect and righteous character is instilled in man, and man converted from mortal flesh to immortal spirit, then is to come the INCREDIBLE HUMAN POTENTIAL—man being BORN INTO the divine FAMILY of God, restoring the government of God to the earth, and then participating in the completion of the CREATION over the entire endless expanse of the UNIVERSE! That incredible potential of man will be fully explained in the pages that follow in this volume. God shall have reproduced HIMSELF untold millions of times over!

So, on the sixth day of that re-creation week, God *(Elohim)* said, "Let us make man in our image, after our likeness" (Gen. 1:26).

Man was made to have (with his assent) a special relationship with his Maker! He was made in the form and shape of God. He was given a spirit (essence in form) to make the relationship possible. Much more of that a little later.

The Soul Is Mortal

But God made MAN of MATTER! This was necessary for the supreme accomplishment God willed.

"And the Lord God formed man of the dust of the ground, and breathed into his nostrils the breath [air] of life; and man became a living soul" (Gen. 2:7). Man, formed from material dust of the ground, upon breathing air, BECAME a living soul. It does not say man is, or has, an *immortal* soul. What was formed from material ground BECAME a soul.

The word "soul" is translated from the Hebrew in which Moses wrote, from the word *nephesh*. The Hebrew *nephesh* merely means a breathing animal. Three times in the first chapter of Genesis animals are called *nephesh*: Gen. 1:20, "moving creature" (Hebrew, *nephesh*); Gen. 1:21, "great whales, and every living creature" (Hebrew, *nephesh*); Gen. 1:24, "living creature" (Hebrew, *nephesh*). The translators in translating into the English language used the English word "*creature*," but in Genesis 2:7 they translated the same *nephesh* into the English word "soul"—man became a "living soul" (*nephesh*).

Therefore the SOUL is physical, composed of matter, and can die. This is a TRUTH believed by very few denominations, and probably by no other religions—another PROOF that identifies the one true Church of God!

How Human Mind Functions

Now we come to another truth, so far as I know, exclusive to the one true Church.

Did you ever wonder about the vast difference between human mind and animal brain? This, incidentally, is another PROOF of the falsity of the theory of evolution!

The physical brain of the higher vertebrates in the animal kingdom is essentially the same in physical form, design, constituency, as human brain. The brains of whales, elephants, dolphins are larger—and chimp almost as large. Yet the output of the human brain is indescribably greater. Few indeed know WHY!

Many passages of Scripture show that there is a spirit *in* man. Spirit is *not* matter, and man is matter. To distinguish it from God's Holy Spirit, I designate it as the "human" spirit. Nevertheless, it is spirit and not matter.

This "human" spirit imparts the power of intellect to the human physical brain. The spirit cannot see, hear, taste, smell or feel. The *brain* sees through the eye, hears through the ear, etc. The "human" spirit cannot of itself think. The physical brain thinks.

What, then, is the function of this "human" spirit? It is NOT a "soul." But, 1) it imparts the power of intellect—of thinking, and of MIND power, to the human brain; and 2) it is the very means God has instilled, making possible a personal relationship between human MAN and divine GOD.

What Is the Real Value of a Human Life?

Philosophers, humanists, speak loftily of human worth as of supreme value in itself. They speak of the "god" within you—of tapping the innate hidden resources within yourself. They teach SELF-reliance, self-glorification.

They are smugly ignorant and unaware of the TRUE VALUES and the incredible but real human potential.

Human life is at once of infinitesimally less value than they suppose, and at the same time of supremely greater potential than they know.

Real truth is revealed. Unless revealed it remains a mystery, utterly unknown to the deceived and vain intellectuals. I repeat, Jesus said in prayer: "I thank thee, O Father, Lord of heaven and earth, because thou hast hid these things from the wise and prudent, and revealed them unto babes" (Matt. 11:25).

What is the real truth concerning human worth? What is the real value of a human life? It is grossly overestimated in its own reality, and astoundingly undervalued in its supreme potential. The truth indeed is staggering.

You look upon a sweet, innocent babe a few hours old, or upon a life-fulfilled elderly person of 80 and ask yourself, "Just how valuable is that life?—one just beginning, the other already spent." Could you supply the correct answer?

Let's UNDERSTAND! Right here is the point of difficulty. Right here is the jumping off point where the world's educated jump the track. Science and advanced education today almost universally assume nothing exists but matter. They deny the existence of spirit. Which is to say, whether admitted or not, they deny the existence of God.

We come to the modern science of brain research. We learn that the human brain exercises many functions impossible in animal brain, yet we learn there is virtually no significant difference, physically. The animal cannot think, reason, study, make decisions apart from instinct. It cannot know what the human knows. It does not have attitudes of judgment, wisdom, love, kindness, cooperation, nor is it aware of competition, conspiracy, envy, jealousy, resentment. It has no appreciation of music, art and literature. It has no spiritual qualities or characteristics.

Yet science and higher education insist the faculty of intellect in humans is solely physical.

I had to PROVE to myself rationally that God exists and is in fact more REAL than matter. I had to PROVE that the Holy Bible is in fact the authoritative word of God, by which he communicates to man, reveals truth otherwise inaccessible to man. And I found revealed PURPOSE, DESIGN, MEANING that is hidden from the self-professed scholarly. I found revealed the reason for mounting evils in a progressive world.

Can the human, who has been designed, created and made, say to his Maker, "WHY did you make me thus?—and for what PURPOSE?" And can he instruct his Maker? Should he not, rather, open his mind, and listen when his Maker reveals to him the very reason for his being?

The Creator reveals and instructs in a highly coded book,

the Holy Bible. Its profound message is opened to human understanding through the presence and in-dwelling of the Holy Spirit injected into the human mind that has surrendered and yielded completely to the revelation in belief and obedience. To such a one the TRUTH is made plain—wonderful beyond description.

But mark well this question! Think on this! If man had only the physical brain, like the dumb vertebrates, how could the great Spirit God inject into the animal brain these marvelous spiritual truths? The answer is plain. God does not. The dumb animals have no awareness of God or of spiritual knowledge.

But the human spirit in mortal man makes possible a direct contact from the great Spirit God. There is no direct channel of communication between the dumb animal brain and the mind of the Supreme God.

Meditate on this. We humans sometimes speak of how wonderfully God made man, with his brain and the marvelous physical components of his body all functioning together. But without this spirit, imparting the power of intellect to the brain and also opening a channel of direct communication with the mind of the Great God, man would be no more than the dumb brutes. But with the spirit in man, man's creation becomes all the more awesome to contemplate. It is this human spirit in man that makes it possible for man to be united with God, so that man may be begotten of God by God's Spirit uniting with the human spirit, thus impregnating the human person as a child of the Supreme Creator God.

The real value of a human life, then, lies solely within the human spirit combined with the human brain. It should be stated at once that this human spirit is not perceived by the most highly educated psychologists, yet it is the very essence of the human MIND.

The Soul Can Die

The Creator's book reveals, contrary to fallible humanist teaching, that man was made from the dust of the ground, and this dust thus becomes soul, mortal—like all vertebrates. Man has continued to accept the first lie in human history—

Satan's lie to mother Eve that man is immortal and cannot die.

The soul is merely the breathing animal. All animals are biblically called "souls"—in Hebrew, *nephesh*. Therefore, if man is a soul as in Genesis 2:7, so also are the dumb animals. But there is a human spirit *in* the human soul.

This human spirit does not impart human life. Human life, like that of all vertebrates, comes from blood circulation, oxidized by the breath of air. But God reveals there is a spirit within every human. This spirit is not present in animals. The human spirit empowers the human brain with intellect—with ability to acquire knowledge, to think, reason, make decisions, produce attitudes of good or evil.

Human and animal brain are alike. Human mind superiority comes not from superior brain, but from the presence of human spirit within the human brain. Animal brain is supplied with instinct, not intellect.

It may seem shockingly strange, because it is a dimension in knowledge hitherto untaught, but the real value of a human life lies solely in the human spirit, as it works in combination with the human brain.

God formed man of matter, but after his own image and likeness as to form and shape.

But the brute animal and man have the same breath, the same source of life. They die the same death. Human life *is* animal existence, but in the form and shape of God, and with the human spirit added to the brain.

Man's Creation Not Yet Completed

Man was created to have a relationship with his Maker. Therefore he was made in his Maker's form and shape, with contact and relationship made possible by the presence within him of the human spirit.

But man's creation was not completed. He was made mentally and spiritually only "half there." He needed the addition of God's Spirit to unite with his spirit, begetting him as a child of God—uniting him with God—ultimately enabling him to be born into the very GOD FAMILY.

Pause here a moment. Notice once again the duality in God's creative process. The first man Adam was a physical creation with the human spirit added. When man's creation is finally complete, he will be a spiritual creation, formed wholly of Spirit.

When man receives the Holy Spirit of God the very Spirit and mind of the immortal God is injected into him. It joins with his human spirit. The Spirit of God cannot be received by, or injected into, the brute animal because the animal has no spirit within itself with which the Spirit of God could combine.

At this point, let me inject a truth that, at the time this is being written, is probably the most controversial question at issue among the Western world's population—the question of abortion.

The human spirit enters the human embryo at conception. It is this spirit that may, upon adult conversion, be united with the Holy Spirit from the great Creator God, impregnating that human with God-life as a child of the living God, in a state of gestation, though as yet unborn. To destroy an embryo or a fetus in a mother's uterus is to MURDER a potential future God Being.

Therefore, abortion is murder.

Now back to our original question: "What is the only real value of a human life?"

Human life is animal existence but with human spirit empowering the brain with intellect. The human spirit in man makes possible the union with the Holy Spirit and mind and immortality of God. When mortal man dies, the body reverts to dust, and the spirit returns to God.

Life After Death

The departed human spirit at death is in fact a spiritual mold, of itself unconscious, yet in the resurrection bringing into the resurrected body all the memory, knowledge and character as well as form and shape of the person before death. The human spirit of itself cannot see, hear, think or know. The only real LIFE, inherent and self-containing, lies in the Holy Spirit of God, united with the human spirit. The value of a human life lies in the human spirit and its potential of being united with God's Spirit—which is God-mind and God-life.

Philosophers think of human worth as of supreme value in itself alone. They speak of "human dignity." They speak of the innate "god" powers within each human. They advocate SELF-confidence, self-glorification. They make mortal man to think of himself as immortal God.

Much to the contrary, the sole value of human life lies in the human spirit and the potential of being begotten of God, later to be born VERY GOD, a child in the GOD FAMILY.

Man is not "god" within himself, but only mortal flesh and blood with a brain empowered with intellect by the human spirit.

Therefore, man of himself is infinitesimally of less value than the self-professed wise of this world suppose. But, once begotten by the Supreme God through the very LIFE and Spirit of the living God dwelling in him, a human being's potential is of infinitely greater value than the world has understood.

God creates, as previously explained, by the principle of DUALITY. So it is with the creation of MAN. It is accomplished in TWO STAGES: 1) the physical phase, which began with the first man, Adam; and 2) the spiritual state, which begins with the "second Adam" Jesus Christ (I Cor. 15:45-46).

So also, man was made from his creation (and birth) with the one "human" spirit that became an integral part of man. But he is mentally and spiritually INCOMPLETE; he was made to need *another* Spirit—the HOLY SPIRIT of God—and when that gift of God is received, God's "Spirit itself beareth witness with our spirit, that we are the children of God" (Rom. 8:16)—in the begotten (or first stage) of man's *spiritual* creation.

This is clearly explained in I Corinthians 2. ". . . Eye hath not seen, nor ear heard, neither have entered into the heart [mind] of man, the things which God hath prepared for them that love him" (verse 9)—spiritual knowledge.

The natural mind can receive knowledge of material and physical things. Also it can have a sense of morality, ethics, art, culture not possessed by the dumb animals. But in the realm of good and evil it can know and perform what is good only on the human level, made possible by the human spirit within man. But this sense and performance of good is limited to the human level of the human spirit that is innately selfish. It can possess and express love on the human level, but without the Holy Spirit of God it cannot possess or express love on the God level, nor can it acquire knowledge of that which is spiritual, as revealed in I Corinthians 2.

Only God Reveals

"But God hath revealed them [spiritual things] unto us by his Spirit . . ." (verse 10). Notice particularly spiritual knowledge is not revealed by a Person called the Holy Spirit. It is revealed by God, and to us today through God's Spirit, which may be received only as God's gift through his mercy and grace. God is the revealer. The Holy Spirit is the instrumentality by which we may comprehend that which only God can reveal.

"For what man knoweth the things of a man, save the spirit of man which is in him? . . ." (verse 11). If the Holy Spirit is the third Person of a Trinity, then is not the spirit in man also another man? A cow, sheep or dog cannot know the things a MAN knows—and neither could a man, except by the spirit of man that is *in* him. For example, such knowledge as chemistry, physics and technological and scientific knowledge. Likewise, the natural man with this one spirit is *limited*—"even so the things of God knoweth no man, but the Spirit of God."

ONLY when the Holy Spirit enters, combining with the "human" spirit, can a man come to really comprehend that which is spiritual—"But the natural man receiveth not the things of the Spirit of God: for they are foolishness unto him: neither can he know them, because they are spiritually discerned" (verse 14).

The most highly educated view all things through the eyeglasses of evolutionary theory. Evolution is concerned solely with material life and development. It knows and teaches nothing about spiritual life and problems, and all the evils in the world are spiritual in nature.

That is WHY the most highly educated are, overall, the most ignorant—they are confined to knowledge of the material, and to "good" on the self-centered level. Knowledge of God and the things of God are foolishness to them. But, of course, God says, "The wisdom of this world is foolishness with God" (I Cor. 3:19).

World Cut Off from God

Now back to the first human, Adam.

Remember God's PURPOSE in creating man on the earth: 1) to restore the GOVERNMENT OF GOD on earth, and by regulating human life through that GOVERNMENT, a) complete the physical creation of earth where angels turned it to ruin, and b) in the process complete the creation of MAN by developing righteous spiritual CHARACTER; and 2) to establish the KINGDOM OF GOD, and eventually the incredible human potential of finishing the creation of the vast UNIVERSE!

This supreme PURPOSE required: 1) that MAN reject Satan's WAY, embracing GOD'S WAY of LOVE, based on God's spiritual law; and 2) that man be made first of matter so that, if he was led into Satan's way of "GET," he could be CHANGED, converted to GOD'S WAY of LOVE, or if he refused to change, his life would be blotted out without further or continuous suffering just as if he had never been.

Spirit beings, once a finished creation (as were the one third of the angels who became evil characters), *could not be changed!* Spirit, once its creation is completed, is constant and eternal—not subject to change. But physical matter is constantly *changing.*

Through God's master plan for his spiritual creation, to be covered later, it had been master-planned by God and the Word that the Word would divest himself of his supreme glory, and in due time take on him the likeness of human flesh, as Jesus Christ, making possible the spiritual phase of the creation of MAN—God REPRODUCING HIMSELF! What a MASTER PLAN for the extreme ULTIMATE in creative accomplishment! How GREAT is our God, in mind, purpose, planning, designing, as well as CREATING—from the tiniest germ or insect to the most huge sun, dwarfing our own great sun to insignificance!

And the incredible human potential is that the GREAT MAJESTIC GOD is, in MAN, reproducing himself—man can be born into the GOD FAMILY!

The first human, Adam, was created with the potential of

qualifying to replace Satan, the former Lucifer, on earth's throne, restoring the GOVERNMENT OF GOD.

But it was necessary that he resist, and reject Satan's "GET" way, which was the foundation of Satan's evil government, and choose GOD'S WAY of his law—the way of LOVE (GIVE), the basis of God's government!

His Maker talked first to Adam and Eve—instructed them in the GOVERNMENT and spiritual LAW of God—though in Genesis 2 only the most condensed summary of God's instruction to them is revealed. Satan was restrained from any contact with them until God first had taught them.

The Two Symbolic Trees

In the gloriously beautiful garden of Eden in which God placed them were two very special symbolic trees. Little has been heard about these trees and their tremendous significance, except what most people have heard about "Adam's apple." The forbidden tree, however, probably was not an apple tree.

The real significance of these two symbolic trees explains the very foundation of the world. In them is the answer to the great mystery of our time in this modern twentieth century. Today we live in a world of awesome progress and advancement, yet paradoxically of appalling evils. The baffling question today is, Why cannot the minds that can learn to fly to the moon and back, transplant hearts, produce computers and technological marvels, solve their own problems? Why no peace in the world?

We cannot understand the mystery of today's events and conditions unless we go back to the very foundation of the world, and learn what developed from its origin to the pulsating, confused present.

The world began at the time of these two special trees. We hear virtually nothing in the biblical misteaching of today about the tree of life, and almost nothing about the forbidden tree.

But now consider. God had created a man out of the dust of the ground. But God creates in dual stages. The man was not yet physically complete. God wanted him to "multiply and replenish the earth." But the man could not do that because he was not yet physically complete. So God put him into a deep sleep (anesthesia) and performed an operation, removing a rib and forming a woman from it. They became one family. The physical creation of man was completed. They could reproduce their kind.

But the man God created was mortal. He had only a temporary physicochemical existence kept alive by circulation of blood, oxidized by the breath of air, and fueled by food and water from the ground. He did not have LIFE inherent—self-containing life. But he did have a human spirit that, united with God's Holy Spirit, could beget him with eternal life.

Immortal Life Offered

But God offered to him immortal LIFE through this symbolic tree of LIFE. God did not urge or compel him to take it—he merely made it freely accessible. Adam could eat of all the trees of the garden except the one forbidden tree, of "the knowledge of good and evil."

What if Adam had taken of the tree of LIFE? You probably never heard that question answered. That symbolic tree is offered today to those called and drawn by God to Jesus Christ. There is one difference between the original Adam and the called Christian. Adam had not yet sinned and no repentance was necessary if he had chosen the tree of life. Otherwise the repentant and believing Spirit-begotten Christian is in the same position Adam would have been had he taken of the tree of life.

Adam would have received the Holy Spirit of the immortal God to join with his human spirit. Of course, since Adam was required to make a choice, he would have rejected the way of Satan by taking the tree of life.

But again, what would have happened, had Adam taken the tree of life?

He would have received the Holy Spirit of God to unite with his human spirit. The man was not mentally or spiritually complete until receiving the Spirit of God. This would have united him, mentally and spiritually, with God. He would have been begotten as a child of God, just as is the converted Spirit-begotten Christian.

He would have received the Holy Spirit of God to join with his human spirit, begetting him as a son of God, imparting to him the earnest of immortal life, and making him at one with God.

As in the case of the Spirit-begotten Christian today, where "Christ in [us is] the hope of glory" (Col. 1:27). And again, the mind of Christ is in us (Phil. 2:5), so the very mind of the Eternal would have been in Adam. But instead the mind and attitude of Satan entered into him and worked in him, even as it has in all his children that have composed this whole world. We read in Ephesians 2:2, that Satan, as prince of the power of the air, does indeed actually work within humans.

At this juncture, we explain a point that might be misunderstood. In the temptation by Satan, Eve was deceived, but Adam was not (I Tim. 2:13-14). Adam disobeyed God and sinned deliberately. But even though he was not deceived in this original temptation, his deliberate disobedience of God's explicit command cut him off from God, producing a state of mental perversion and opening his mind to the deceptions of Satan. From that moment, Adam and all his children after him were receptive to the sway of Satan. Satan began to work in the mind of Adam, even as God would have worked in his mind had he taken of the tree of life.

A World Held Captive

Thus, from that moment, Satan had spiritually kidnapped Adam, and all his human family has ever since been held captive by Satan.

God would have revealed to Adam God's way of life—which is God's spiritual law. That law is the way of outflowing love—but it would have been "the love of God . . . shed abroad in [human] hearts by the Holy [Spirit]" (Rom. 5:5). Human natural carnal love cannot fulfill God's holy law.

But, even as a human embryo has been begotten by human parents, and just as the embryo must develop through the process of gestation before being born, so is the Spirit-led Christian, and so would have been Adam.

But he would have experienced a direct connection and contact with God.

I like to compare this to the umbilical cord connecting the newborn baby with its mother. Its human life and physical nourishment has been supplied during gestation from the mother to the child. God's spirit LIFE is imparted to the Christian through the Holy Spirit. Also, spiritual knowledge is imparted by God but through the indwelling of the Holy Spirit (I Cor. 2:10). Full comprehension of God's LAW (his way of life) is imparted by God through the Holy Spirit. But the law of God requires action and performance, and LOVE is the fulfilling of God's law (Rom. 13:10), and it can be fulfilled only by the love of and from God (Rom. 5:5).

So Adam would have had the in-depth spiritual knowledge to live God's way, and also would have been supplied with the divine love that, only, can fulfill that perfect law of love and put it into action.

He would also have received by the Spirit of God the very FAITH of God. He would have received knowledge, guidance and help from God. He would have had reliance on God to intervene in matters beyond his control. In such matters God supernaturally does for us what we are unable to do for ourselves. In other words, God fights our battles for us.

Rejecting God's Law and Government

But instead Adam chose a different kind of knowledge— he took TO HIMSELF the knowledge of good as well as evil. He relied wholly on himself—both for the KNOWLEDGE as well as power of performance of good as well as evil. He REJECTED reliance on God and chose the course of SELF-reliance. The only righteousness he could acquire was SELF-righteousness, which to God is like filthy rags.

Adam and Eve took of the tree of "the knowledge of good and evil." Taking of its fruit was taking *to themselves* the knowledge of what is good, and what is evil—deciding for themselves what is right and what is sin. This, of course, meant rejection of GOD'S LAW, which defined *for them* the right and the wrong.

The glorious archangel Lucifer, as God originally created him, was the pinnacle of God's creative power in a single being. Few today remotely realize the great power, now turned to cunning deception, possessed by Satan. Apparently Adam completely underestimated him.

The wily Satan got to Adam through his wife Eve. He did not say, "CHOOSE MY WAY!" He appeared as a subtle serpent. He cleverly deceived her.

He put DOUBTS in her mind about God's veracity. He put a sense of injustice and resentment within her. He deceived her into believing God had been unfair—selfish. He subtilely injected vanity of mind. He misled her into thinking it was *right* to take of the forbidden fruit.

Adam, not deceived, nevertheless went along with his wife. With her, he took to himself the determination of what is right and what is wrong—thus DISBELIEVING what his Maker had said, REJECTING God as Savior and Ruler—rejecting God as the source of revealed BASIC KNOWLEDGE. He believed and followed Satan's WAY!

Adam's World Sentenced

When God "drove out the man" from the Garden of Eden, and barred reentrance—*lest* he go back and receive eternal life *in sin* (Gen. 3:22-24)—God PRONOUNCED SENTENCE!

God said, in effect: "YOU have made the decision for yourself and the world that shall spring from you. You have rejected me as the basic source of knowledge—you have rejected power from me through my Spirit to live the righteous way—you have rebelled against my command and my government—you have chosen the 'GETTING,' 'TAKING' way of Satan. Therefore I sentence you and the world you shall beget to 6,000 years of being *cut off* from access to me and my Spirit—except for the exceedingly FEW I shall specially call. And that FEW shall be called for special service preparatory for the kingdom of God. They shall be required to do what you have failed to do—reject, resist and overcome Satan and his WAYS, and follow the ways of my spiritual LAW.

"Go, therefore, Adam, and all your progeny that shall form the world, produce your own fund of knowledge. Decide for yourself what is good and what is evil. Produce your own educational systems and means of disseminating knowledge, as your god Satan shall mislead you. Form your own concepts of what is god, your own religions, your own governments, your own life-styles and forms of society and civilization. In all this Satan will deceive your world with his attitude of SELF-centeredness—with vanity, lust and greed, jealousy and envy, competition and strife and violence and wars, rebellion against me and my law of LOVE.

"After the world of your descendants has written the lesson in 6,000 years of human suffering, anguish, frustration, defeat and death—after the world that shall spring from you shall have been brought to confess the utter hopelessness of the way of life you have chosen—I will supernaturally intervene. By supernatural divine power I shall then take over the government of the whole world. With reeducation, I will produce a happy world of PEACE. And on repentance, I shall then offer eternal salvation to all. After a thousand years of that happy world to come, I will resurrect from death to mortal life all who have died uncalled during this present 6,000 years. Their judgment shall then come. And on repentance and faith, eternal life shall be offered them.

"During this 6,000 years, when I myself shall cut them off from me, they shall not be eternally judged. Only, as they sow during their lifetimes, they shall reap. But *when* I open eternal salvation to them, there shall be no Satan to hinder or deceive them—no Satan for them to overcome. Those few called during this first 6,000 years shall have to reject and resist Satan's pulls and overcome. But those who overcome shall sit with me in my throne, and have power under me to rule all nations under my Supreme Rule."

Origin of Self-Reliance

What does all this mean?

Adam the first human rejected knowledge from and reliance on God. He chose to rely on his own knowledge and abilities.

The modern world, developed from Adam, relies wholly on human self-reliance. The psychology taught in our day is self-reliance. Rely on the innate powers within you, they teach. An atmosphere of self-reliant professionalism pervades most modern university campuses. It is the spirit of vanity.

The university student is induced to think of himself as becoming a professional—that is, he considers himself elevated above those who have not had his brand of education. Through the basic concept of the evolutionary theory, he feels himself completely above those who believe in God and the Lord Jesus Christ. He regards them with disdain.

Salvation Closed Off

Upon Adam's making this fateful and fatal decision, God CLOSED OFF THE TREE OF LIFE (Gen. 3:22-24) from the world sired by Adam, for 6,000 years. That is, except in the case of chosen prophets for the writing of the Bible, and of the Church called out of this world by Jesus Christ. But even Jesus said plainly: "No man can come to me, except the Father which hath sent me draw him" (John 6:44).

God thereupon, at the very foundation of this world, laid out a 7,000-year master plan for accomplishing his purpose.

It was Satan who deceived Eve. Adam then sinned deliberately in partaking of the forbidden fruit. The whole world since has been deceived (Rev. 12:9).

Let us pause here momentarily. Let us realize this was the very foundation of the world in which we still live. At this point, Satan must have gloated. He must have believed God was defeated—that God through Adam had failed to overthrow Satan's rule on the throne of the earth.

But God says, "My purpose shall stand."

God's 7,000-year plan will accomplish God's purpose in overwhelming and magnificent glory.

Understand this point, which has been a mystery to the world. When God closed off the tree of life, he closed off the redemption and salvation of mankind for 6,000 years, until the second Adam, Jesus Christ, after 6,000 years should return to earth in supreme power and glory to unseat Satan from his throne and to rule all nations of mankind.

The first man Adam had been given the opportunity to choose God's government, to restore that government to the earth, and to unseat Satan from the throne of the earth. Since he failed, salvation cannot be opened to humanity generally, until Jesus Christ, the second Adam, has accomplished what the first Adam failed to do—namely, to unseat Satan and to sit on the throne of the earth, restoring the government of God to this earth.

The closing of the tree of life from the human family marked the foundation of the present world still ruled invisibly by Satan. How, then, was God going to accomplish his purpose? At that very foundation of this world it was determined by God that the Word would be born on earth as the sacrificial lamb of God to redeem mankind from the rule of Satan the kidnapper (Rev. 13:8).

But how, then, was God ever to accomplish his purpose of reproducing himself through the humans to be born during that next 6,000 years?

Salvation Through Resurrection

At that very foundation of Satan's world it was also decreed (Heb. 9:27) that God had appointed that all humans should die once, and after that, by resurrection from the dead, would come the judgment. Meanwhile mankind as a whole would not as yet be brought to judgment—neither condemned nor saved. It was at that time decided that as in Adam all humans should die, so in Christ the same "all" should be brought back to life by a resurrection to judgment (I Cor. 15:22). This very resurrection of all who died in Adam has been a mystery to the whole world deceived by Satan. Even today traditional Christianity celebrates the resurrection of Jesus on the pagan Easter every spring, but says nothing about the future resurrection of the billions who have died in Adam. That resurrection will be explained later in this volume.

Meanwhile, when Christ should come as humanity's sinbearer, he would found the Church of God. The purpose and function of the Church will be fully covered in chapter six of this book.

Pause right here! Understand what Satan has blinded the entire world from seeing. Realize what a deceived traditional Christianity has not understood.

This is of supreme importance!

The world of traditional Christianity has been deceived into supposed Christian teaching of the immortality of the soul, of those who "profess Jesus" going immediately upon death into a heaven of eternal idleness, freedom from responsibility and bliss in ease and laziness; in those who fail to "accept Jesus" going at death to a definite place of eternal continuous burning fire called hell where they shriek and scream in indescribable pain and agony forever and ever without hope.

The teaching has been that man is an immortal soul and already has eternal life. It denies (Rom. 6:23) that the penalty for sin is death and that man can have eternal life only as the gift of God. The false traditional Christianity teaching might be compared to taking a one-way railroad trip. This trip is your life's journey. At the end of the line a switch is automatically set that will send you straight to a lasting burning hell of indescribable pain and torture. But if, at any time during life's journey, you profess to "accept Christ," the switch at the end of the line, at that point, is turned to shoot you straight to heaven.

Much supposed "Christian" teaching has been that God created the first man a perfect immortal being, but that when God was not looking Satan stole in and wrecked this wonderful handiwork of God. Salvation is then pictured as God's effort to repair the damage, and to restore mankind back to a condition as good as when God first created him.

In doctrine after doctrine they have believed and taught the diametric opposite of the truths plainly revealed in the Bible.

Satan's First Lie

They have taught Satan's first lie that man is an immortal soul. This teaching, when one stops to give it thought, is that "saved mothers" who have died and gone to heaven are continually conscious of their lost sons who are shrieking and screaming in indescribable torture of hell fire.

But what is the real truth of God's holy Word? Do the dead know what the living are doing? My wife told me shortly after our marriage that after her mother died, when she was only 12 years of age, she thought her mother in heaven was seeing everything that she did.

I quote now from an article in *The Plain Truth* March 1985: "Scripture plainly reveals that when you die you are dead. According to the Bible, the dead don't hear anything, see anything, think anything or know anything. The dead have absolutely no awareness of any kind: 'For the living know that they shall die: but the dead know not any thing, neither have they any more a reward; for the memory of them is forgotten. Also their love, and their hatred, and their envy, is now perished ...' " (Eccl. 9:5-6).

The Bible's message is clear on this point. Death is death beyond any shadow of doubt. The apostle Paul wrote that "the wages of sin is death" (Rom. 6:23). Death, by definition, is the absence of life—not just separation from God.

Scripture even warns us to make the most of life now while we have the opportunity: "Whatever your hand finds to do, do it with your might; for there is no work or device or knowledge or wisdom in the grave where you are going" (Eccl. 9:10, Revised Authorized Version).

It couldn't be more plain. But what about those who want to cling to the cherished belief in floating off to heaven after death if good, or sinking to hell if bad?

Listen to the apostle Peter's response. If anyone deserved to go to heaven, it would certainly be someone after God's own heart, wouldn't it? David was such a person (Acts 13:22). But Peter was inspired by God to say, David is "both dead and buried, and his tomb is with us to this day" (Acts 2:29, RAV), and further, "David did not ascend into the heavens" (Acts 2:34).

Jesus himself also said that "no man hath ascended up to heaven," where God's throne is (John 3:13).

Will We Each Live Again?

But there is more to this life than living for the present life. The Great God put humans here on this earth for a marvelous, eternal purpose, not even understood by this world's humanly devised religions.

We are on this earth for a wonderful reason. It involves the answer to why we humans were made mortal and suffer through the gamut of emotions and troubles, or experience the good times of human life.

Even though when we die we are dead, we will not remain dead forever. The dead in their graves will live again! Read what Jesus says: "Do not marvel at this; for the hour is coming in which all who are in the graves will hear His voice and come forth—those who have done good, to the resurrection of life, and those who have done evil, to the resurrection of [judgment]" (John 5:28-29, RAV).

There is an accounting for our behavior in this life! Every human being who has ever lived will ultimately give an accounting and be in a resurrection.

I have explained earlier that the spirit in man of itself does not see, cannot hear, cannot think. The brain sees through the eye, hears through the ear, and thinks as it is empowered by the spirit. At death, "Then shall the dust return to the earth as it was: and the spirit shall return unto God who gave it" (Eccl. 12:7).

The spirit is the depository of memory and character. The spirit is like a mold. It retains even the human form and shape of the deceased, so that in the resurrection to judgment those who have died shall look as they did in life, retain whatever character they established in life, remember everything that was stored in their memory. But in the meantime, in death, there is no consciousness—they "know not any thing" (Eccl. 9:5).

The most universal false teaching, believed by virtually all churches called Christianity, except the one and only true and original Church of God, is that ALL are automatically *"lost" unless they profess* Jesus Christ as Savior—and that now is the *only* day of "salvation." But the truth is that those cut off from God are NOT YET JUDGED!

Few UNDERSTAND this basic master plan of God. The reader cannot possibly be more surprised at the truth revealed in this volume than was the author, more than 58 years ago. The WHOLE WORLD has been deceived, as God's Word foretold! One deceived is not aware of the deception! Don't underestimate Satan!

Humans, Cut Off from God?

One, reviewing the multiplied evils in the world today, might think MAN has cut himself off from God. But it is GOD who cut off mankind from him. And WHY?

Does that seem to make God appear unfair? Quite the opposite!

Let us make that point clear. Adam, by choosing to take

of the forbidden tree, cut off himself and his family after him from God. Yet because all humans born from Adam have sinned, each human has in fact cut himself off from God (Isa. 59:1-2).

The Person in the God family who spoke with Adam was the *Logos* or "Word" who was later born as Jesus Christ. Adam had no contact with God the Father. When the WORD closed the tree of life, all mankind was cut off from God the Father until Christ would come to earth in supreme power and glory to take from Satan the throne of the earth and to restore the government of God over the entire earth. Meanwhile Christ, the second Adam, came at his first appearing to *reveal* the existence of God the Father (Luke 10:22). Until that time, the world had no knowledge of the existence of God the Father. That is one reason the religion of Judaism had believed that God consists of ONE PERSON ONLY. That is the reason theologians have lost, or rather never possessed, knowledge of the fact GOD is a FAMILY into which we may be born as part of that very God family. That, also, explains why, on reading in the New Testament of God the Father, and also of Jesus being God, they came up with the false theory of the Holy Spirit being a "Ghost," or third Person of a Trinity, thus blaspheming the Holy Spirit and LIMITING God and doing away with all knowledge that converted humans can become members of the very divine God FAMILY. Thus Satan blinded "Christianity" from the truth and purpose of the gospel of Jesus Christ.

They have overlooked a most important truth: the resurrection from the dead.

They celebrate a pagan Easter acknowledging the resurrection of Jesus Christ from the dead. But they overlook entirely the plain biblical teaching that all who ever lived are to be resurrected from the dead, although in the time order of three distinctly different resurrections. The only hope the Holy Bible gives for the vast humanity of this dying world is the hope of a resurrection from the dead, but that is a positively sure hope. All this will be completely covered and the full scriptures given in the chapters to follow.

What a tragedy that, as plainly stated in Revelation 12:9, this whole world has been deceived and blinded from the truth by Satan the devil, still sitting on the throne of the entire earth.

The real truth is startling, but you will find it plainly revealed in your own Bible. Follow it as you carefully read this book.

Consider! When God drove Adam and Eve out from the Garden of Eden, He set angels to bar mankind from reentering. Suppose the Eternal had left the gate into Eden open. Man had already taken of the forbidden tree. Man had already turned to sin. What would have happened? Probably the whole of sinning mankind would have surged back in to take of that tree of LIFE! Without any repentance—without even FAITH in God or in Christ—mankind would have helped himself to RECEIVING ETERNAL LIFE.

THINK a moment!

God Not Unfair

How UNfair would God have been, had he allowed that! Man, with all his sins—and sin has a habit of increasing in the one who indulges in it—would have become immortal —living *forever* while *suffering* the pains, mental, physical and spiritual, that sin would bring on him!

Man does not seem to realize that he now is the SLAVE of sin. Sin has cut him off from God the Father. Few understand that we are not saved by the death of Christ. We are reconciled to God the Father by Jesus' death. We are saved by his life (Rom. 5:10). Man does not realize that only a real repentance—turning *from* sin—and the living FAITH of Jesus Christ can FREE him from that penalty! Sin enslaves! It punishes! It brings sorrow, remorse, anguish. It inflicts physical injury, sickness and disease. It produces frustration and hopelessness.

The most UNfair, UNkind, cruel thing God could have done once Adam and Eve had taken the forbidden tree would have been to leave the way open into the garden, with free access to all comers to the tree of LIFE—symbolic of the gift of ETERNAL LIFE!

But what *did* God do? He drove out the man and the woman. He barred reentrance.

He, however, made salvation and eternal life in extreme

happiness and bliss become available to ALL the human family. But, with godly wisdom, he set a time-order and conditions! For the first 6,000 years—now almost completed—all but the predestined FEW were cut off.

On this point the entire world of traditional Christianity has been deceived. Here is a most important truth: Satan sitting on earth's throne tried to kill the Christ child. He then tried to tempt and disqualify Jesus just before the Christ started his earthly ministry (Matt. 4). Satan caused the martyrdom of most of the apostles. He caused intensive persecution against the Church. He caused a violent controversy to flare up in the early months and years of the Church disputing whether the gospel to be proclaimed was the gospel *OF* Christ, or man's gospel ABOUT Christ. Satan caused the latter to win out, and in less than 20 years a false and counterfeit gospel ABOUT Christ was being proclaimed by all but the persecuted FEW who loyally remained as the small and persecuted true original Church of God.

Is Now the Only Day of Salvation?

These deceived "Christians" taught, and still teach, that now is the ONLY day of salvation, and that their counterfeit salvation of just "accepting" Jesus Christ, without the repentance of turning from sin and the obeying of God's law, would send people as "immortal souls" immediately to heaven upon death.

Satan has blinded the minds of those of "traditional Christianity" to the fact that God closed off the tree of life until the glorified Jesus Christ comes in supreme power and glory to restore the government of God over the whole earth. It was decreed, I repeat, that it was appointed to humans once to die, and after death is to come the resurrection to judgment (Heb. 9:27). Meanwhile the world of Adam is not being judged, though in the final judgment all shall be held to account for their sins.

But, meanwhile, God has made certain exceptions for a definite purpose. God raised up prophets for the very purpose of being part of the foundation of the Church. Jesus called disciples OUT OF THIS WORLD to be taught to teach others and in the coming millennium of the restored kingdom of God, to rule and teach under King of kings Jesus, when the tree of life will be opened to all flesh.

The Church was called to be trained to become rulers and teachers in the kingdom of God WHEN the tree of life shall be opened. Meanwhile the Holy Spirit has been closed to all but the prophets and the called-out-ones of the true Church. The prophet Joel foretold it shall come to pass afterward—after the 6,000 years of this world of Satan, that God will pour out of his Spirit upon all flesh (Joel 2:28).

Meanwhile it was necessary for God's purpose that the Holy Spirit be given to the prophets and those specially called out for training to become rulers and teachers under Christ, when the government of God is restored to the earth over all nations.

In calling out the Church, Jesus said plainly, "No man can come to me, except the Father which hath sent me draw him . . ." (John 6:44). The Church is merely the "first-fruits" of salvation. This entire truth will be made more clear in chapter six.

Why the Second Adam?

To review: Approximately 4,000 years from Adam, God sent Jesus Christ to live a perfect life, overcoming Satan, *qualifying* where the first Adam failed, to replace Satan as RULER on the throne of the whole earth. Those who, as Jesus did, overcome Satan, their own selves and sin (the "called," that is), will sit *with Christ* in his throne *when* he comes to set up THE KINGDOM OF GOD and to restore the GOVERNMENT OF GOD, which the former Lucifer rejected and ceased to administer!

Those *very* few called, beginning with "righteous Abel" up to now and on to Christ's return to earth, have had to do what Adam refused to do—REJECT THE WAY OF SATAN, who rebelled against the GOVERNMENT OF GOD!

Who, then, is a *real* Christian? Only those who have been, and are being, led by the Holy Spirit of God (Rom. 8:9, 11, 14). And none can receive the Holy Spirit until that person 1) REPENTS—of his sins, his transgressions of God's law; and 2) has complete faith in Jesus Christ—relying on Christ—which includes BELIEVING Jesus Christ. I mean, believing what he says—his WORD, the Holy Bible!

Thus, the called-out-ones after real repentance and belief Christ reconciles to God the Father and we receive the Holy Spirit impregnating us as children of God.

At this point let us clear up another question. Why could not Cain, Abel and Seth, the firstborn children of Adam, have repented and purely on that repentance have received the Spirit and life of God? God's law could not be a law except there be a penalty for its infraction. Adam had sinned. All his children had sinned and incurred on them the death penalty. They and no person after them could be freed from the penalty of that law until Christ, their very Maker, had paid that death penalty in their stead. Therefore, no salvation was possible until the crucifixion of Christ. Only Jesus' atonement could reconcile any human to God the Father.

Now, what of these and all the others—the THOUSANDS OF MILLIONS? Up to now, unless called and *drawn* by God, they simply have not yet been judged! I do not mean they shall not have to give account for their sins. They shall, indeed! But their judgment is COMING. Judgment has begun in the true Church of God (I Pet. 4:17). Jesus said, "No man can come to me, except the Father ... draw him ..." (John 6:44). No MAN *CAN* come to Christ otherwise! But the Church is merely the FIRST harvest.

In Satan's deceived world many have come to a counterfeit Christ who is supposed to have done away with his Father's commandments. They even worship Christ. But Jesus himself said plainly: "Howbeit in vain do they worship me, teaching for doctrines the commandments of men. . . . And he said unto them, Full well ye reject the commandment of God, that ye may keep your own tradition. . . . Making the word of God of none effect through your tradition, which ye have delivered: and many such like things do ye" (Mark 7:7, 9, 13).

Deceived millions do not realize that they are worshiping Christ in vain. They have been deceived into worshiping "another Jesus."

Every Human Shall be Called

When Christ comes as KING OF KINGS and LORD of lords, he will reign for the next thousand years. EVERYBODY living from his coming will be called.

After that thousand years shall occur the "Great White Throne Judgment" of Revelation 20:11-12. All who ever lived from Adam on, who were uncalled by God, shall be resurrected MORTAL in human flesh and blood as they were in their first life. *Then* they shall give account for the sins of their former life. The penalty of those sins is death. They shall then learn that Jesus Christ had paid that death penalty in their stead. But on real repentance and faith they shall be forgiven and receive God's Holy Spirit, begetting them to ETERNAL LIFE.

GOD'S WONDERFUL MASTER PLAN WILL CALL EVERYONE WHO EVER LIVED TO RECEIVE ETERNAL SALVATION, but on real repentance and belief of God's truth. But, there is a time-order in resurrections (I Cor. 15:22-23). "For as in Adam all die, even so in Christ shall all be made alive. But every man in his own order: Christ the firstfruits; afterward . . ." (two other resurrections revealed in Revelation 20:11-13 are not covered in I Corinthians 15).

Those called in the millennium, and those in the Great White Throne resurrection and judgment, shall NOT have Satan, then, to overcome.

How WONDERFUL are God's ways—even though hidden now from most of humanity bringing so much suffering on themselves! As the apostle Paul exclaimed: "O the depth of the riches both of the wisdom and knowledge of God! how unsearchable are his judgments, and his ways past finding out!" (Rom. 11:33).

In MAN, God is reproducing himself! The word for God in Genesis 1:1 is *Elohim* in the original Hebrew. It is a name, like church or family or group. God said, "Let US"—not ME—"make man in OUR image." God truly is a family into which we, *literally,* may be born!

WHAT, then, is man? He is a living being made from the dust of the ground. He is CLAY, and GOD is the Master Potter, molding, shaping, forming our CHARACTER—if we respond when he calls and draws us to him. With our willingness he is infusing into us HIS VERY OWN SPIRITUAL HOLY, RIGHTEOUS and PERFECT CHARACTER!

WHY is man? God created man on the earth to build in us what the sinning angels refused to let God build in them—his perfect CHARACTER! He is, in his time-order and way, developing us to become VERY GOD—each of us—and to finish the creation of the unfinished UNIVERSE! But, for NOW, we still live in this deceived world led by Satan.

MYSTERY
OF CIVILIZATION

FEW stop to think about it, but when you do, could anything be wrapped in more mystery than this world's civilization? How explain the astonishing paradox, a world of human minds that can send astronauts to the moon and back, produce the marvels of science and technology, transplant human hearts—yet cannot solve simple human problems of family life and group relationships, or peace between nations?

The developed nations have made awesome progress. They have produced a highly mechanized world providing every luxury, modern convenience and means of pleasure. Yet they are cursed with crime, violence, injustice, sickness and disease, broken homes and families. At the same time more than one-half the world is living in illiteracy, abject poverty, filth and squalor. Violence and destruction are rapidly multiplying. Many ask, "Why, if God exists, does he allow so much violence and human suffering?"

We were born into this twentieth-century world as it is. We take it for granted. But we can't explain it. It's like viewing a movie at a point already near the end. We see what is occurring at that point, but, not having seen it from the beginning and not knowing how events developed to the point of viewing, we simply cannot understand what we are seeing. A fiction writer wrote about a time machine that could transport one back to some time in history. If we had such a time machine, we should now transport ourselves backward 6,000 years where we could actually see what was transpiring in that original Garden of Eden, at the foundation of the world. That's where this civilization started. Then we may better understand why there is now talk of the imminent end of the world.

How did our civilization develop to our twentieth-century state? What a mystery that is to thinking people! Of course most are not thinking people and never ask themselves that question. But if one does, he finds the question enveloped in mystery. So let us understand.

It has already been explained in this volume how God created man for the supreme purpose of reproducing himself. But this supreme purpose necessitated the creation in us with our own assent, diligence, effort and joy, the supreme spiritual character of God. But in so doing, why did God place man on the earth? Why this particular planet?

The Unfinished Earth

God placed man here to restore the government of God to the earth. Lucifer and his angels had been placed here originally. God had put them here on an unfinished earth. Remember, God creates in dual stages. Like a woman baking a cake, she bakes first the body of the cake, but it is not finished until she puts on the icing. The substance and body of the earth had been created before the angels were placed here. But God intended for the angels to develop the surface of the earth, to beautify and improve it. For this purpose he gave them his government to regulate their conduct and performance together in so doing.

But Lucifer, on the throne to administer the government in cooperation and harmony for their world, rebelled. He turned cooperation and harmonious activity into competition, evil, rebellion and destruction. Light on earth was turned to darkness. Wasteness, decay and ruin came to the surface of the earth.

Then in six days (Ps. 104:30) God sent forth his Spirit and renewed the face of the earth for man.

But still "the icing on the cake" had not been added. God placed man here to do that which sinning angels had not done.

Man was to finish the beautification of the earth. God is not the author of confusion, ugliness or decay, but of beauty, perfection, character, the best in quality.

Look at the description of God's heaven—the seat of God's throne—where, we might say, God lives as described in the fourth chapter of Revelation. God sits on a throne surrounded by brilliant splendor, quality and beauty and character. More dazzlingly and gloriously beautiful than anything human eyes have ever seen.

God intended man to work this earth, improve it, beautify it, give it glorious character—and in so doing to build into his own life the "beauty of holiness" (I Chron. 16:29). God never intended humans to live in poverty, filth and squalor or ugliness. Man should have beautified the earth, and developed man's character in so doing. His civilization should have been a "heaven on earth."

What Man Has Done

But what has man done on the earth where God placed him? Man has made ugly, polluted, defiled, profaned everything his hands have touched. He has polluted the air, befouled the water in the rivers, lakes and seas. He has deteriorated the land, denuded the forests, thus altering rainfall and causing the expansion of deserts. He has worn out the soil by neglecting to give it its sabbaths of rest every seven years. Man has built cities and allowed them to deteriorate into slums, filth and squalor.

All because the very first human rejected and turned from God, relying solely on himself—and all Adam's children have done likewise.

Thus man has built a man-made and Satan-influenced civilization. Man not only has ruined the earth he should have developed and improved, he has destroyed his own health by wrong living, and degraded and perverted his own spiritual character. Now, at last, as we near the end of the 6,000 years God has allowed him this free rein, man has created the Frankenstein of weapons of mass destruction that can destroy all mankind utterly—unless a merciful God intervenes to save us from ourselves.

A Modest Foretaste

We now live in the era biblical prophecy calls the last days—the last generation before the coming of Christ to rule and accomplish on earth what mankind should have done. In these last days, according to biblical prophecy, knowledge, spiritual as well as material, was to be increased. The true Church of God was to be set back on the track, restoring the glorious knowledge of the faith once delivered to the saints in the days of the original apostles.

Jesus Christ, through the Church, built three colleges—two in the United States and one in England. The three campuses, in material beauty, have mutually excelled each other, as a high character physical setting for the development of God's righteous character in students. The beauty of godly character in these students has excelled the physical beauty of the campuses. A royal Queen on a recent six-day visit to the headquarters campus in Pasadena, California, on touring the campus, exclaimed, "I have just been in heaven."

Three times this campus has won the award of being the most beautiful, best landscaped, and best maintained campus in the United States. These campuses are an example of what mankind should have done, and a modest foretaste of the beauty that will blossom forth over the whole earth after Christ and his saints in his kingdom are ruling the earth in the wonderful world tomorrow.

Deteriorated, former millionaire mansions have been restored. An area behind them that had deteriorated into Pasadena's slum has been cleaned out and been built into the most beautiful area in Pasadena.

What If Adam Had Taken the Tree of Life?

How did this material and human character degradation start?

Had Adam taken of the proffered tree of life the whole course of civilization would have been entirely different.

Peace, happiness, joy, health and abundance would have spread over the earth.

But what did result?

Adam took to himself the knowledge of good as well as evil. But it was only human good, no higher than the carnal human level of the human spirit within him. He rejected reliance on God and relied on himself for knowledge, ability and power—all limited to the fleshly human plane, deceived and led by the perverted Satan.

Had he taken of the tree of life, he himself undoubtedly would have succeeded Satan on the throne of the earth, restoring the government of God, empowered, influenced and led by the Eternal God. But he allowed Satan to enter within his mind. He was, as it were, kidnapped and held captive by Satan.

Thus the first created human disbelieved God, disobeyed God, chose to go HIS OWN WAY, do his own thing. Adam did it willingly, but not apparently willfully or with malicious intent.

Willingly, Adam was led into captivity by Satan. He had willingly gone along with Satan, the archkidnapper of all time.

A World Held Captive

Adam had been created with the potential to be born a son of GOD. Even though not as yet even a begotten son of the GOD FAMILY, he had been created as potentially just that. Once he succumbed to Satan's WAY of choosing to "do his own thing," in rebellion against a deliberate command of God, he became spiritually the property of Satan. He actually had succumbed to the GOVERNMENT of Satan, choosing the LAW of that government—the law of vanity, self-centeredness—leading automatically into attitudes of self-glory, coveting, competition, desire to GET rather than God's way of GIVE.

All humanity came out of Adam and Eve. The present world was FOUNDED in them. The WORLD has ever since been HELD CAPTIVE! The world had thus chosen THE WAY of the kidnapper, rather than of the potential Parent!

But God the Father was to pay the ransom price and even

yet bring his potential spiritual children back to him. God did not choose to redeem, correct and restore humanity to him at that time.

At the Foundation of the World

Upon Adam's sin, God closed off the tree of life to the world as a whole until the second Adam, Jesus Christ, shall have deposed Satan and taken over the throne of the earth.

There cannot be a law without a penalty. The penalty of human sin is DEATH.

The penalty of death had passed on Adam and all his children. That penalty had to be paid. There was no escaping it. Satan must have gloated, believing he had totally defeated God's purpose of restoring God's government and unseating Satan on earth's throne. Truly all Adam's children would come under the penalty of death, for all would sin.

But what even Satan probably did not realize, God's plan was yet to save humanity, and remove Satan from earth's throne.

At this very foundation of the world, it was determined that Jesus Christ, as the "Lamb of God," should be slain in payment of the penalty for all human sin (Rev. 13:8), which substitute sacrifice is effective only upon repentance and faith. It was also determined by God at that time that all Adam's children should die, but after dying be resurrected to judgment (Heb. 9:27). But as in Adam all must die, so in Christ the same ALL shall be made alive by a resurrection from the dead to be judged (I Cor. 15:22).

But still, none could ever be born of God until God's holy and perfect spiritual character had been instilled within, by individual choice and proof by performance.

God set apart a 7,000-year period to complete his original SUPREME PURPOSE of reproducing himself through man. It was a masterminded MASTER PLAN for working out the PURPOSE here below.

For almost 6,000 years a civilization has developed, which we call the world. But it has been a world held captive. It has become SATAN'S WORLD though millions have been deceived into believing it is God's world. To this day Satan is still on that throne of the earth.

Meanwhile Satan has worked IN all humans. He has injected into the world enormous EVILS.

But how has Satan injected those evils into the minds of all humans, even of the most scholarly and advanced in education, science, government and areas of awesome human accomplishment? Even that question is a mystery understood by almost no one.

Satan—the Master Broadcaster

In Ephesians 2:2, Satan is called the prince of the power of the air, working in—inside the minds of—people. I could never have understood this until: 1) I had understood how radio and television sounds and pictures are transmitted through the air; and 2) I had learned the truth about the human spirit in the human brain. If your radio is set on the proper radio wavelength, or television set is tuned to the proper channel, the broadcaster's message comes through clearly. Satan as prince of the power of the air broadcasts— not in words, sounds or pictures, but in attitudes, moods, impulses.

For example, we read in Ezra 1:1, when King Cyrus of Persia issued a proclamation to send a colony of Jews back to Jerusalem to build the second Temple, he was moved to do so because God stirred up his human spirit—in other words, put the suggestion and impulse in his mind, and the king acted on it. In the same manner Satan moves on the human spirit within people to move them in attitudes of envy, jealousy, resentment, impatience, anger, bitterness and strife. People have no realization of the tremendous power of Satan. The human spirit within each human is automatically tuned to Satan's wavelength. It seems as if Satan has surcharged the air over the entire earth with his attitude of self-centeredness and vanity.

And so a world—a civilization—developed from the original Adam and Eve. When God shut off the tree of life, that act marked the foundation of the world. It was founded on rejection of God, on disobedience to God's law, which defines God's way of life. And all the evils, sorrows, pain and suffering in 6,000 years of human civilization have resulted.

God had designed a 7,000-year master plan for accomplishing his tremendous purpose. The first 6,000 years were allotted to allow Satan to remain on earth's throne, and for humanity to learn the bitter lesson, through experience, that Satan's way of self-centeredness in opposition to God's law leads only to pain, suffering, anguish and death.

The whole world of humankind has been deceived into preferring this "getting," self-centered way of life.

At this point, remember, the world had never known of the existence of God the Father until Jesus came and revealed the Father (Matt. 11:27).

The world, from its foundation, was cut off from God the Father. Jesus came to reconcile repentant believers to the Father (Rom. 5:10).

The Beginning of Civilization

But notice briefly how human civilization developed.

God created the first humans, perfect specimens physically and mentally. Physically this perfectly created pair had no chronic ailments or tendencies toward diseases or illnesses. That is testified in part by the fact that Adam lived to be 930 years old. And for nearly 2,000 years the human life span from Adam to Noah averaged close to 900 years.

Think of it! The first man lived nearly one sixth of all the time from human creation until now!

Adam and Eve had two sons, Cain and Abel. When they were grown, perhaps still in their teens, Cain became envious and hostile against his brother Abel. Even though by the closing off of the tree of life they were cut off from God the Father, the "Word" (the "Lord" or the "Eternal" in English) spoke to Cain and warned him. But Cain was being led by Satan. This prince of the power of the air stirred Cain to an attitude of resentment, anger and hostility. Cain slew his younger brother, and when the Eternal asked him about his brother, he lied to God about it. The very first human ever born was moved by Satan to become a murderer and a liar.

God sentenced him to become a vagabond and a fugitive.

But even though the human family had rejected God, chosen to rely on self even as swayed by Satan, the human mind was capable of working with material substance. In a few generations a son of Cain was making harps and organs and musical instruments (Gen. 4:21) and another, an artificer in brass and iron.

Mankind was making progress in material development, even though growing further from God spiritually. But remember at this point, that "except the Lord build the house, they labour in vain that build it" (Ps. 127:1). Also in Matthew 7:24-27, a house built on a faulty foundation is bound to fall. Civilization as we know it was built, not on the foundation of God and his direction, but on man's self-reliance under the deception and sway of Satan.

The Bible tells us little of human development prior to Noah, but after 1,500 to 1,600 years human civilization had become so evil that only one man, Noah, remained righteous. There was a population explosion, but humanity had turned to evil continually. After 100 years of warning by Noah, God sent the Flood to drown all living except Noah, his wife, three sons and their wives—eight people.

The Extent of Evil

Notice to what extent humanity had been turned by Satan to evil. In Genesis 6:5, "God saw that the wickedness of man was great in the earth, and that every imagination of the thoughts of his heart was only evil continually." The earth was filled with violence. Man's thoughts, contemplations and plans were continually on self-centered, lustful and evil objectives.

This violence had become so universal that God determined to spare humanity from suffering longer in mounting misery and anguish.

God took away their miserable lives, by the earthwide Flood, *to be resurrected in the next second of their consciousness* in the "Great White Throne" resurrection (Rev. 20:11-12). They will be brought back to life in a time when Christ is ruling the earth in righteousness, peace and happiness. Satan will be gone. Their minds then will be opened to God's TRUTH, and eternal salvation will be opened to them.

But God intended to preserve human life—to give humanity a new and fresh start.

God found only one man, of all the millions, who was

walking with God. Two can't walk together except they be agreed. Noah alone agreed with God and God's way of life. God used Noah as a preacher of righteousness (II Pet. 2:5). For 100 years Noah warned the unheeding world, from age 500 until he was 600 years old.

Noah was "perfect" in his generations. That is, his heredity, ancestry (Gen. 6:9).

Proof of this lies in the meaning of the Hebrew word translated "perfect." It may refer either to spiritual character (Gen. 17:1) or to *physical characteristics* (Lev. 22:21). Therefore Genesis 6:9 allows the translation that Noah was either "blameless" or of "pure strain."

The context (Gen. 6:2) clearly indicates the latter is the intended meaning of the Hebrew word translated "perfect." So a good rendering of Genesis 6:9 is that Noah was the only "just" man (in spiritual character), and also of "pure strain," unmixed (in his genetic heritage) among his contemporaries.

End of the Antediluvian World

The subject matter of the chapter is the generations ancestry of Noah. Exceeding wickedness had developed through those generations, by Noah's generation reaching a climactic crisis that *ended* that world.

What was this universal evil and corruption? Jesus described that universal, corrupt evil as "eating and drinking, marrying and giving in marriage" (Matt. 24:38). Eating food and drinking is not evil. Marrying is not evil in itself. There had to be *wrong use* and *excess* in eating, drinking and marrying—the evil was *in the manner,* and in *the extent* of eating, drinking and marrying.

It could only be eating improper food, drinking excessively of alcoholic drinks, revelings (Gal. 5:21), rioting, violence. Marrying, to be evil, had to be as in Genesis 6:2, when men "took them wives of all which *they* chose." There was interracial marriage—so exceedingly universal that *Noah, only,* among males, was unmixed or of pure strain in his generations—his ancestry.

It is amply evident that by the time of Noah there were at least the three primary or major racial strains on earth, the white, yellow and black, and in addition interracial marriage produced many racial mixtures much as we have in today's world.

God does not reveal in the Bible the precise origin of the different races. But it is a fair conjecture that in mother Eve were created ovaries containing the yellow and black genes, as well as white, so that some of the children of Adam and Eve gave rise to black, yellow, as well as white.

The one man God chose to PRESERVE the human race alive after the Flood was *unmixed in his generations*—all his ancestry back to Adam was of the one strain.

If you are a livestock breeder, planning to enter your prize animals in a livestock show—perhaps at a state or county fair—you will be sure to enter only thoroughbred or pedigreed stock! Mixing the breed alters the inheritable characteristics.

God originally *set the bounds* of national borders, intending nations to be SEPARATED to prevent interracial marriage. Notice, "When the most High divided to the nations their inheritance [speaking of land or geographical boundaries], when he *separated* [notice—he *separated*] the sons of Adam, he set the bounds of the people..." (Deut. 32:8).

But people wanted to intermarry—thinking they would become only ONE RACE!

That desire seems still inherent in human nature today!

Noah was of unmixed lineage in his generations and undoubtedly that happened to be white—*not* that white is in any sense superior. His wife and three sons were of that same white strain. But Japheth evidently had married an Oriental woman, and Ham a black. That is how God chose to preserve the primary races through the catastrophe of the Flood.

We know little more than stated above about civilized development prior to the Flood.

Mankind should have learned its lesson by the Flood, but man cut off from God, and swayed by Satan had not, and has not to this present day. But once again, "as it was in the days of Noah," Jesus said in a prophecy, there is a population explosion, and evils are multiplying. This time worldwide nuclear war will threaten to erase all humanity from the earth. But, for the sake of the "elect" of God's true Church (Matt. 24:21-22), God will cut the destruction short—and this time send Jesus Christ as King of kings to replace Satan and sit on earth's throne.

Origin of Cities

It was only the second generation after the Flood until a man named Nimrod organized people into cities. First was the tower of Babel and the city of Babylon. Then Nineveh and other cities, which became city-states.

God had set the bounds of the nations, intending geographical segregation of the races.

At this point I quote from *Satan's Great Deception,* a thesis by C. Paul Meredith (pages 14-16):

> *Everyone on earth after the Flood knew of God* and why he had drowned the wicked. They feared to do evil—at first. . . . Men lived . . . without cities and without laws, and all speaking one language. . . .
>
> This group, composed of the *only people on the earth* (for the others had all been destroyed by the great Flood), began migrating from the mountains of Ararat (Gen. 8:4) where the ark had landed: "And the whole earth was of *one language,* and of one speech. And it came to pass, as they journeyed from the east, that they found a plain in the land of Shinar; and they dwelt there" (Gen. 11:1-2). These people, now known as Sumerians (Miller's *Ancient History in Bible Light,* page 51), pushing through the mountains of the east, came upon a prodigiously fertile plain built up by the deposits of the Euphrates and the Tigris rivers. This land of Shinar is now known as ancient Babylonia (J. H. Breasted's *Ancient Times,* page 107). Here was a land that would produce all they desired in abundance. . . .
>
> These people, like Adam and Eve, disobeyed God and brought trouble upon themselves. The land was productive, but the wild animals were multiplying faster than the people due to the destruction of the former civilization by the great Flood. Because of their primitive weapons, there was a great danger to life and possessions (Ex. 23:28-29). What could be done about it?
>
> Nimrod, the son of Cush, was a large, powerfully built man who developed into a great hunter. It was he who

gathered the people together and *organized* them to fight the wild ferocious beasts. "He was a mighty *hunter before the Lord*" (Gen. 10:8-9). In other words, the name of Nimrod was known everywhere for his might. He emancipated the people of the earth after the Flood from their fear of the wild animals. His prestige grew. He became the leader in worldly affairs. He was ambitious.

First City—Babylon

There was a better way to protect the people from the wild animals that roamed the earth than by constantly fighting them. Nimrod built a city of houses and surrounded this city with a high wall and gathered the people therein. Thus the people were protected and Nimrod was able to *rule* over them. This arrangement was agreeable to the people for "They said ... let *us* build *us* a city and ... make *us a name,* lest we be scattered abroad" (Gen. 11:4).

The people not only protected themselves from the wild animals by building a walled city but also established authority *of their own*—"let *us* make *us* a name." This was to be a central place of *mankind's* authority—*the necessity of their obedience to God was not going to be recognized!* Nimrod was their leader. Also they built a tower whose top was to "reach *unto heaven."* With a tower this high they could do as they wished—disobey God and still be safe from his *punishment* which had drowned the inhabitants of the earth before. This was mankind's first act of open rebellion against God after the Flood—they thought they had placed themselves out of God's reach if they wished to *disobey him.* They, like Satan, thought that if they could "ascend above the heights of the clouds," they could "be like the most High" (Isa. 14:14). Cush, Nimrod's father, also had much to do with the building of this tower and city (*The Two Babylons,* by Alexander Hislop, page 26).

These people were not only of one language, they were of three races or families—white, yellow and black. Just as God created varieties in many species of flowers and of animals— for example, many varieties and colors of roses—for greater beauty, so God created the three races and colors of human skin.

They wanted to become amalgamated through intermarriage of races.

As mentioned before, God had set the bounds of the races, providing for geographical segregation, in peace and harmony but without discrimination. But the people thought they had found a better way. One purpose for the tower of Babel was to unite them, and to prevent them from being scattered in geographical segregation.

They built the tower, "lest we be scattered abroad upon the face of the whole earth" in geographical segregation (Gen. 11:4). But God looked upon their building of the tower and said, "Behold, the people is one, and they have all one language; and this they *begin* to do: and now nothing will be restrained from them, which they have imagined to do" (Gen. 11:6).

What has mankind "imagined to do"? By this twentieth century man has gone into outer space, flown to the moon and back, invented and produced the most intricate machines, computerized instruments, transplanted hearts, and even attempted to produce life from dead matter. The human mind's capacity for material accomplishment seems unlimited. But his problems are not material, but spiritual. And before them he is still helpless without God.

So God confounded their languages and "scattered them abroad . . . upon the face of all the earth" (Gen. 11:8).

Continuing from C. Paul Meredith's thesis, now out of print (pages 16-17, 25-29):

> Then it was that Nimrod "began to be a *mighty* one" and a "*mighty* hunter *before* the Lord" [Gen. 10:8-9] in a *ruling* sense (the Hebrew word for "mighty" is *gibbor,* which means "tyrant," *Strong's Concordance of the Bible*). Nimrod became a tyrant over the people. *He* made the laws. Not only that but he was "mighty . . . *before*" the Eternal. (The Hebrew word *paniym* translated "before" here, should be translated "against"—*Strong's Concordance of the Bible*.) The Bible says Nimrod was against God! . . .
>
> Nimrod kept growing in power but the inborn desire of the people to worship must be satisfied. Nimrod and his followers had turned against the *true* God. They wanted to glorify God *in their own way!* They "*changed* the glory of the *uncorruptible* God into an *image* made like . . . *creeping things*" (Romans 1:23)—the snake, and other things God

had created. (They should have worshiped God in spirit and in truth and not through idols—John 4:24 and Ex. 20:4-5.) With the civil power he wielded, Nimrod set himself up as the priest of the things worshiped by the people, to obtain a still stronger hold on them and gradually put himself in place of the true God....

[But] Noah, the preacher of righteousness (II Pet. 2:5), did stand fast and gained a staunch supporter in his son Shem. While Nimrod was expanding his kingdom so rapidly, there was opposition to Shem, the representative of *Noah*.... Nimrod became the representative for the forces of evil in opposing Shem....

Shem, a very eloquent person, is said to have obtained the aid of a group of Egyptians who overcame Nimrod.

The death of Nimrod seemingly halted the counterfeit pagan worship which he started.

Semiramis . . .

[If] Nimrod had been a man of unbounded ambition, the ambition of ... Semiramis—the future "Queen of Heaven" (Jer. 7:18)—exceeded even his. Nimrod ... had become the greatest and most powerful figure in the world. He was dead. She clearly saw that if she were to ... have the great position and power ... of the most powerful man on earth, something must be done to assure ... her power.

Nimrod's kingdom, which consisted of most of the populated world of that time, had fallen to her. *Much of Nimrod's power had come from his setting himself up as the human representative of the Sun-God.* She must retain this world rule by any and all means. The *religious control* which had given so much power to [Nimrod] must be used by her also if she were to retain the maximum hold on her subjects.... In life [Nimrod] had been honored as a hero; in death she will have him worshiped as a god....

Semiramis was actually the founder of much of the world's pagan religions, worshiping false gods. Even such so-called Christian observances as Christmas, New Year's and Easter emerged from the false religious system she developed. For details of this the reader is referred to *The Two Babylons*, by Alexander Hislop.

Today, the English language is fast becoming the chief

international language. Men are starting to get back to one worldwide language.

Present Evil World Develops

The only survivors of the great Flood on earth composed the one family, that of Noah. It consisted of Noah, his wife, their three sons Shem, Ham and Japheth and their wives. The whole human population came from that one family.

The Bible speaks of three worlds—the world that then was being overflowed with water, this present evil world, and the world to come.

As the flood waters evaporated the whole earth consisted of the one family of Noah. But Shem, who was white and married to a white woman, started his own family. Ham, married to a black woman, had children and began his own family. Japheth, married to a yellow or Oriental woman, started his own family, which inherited yellow extraction. The early history recorded in the Bible speaks of "families," rather than "races."

At the incident of the tower of Babel, God divided the speech of the people so that they were able to communicate each one only in his new and different language.

And so as time passed, the families grew, each family speaking its own language in its own local geographic area.

Nimrod built a number of cities—Babylon, Erech, Accad, Calneh, Nineveh, etc. There developed city-states, each with its own local government. As time passed, nations arose with national governments. Among these were Babylon (which became known as Chaldea), Egypt, Assyria. The religion started by Semiramis was carried into the different nations in the language of each. Semiramis and Nimrod were also identified with the names Isis and Osiris in Egypt. Each nation had its own names for its gods. But the whole labyrinth of pagan religions developed from that which originated with Semiramis.

As the generations of humanity continued, this world's civilization developed. It started with a government system started by Nimrod, through a religious system that stemmed from Nimrod and Semiramis. The modern system of academic educations was started by Plato, taught by Socrates.

Systems of commerce, industry, finance and banking developed—but none of these Satan-influenced and humanly devised systems originated with God. All laws were made by humans—either decrees by kings and despots, or human lawmaking groups, such as city councils, state legislatures, national congresses, parliaments, diets, or whatever. Social customs developed and all facets of civilization up to the chaotic present.

In such a world God called out a special nation of his own, not a favorite nation for special favors, but a nation chosen for a special purpose that that nation failed to perform.

After the Flood profane history implies that Shem continued more or less in the knowledge and way of God. But no man really walked with God until Abraham. To Abraham, God made all the promises on which ultimate human salvation depends, as well as the material and economic prosperity that has come to the United States and the British.

Summation of Human Civilization

Humanity was created on earth for a glorious and wonderful purpose. God was reproducing himself. Stated another way, God's purpose was to create humanity to become supremely happy and joyful in peace and perfect comfort, to become productive, creative, joyfully successful with eternal life.

This meant the supreme perfect spiritual character of God—perfect utopia. This purpose shall be accomplished.

But to accomplish it, humanity must make its own decision. The former cherub Lucifer had chosen a course of action and being that led in the diametrically opposite direction. The first man had to choose either to accept and live the way of God's purpose, or Satan's way of self-reliance in the opposite direction. The first man Adam chose to take to himself the knowledge of good and evil. He started his human family relying on self for good on the human level, mixed with evil, and relying on human self not only for knowledge of the way, but for the solution of all problems that might arise. He rejected spiritual knowledge from God and reliance on God for power to live the way of utopia.

Man built his world on self-sufficiency without God.

God set in motion a master plan for accomplishment of his purpose, consisting of a duration of 7,000 years. Satan was allowed to remain on earth's throne for the first 6,000 years. God purposed that man must learn his lesson, and come voluntarily to accept God's way and character.

For nearly 6,000 years mankind has been writing that lesson. But even at this late hour he has not yet learned it. He has not yet given up on his own self-centered way and come to accept God's way to his ultimate happiness. God is letting the law of cause and effect take full toll. Man's society, deceived and misled by Satan, has not even yet brought man to admit failure of his course of self-sufficiency.

Today man's world is reeling on its last legs. Wars, violence, destruction, terrorism engulf the entire world. Half the world exists in ignorance, illiteracy, poverty, living in filth and squalor. The developed half is sick with ill health, disease, mental stress, fear, frustration, wracked with crime, alcoholism, drug abuse, perverted and misused sex, broken homes, hopelessness in frustration.

Mankind is nearing the end of his rope. But even now, God will not intervene to save this defiant humanity from itself until man is finally brought to the point where, if God delayed longer in intervention, man would annihilate himself. God will not intervene and usher in the next world under the kingdom of God until the remnant of mankind has been brought to fully realize human inability to solve problems or bring worldwide peace in happiness and joy. Man must be brought to realize his helplessness and futility without God.

At last the weapons of mass destruction have been invented and produced that can erase all life from this planet earth. In these last days of mankind's last gasping of breath, Jesus foretold how it would all end. After Jesus' gospel had been suppressed, replaced with a false gospel of men about a different Jesus, he said, "This gospel of the kingdom shall be preached in all the world for a witness unto all nations; and then shall the end [of this world] come."

This gospel now has been preached into every nation. During its 50 years of proclamation, nuclear energy has developed with capacity for the first time in history to destroy every human alive on earth. Next, Jesus foretold the great tribulation—a time of trouble so great that, unless God does intervene, no human being would be saved alive. But, for the sake of his Church, God will intervene supernaturally before total destruction of humanity. Mankind will be brought to acknowledge human insufficiency without God. Immediately after, Christ will come in the clouds in supreme power and glory to unseat Satan, and start God's own new civilization toward utopia (Matt. 24:14, 31-41).

These are the very last days of Satan's evil world. God's utopian civilization will be started with the present generation.

MYSTERY OF ISRAEL

D ID IT EVER STRIKE you as most unusual that the Great
God should have raised up the ancient nation Israel to
be his *chosen* people?

Consider these seemingly paradoxical facts:

God says he is not a respecter of persons. Is he, then, a respecter of nations? Does he have a *favorite?*

Did you ever realize that God denied his chosen people salvation—save only their prophets? That the chosen nation was given only material and national promises—that God's Holy Spirit was inaccessible to them?

Did it ever occur to you that the Holy Bible is the book of and concerning only that one people Israel? And that other nations are mentioned only if and as they came into contact with Israel?

And here's another shocker!—almost totally unrealized today by Christianity—even by Judaism and not recorded or understood by historians! The northern kingdom of Israel *was not Jewish!* The first place in the Bible where the word *Jews* occurs is in II Kings chapter 16 and verse 6, where the nation Israel was at war, in an alliance with Syria, against the Jews!

The truly amazing truth about Israel is a mystery totally unknown by any religion—by Christianity—by even Judaism!

It is indeed true that the nation Israel was God's chosen people. But understand: They were not chosen as "teacher's pet" nor for special favors. They were chosen for a special PURPOSE *preparatory to the ultimate establishment of the kingdom of God!*

It is an intriguing story! The answer to this chapter title, "Mystery of Israel," has great significance in God's PURPOSE for all peoples! One cannot understand the real purpose and incredible potential of man without this vital knowledge.

Supreme Master Plan

The Creator God is *reproducing himself* in and through man! God's ultimate transcendent PURPOSE is breathtaking beyond words. The establishment of the ancient nation Israel is an integral part of the supreme master plan.

Seven generations after the Flood, the Eternal found a man who would obey him. His name was Abram. He lived in Haran, in Mesopotamia. This man was to become a type of God the Father. It was from him that the nation Israel descended. Through this nation God raised up his prophets, and in due time God's own Son, Jesus Christ.

Man of Destiny

Abram, as he was originally named, was not seeking God. But God chose to call and test Abram. This ancient patriarch, later in Scripture, is called the father of the faithful. God was calling him for a very special purpose. That purpose was not to "give him salvation" or "get him into heaven." God was calling him because he had seen in this man the potentialities of obedience to God and of leadership. God was calling him to be prepared for special service and ultimately high position in the kingdom of God—the coming world tomorrow. I quote now from a book I wrote more than 50 years ago, *The United States and Britain in Prophecy*, commencing with page 16:

> To this man, Abram, God commanded: "Get thee out of thy country, and from thy kindred, and from thy father's house, unto a land that I will shew thee: and I will make of thee a great nation" (Gen. 12:1-2).
>
> Here was a command, which was a *condition* and a PROMISE, provided the condition of obedience was met.

And so now, as God had started the whole world with one man, he started his own peculiar nation in the world from one single man—Abraham. As the world, which has strayed far from God and the blessings of God's worship and rule, was started with one man who rebelled against God and rejected his rule, so God's own flesh-born nation, from which is to be reborn the kingdom of God, was started with one man who obeyed God without question, and accepted his divine rule.

Did Abram stop to argue and reason? Did he say: "Let's reason this out a bit first; here I am in Babylon, in the very center of all this world's commerce, society and gaiety. Why can't you just as well give me this promise right here, where everything is pleasant and alluring? Why must I leave all this and go over to that uncivilized land?"

Did Abram quibble, resist, argue, rebel?

He certainly did not!

The inspired Scripture account states simply: "So Abram departed." There was no arguing with God. There was no human reasoning that God was all wrong. There were no foolish questions: "Why must I leave here?" "Can't I do as I please?" There was no stopping to say, "Well, here's the way I look at it."

"Abram departed." Just plain, unquestioned obedience!

Here again we see the principle of duality. Abram was in the very center of this world's developing civilization. Remember, it was a world held captive—a world developing on Satan's pattern. God had chosen Abram to become the patriarch of his nation Israel, the congregation or Church of the Old Testament. The principle of duality is interwoven all through the workings of God in fulfilling this great purpose through humanity on earth. There was the physical congregation of Israel under the Old Testament and the spiritual Church of God under the New Testament. The word *church* as originally written in the Greek of the New Testament was *ekklesia*, which means called-out-ones.

As Israel of the Old Testament was the physical forerunner and type of the Church of the New Testament so God now called out the progenitor of the nation Israel from Satan's world. Abraham later regarded himself as a stranger, a sojourner and a pilgrim in the earth. This was not his world:

"These all died in faith, not having received the promises, but having seen them afar off, and were persuaded of them, and embraced them, and confessed that they were strangers and pilgrims on the earth. For they that say such things declare plainly that they seek a country [a different civilization]. And truly, if they had been mindful of that country from whence they came out, they might have had opportunity to have returned. But now they desire a better country, that is, an heavenly: wherefore God is not ashamed to be called their God: for he hath prepared for them a city" (Heb. 11:13-16). Seeking a better country, a heavenly country, which will be the kingdom of God filling the earth.

And God established this man [Abram], whose name he later changed to Abraham, as the *father* of his nation, *Israel!* To Abraham and his descendants were all the promises of God made. And we must become like Abraham, and through Christ, one of his children, if we are to inherit the promise of eternal life in God's kingdom.

Of his peculiar flesh-born nation, Israel, the Eternal said: "This people have I formed for myself; *they shall* shew forth my praise" (Isa. 43:21). That prophecy shall yet—and soon—be fulfilled!

Dual Promises to Abraham

Few have realized it, but a duality runs all the way through the plan of God in working out his purpose here below.

There was the first Adam, material and carnal; and there is Christ, the second Adam, spiritual and divine. There was the Old Covenant, purely material and temporal; and there is the New Covenant, spiritual and eternal. God made man mortal, physical, of the dust of the ground and of the human kingdom; but through Christ he may be begotten of God to become immortal, spiritual, and of the kingdom of God.

And in like manner there were two phases to the promises God made to Abraham—the one purely material and national; the other spiritual and individual. The spiritual promise of the Messiah, and of salvation through him, is well known by the most superficial Bible students. They know that God gave the spiritual promise to Abraham of Christ to be born as Abraham's descendant—and that salvation comes to us through Christ. But—and this will sound unbelievable, yet it is true—almost no one knows what that salvation is; what are the promises of salvation we may receive through Christ; how we may receive them, or when—incredible though that sounds! But that truth belongs in another chapter.

What is essential to the theme of this chapter is the fact that God also made another entirely different, most amazing national and material promise to Abraham which has been almost entirely overlooked.

Notice now again how God first called Abram, and the *twofold* nature of his promises: "Now the Lord had said unto Abram, Get thee out of thy country, and from thy kindred, and from thy father's house, unto a land that I will shew thee: and I *will make of thee* A GREAT NATION. . . . and in thee shall all families of the earth be blessed" (Gen. 12:1-3).

Notice the twofold promise: 1) "I will make of thee A GREAT NATION"—the national, material promise that his flesh-born children should become a great nation—a promise of RACE; 2) ". . . and in thee shall all families of the earth be blessed"—the spiritual promise of GRACE. This same promise is repeated in Genesis 22:18: "And in *thy seed* shall all the nations of the earth be blessed." This particular "one seed" refers to Christ, as plainly affirmed in Galatians 3:8, 16.

Right here is where those who profess to be "Christians"—and their teachers—have fallen into error and scriptural blindness. They have failed to notice the twofold promise God made to Abraham. They recognize the messianic promise of spiritual salvation through the "one seed"—Christ. They sing the hymn *Standing on the Promises*—falsely supposing the *promises* to be going to heaven at death.

This is a pivotal point. This is the point where professing "Christians" and their teachers jump the track of truth. This is the point where they switch off the track that would lead them to the missing master key to the prophecies. They miss the fact that God gave Abraham promises of physical RACE as well as spiritual GRACE.

But the plain fact that the "great nation" promise refers alone to race—not the "one seed" of Galatians 3:16, who was Jesus Christ the son of Abraham and the Son of God, but to the plural, multiple seed of natural fleshly birth—is made certain by God's repetition of his promise in greater detail later.

Israel to Become Many Nations

Notice carefully! Understand these promises!

"And when Abram was ninety years old and nine, the Lord appeared to Abram, and said unto him, I am the Almighty God; walk before me, and be thou perfect. And I will make my covenant between me and thee, *and will multiply thee exceedingly. . . . thou shalt be a father of* MANY NATIONS. Neither shall thy name any more be called Abram, but thy name shall be Abraham; for a father of MANY NATIONS have I made thee" (Gen. 17:1-5).

Notice, the promise is now conditional upon Abraham's obedience and perfect living. Notice, the "great nation" now becomes many nations—more than one nation. This cannot refer to the "one seed," Christ. The following verses prove that.

"And *I will make thee exceeding fruitful,* and I will make *nations* of thee, and *kings* [more than one] shall come out of thee" (verse 6). Notice, these nations and kings shall *come out of* Abraham—physical generation—multiple seed, in addition to the one descendant *through whom* scattered individuals *may* become Abraham's children by spiritual begettal through Christ (Gal. 3:29). The scattered, individual Christians do not form NATIONS. The Church, it is true, is spoken of as "a royal priesthood, an holy nation" (I Peter 2:9), but Christ's Church is not divided into "many nations." This is speaking of race, not grace.

"And I will establish my covenant between me and thee and thy seed after thee in *their* generations . . ." (Gen. 17:7). The "seed" is plural—"in their generations." "And I will give unto thee, and to thy seed after thee, *the land* wherein thou art a stranger, all the land of Canaan [Palestine], for an everlasting possession; and I will be THEIR God" (verse 8).

Notice, the land—material possession—is promised to the plural seed, of whom he is "their," not "his," God. The plural pronoun "their" is used again in verse 9: "and thy seed after thee in *their* generations."

But now examine this PROMISE carefully!

The future of great nations rests on the promises the eternal Creator made to Abraham. The only hope of life

after death for anyone—regardless of race, color or creed—
is dependent on the spiritual phase of these promises to
Abraham—the promise of grace through the "one seed"—
Christ the Messiah!

How Much Land—What Size Nations?

These are not casual, incidental, unimportant promises.
These are basic—the foundation for the establishment of
the greatest world powers; the basis for any personal
salvation spiritually; for any hope of eternal life for humans.
These are stupendous promises. The future of mankind is
based, by the Creator God, on them.

Jesus Christ came "to confirm the promises made unto
the fathers" (Rom. 15:8)—Abraham, Isaac and Jacob.
These same promises were repromised to Isaac, Abraham's
son, and to Jacob, the son of Isaac.

After 430 years, God raised up his nation Israel—
descendants of Abraham, Isaac and Jacob, whose name God
changed to Israel.

To lead these people out of Egyptian slavery and to the
Promised Land, God called Moses. Moses was not seeking
God. But God had caused Moses to be trained specifically for
this commission by having him reared as a prince in the
palace of the Egyptian pharaoh. So now again, after Moses
had been specially trained for leadership, God called him out
of the world to lead the descendants of Abraham, Isaac and
Jacob out of Egyptian slavery.

Why a Chosen Nation?

So now again we come to the question, WHY did God raise up
this special Hebrew nation as "the chosen people"? WHY,
when God never made accessible to them his Holy Spirit?

One point to notice here. The probability is that these
people were all—or nearly all—of the white racial strain,
unchanged since creation.

After Jacob and his sons and families had come into
Egypt at Joseph's behest, they were kept in the locale of
Goshen—geographically separated from the major population
centers of Egypt.

In this connection, go back momentarily to Abraham. He
prevented his son Isaac, born of Sarah, from intermarrying

among the Canaanites then in the land. He sent his chief servant to his own family in Mesopotamia to find a wife for Isaac. Abraham said, ". . . thou shalt not take a wife unto my son of the daughters of the Canaanites, among whom I dwell" (Gen. 24:3).

The next generation, Jacob married Leah and Rachel, daughters of Laban, nephew of Abraham, who lived in the land of Haran, brother of Abraham. The whole community of Haran, where Laban lived, was of the same family ancestry as Abraham.

Jacob had six sons by Leah, two from Rachel—all of the same original racial stock, and two each from the maids of Rachel and Leah—12 in all. Even the maids of Leah and Rachel undoubtedly were of pure Hebrew stock. These 12 became the progenitors of the 12 tribes of the nation Israel.

But God specially prepared from birth and called Moses, with Aaron his brother to assist as his spokesman. (Moses stuttered.)

In the plagues God caused against Egypt, God was turning the Egyptian gods and objects of worship against them to show them that these were *not* gods. Even the plagues were sent in LOVE for the Egyptians.

The final plague followed the sacrifice of the Passover on the 14th day of the first month of God's sacred calendar—starting in the spring. The Israelites went out of Egypt during the night part of the 15th. They reached the Red Sea. But pharaoh had meanwhile changed his mind and, with his army, pursued them.

The children of Israel had reached the Red Sea, and they were stopped as if dead. There was no bridge. It was too far to swim, with their women and children. Behind them the pharaoh's army was in hot pursuit. There was nothing they could do. They were stopped—HELPLESS! At that point they had to rely on GOD!

In Egypt God had caused their release from slavery by a series of supernatural plagues. Now God caused the waters of the Red Sea to roll back to form a watery WALL on either side, with a wide path on the dry sea floor between.

The Israelites walked on through. On the opposite side they looked back and saw the Egyptians entering the seafloor path. When the Egyptians were all within the seawall passage, God allowed the waters to flow back, drowning the Egyptian army.

Broken Promises

In due time the Israelites pitched tents at the foot of Mount Sinai.

God did not make them his nation, under his theocratic rule, without their consent.

Through Moses, God put to them his proposition. If they would obey his laws of HIS GOVERNMENT, he would prosper them, and make them the wealthiest and most powerful of nations.

Yet God's birthright PROMISES were of a national and material nature—no spiritual salvation.

The people agreed. Thus they became God's chosen nation. BUT WHY?

This we know: God's purpose for them had a definite relation to *preparing for the ultimate KINGDOM OF GOD*—when the GOVERNMENT OF GOD would be reestablished over all the earth, and spiritual salvation would be offered to ALL!

Undoubtedly, one reason was to preserve the original physical strain of Shem's line. But there was much more.

Nations had developed knowledge. Mankind was limited, after Adam's rebellion, to the acquisition of physical and material knowledge.

But, like educated men and scientists today, they were saying, "Give us sufficient knowledge, and we will solve all problems and eradicate all evils—we will create utopia!"

Up to that time, mankind had been denied spiritual knowledge and fulfillment from God. God now decided to give them knowledge of his law—his kind of government—*his way of life!* He was going to prove to the world that without his Holy Spirit their minds were incapable of receiving and utilizing such knowledge of the TRUE WAYS OF LIFE. He was going to demonstrate to them that the mind of MAN, with its one spirit, and without the addition of God's Holy Spirit, could not have spiritual discernment—could not solve human problems, could not cure the evils that were besetting humanity. The nation Israel would be his guinea pig to demonstrate that fact. God had chosen a nation of almost perfect original strain in its generations—its ancestry. Also they had the quality heredity of Abraham, Isaac and Jacob (Israel).

So God entered into a covenant with them, making them HIS NATION. It also represented a MARRIAGE covenant, with Israel the wife, promising obedience to her husband—GOD. It was the physical type of the yet-to-come spiritual NEW COVENANT.

. And what did it prove?

Israel's Heredity and Environment

Here was a people of almost clear racial strain, and the God believing heredity of Abraham, Isaac and Israel. Two requisites make a human whatever he becomes in life: heredity and environment. Heredity involves what has been inherited by birth in such areas as health, intelligence and character tendencies. Environment includes all external influences and self-determined motivations—whether good or evil.

Heredity—if of good and high quality—may start one off at an advantage. An inspiring environment, uplifting influences and right self-motivation may further improvement. Such environment may turn one of inferior heredity into a real success in life.

But a discouraging environment, evil influences and misguided self-motivation may turn one of excellent heredity into failure and an evil nature.

God started his chosen nation off—even though brought out of slavery—with all the natural advantages of a superior heredity. God pulled them out of slavery and gave them a new and fresh start. One might say they had everything God-given going for them.

But now WHY? Why did God so prepare and raise up this nation Israel?

Consider WHY God created mankind in the first place! GOD IS REPRODUCING HIMSELF THROUGH MAN! He is creating in MAN God's own perfect holy and righteous spiritual CHARACTER! And that, in turn, is purposed to *restore* the GOVERNMENT OF GOD over all the earth. And, further, to create BILLIONS OF

GOD BEINGS TO FINISH THE CREATION OF THE VAST UNFINISHED UNIVERSE! And, *beyond that?*

Ah! God has not as yet revealed what he purposes beyond that!

Everything God has done, since the creation of the first humans, has been another progressive step in God's overall supreme PURPOSE!

Type of the Kingdom of God

The immediate purpose, so far in the history of mankind, is to prepare for THE KINGDOM OF GOD, which will RESTORE the GOVERNMENT OF GOD EARTH WIDE!

The kingdom of God is the actual begotten and born FAMILY OF GOD, which will first actually appear by a resurrection and instantaneous translation at Christ's Second Coming! And by begotten and BORN sons of God, emphatically I do NOT mean those deceived into the current "BORN-AGAIN" teaching—that anyone who "professes to receive Christ" is already, in this present human life, "born again." THAT IS A PARAMOUNT DECEPTION by which Satan the devil has DECEIVED those (the many in a so-called "Christianity") who have "accepted" a false conversion. They may be well meaning— but nevertheless DECEIVED! And of course a deceived person does not know he is deceived—he may be wholly sincere!

But now THINK! *HOW* does the Old Testament nation Israel play a part in progressively preparing for the KINGDOM OF GOD?

Government in the Kingdom of God

First, Abraham was a man of very outstanding qualifying abilities. Undoubtedly he, with his sons Isaac and Israel, shall, in the resurrection and kingdom of God, occupy a position next under Christ himself. The kingdom of God will be a spiritual kingdom including both Church and State—earth wide. These, as a team, probably will be next in line of authority under CHRIST—and over both church and state.

Of the nation ISRAEL, Moses, whom God raised up as their leader and lawgiver (though God the Father is the original real Lawgiver) in all probability will be under the Abraham-Isaac-Jacob team, but head over the national governments of the world during the coming millennium. And probably Joshua, who succeeded Moses, will be Moses' assistant in that office of worldwide national governments.

What of the nation Israel as a whole?

They, despite their favorable heredity, *failed utterly to qualify*. When God put the proposal of their formation as his nation before them, they replied, "All that the Lord hath spoken we will do" (Ex. 19:8). But they utterly broke their word and rebelled.

They were in a "husband-and-wife" relation with the Lord God. But the Lord said later of them: "Surely as a wife treacherously departeth from her husband, so have ye dealt treacherously with me, O house of Israel, saith the Lord" (Jer. 3:20).

The nation Israel under Moses was one people divided into 12 tribes.

The Promised Land was then called Canaan. Canaanites had settled in the land. But God had given this land to the descendants of Abraham BY PROMISE! It did not belong to the Canaanites or other national groups settled there.

When God moved his two million-plus Israelites in there, he commanded them through Moses:

"When ye are passed over Jordan into the land of Canaan; then ye shall drive out all the inhabitants of the land from before you, and destroy all their pictures, and destroy all their molten images ... and ye shall dispossess the inhabitants of the land, and dwell therein: for I have given you the land to possess it. ... But if ye will not drive out the inhabitants of the land from before you; then it shall come to pass, that those which ye let remain of them shall be pricks in your eyes, and thorns in your sides, and shall vex you in the land wherein ye dwell" (Num. 33:51-53, 55).

Nationally—Religiously Separate

It's time we UNDERSTAND THIS!

This nation Israel was GOD'S NATION. But they were *a physical, not a spiritual nation*. Yet God gave them HIS Church, as well as national government and religion. GOD INTENDED TO KEEP THEM PHYSICALLY SEPARATE from other nations—both nationally (racially) and religiously.

For them to intermarry with other neighboring people would result in two things: It would lead them into other idolatrous religions and alter their cultural and racial heritage!

The Israelites DID NOT OBEY GOD!

Much later, after the captivities of both Israel and Judah, God sent a colony of Jews from the Judahite slave population in Babylon back to Jerusalem under Zerubbabel as governor of the colony, to build the second Temple.

Among this colony were the prophets Ezra and Nehemiah. Against God's command, the people of the colony began to intermarry with Canaanites, Hittites, Perizzites, Jebusites and other races, "so that the holy seed [of pure strain, for they had not the Holy Spirit] have mingled themselves with the people of those lands . . ." (Ezra 9:2).

The prophet Ezra was ANGRY! He stood up before the congregation and said: "Ye have transgressed, and have taken strange wives, to increase the trespass of Israel. Now therefore . . . separate yourselves from the people of the land, and from the strange wives" (Ezra 10:10-11).

Jesus was born of the tribe of Judah, and it was necessary that HE be of the original genetic strain, even as Noah was.

BUT—nevertheless, the Old Covenant with Israel at Sinai was a type and forerunner of the NEW COVENANT. It will be made with the New Testament CHURCH, which is the *spiritual* Israel and Judah (Jer. 31:31; Heb. 8:6, 10).

Meanwhile, an individual few in Old Testament Israel did obey God and by becoming God's prophets, they became part of the *very foundation* of the New Testament CHURCH OF GOD. The Church is built on the solid FOUNDATION of the prophets (Old Testament) and apostles (New Testament), Jesus Christ himself being "the chief corner stone" (Eph. 2:20).

Among them, Elijah probably will be head, under Christ and Abraham-Isaac-Israel, over the Church, worldwide. John the Baptist may be under Elijah. There are indications that the prophet Daniel will be head over all gentile nations, and under Moses and Christ.

Fulfilling Their Role Despite Themselves

But in what manner did the ancient nation Israel play a part in preparation for the KINGDOM OF GOD?

I have already mentioned how the intellectuals and scholarly of this world feel that, given sufficient KNOWLEDGE, human carnal MAN could solve all problems.

God let many generations of ancient Israel and Judah PROVE by hundreds of years of human experience, that the *best* of humanity, without God's Holy Spirit CANNOT SOLVE HUMAN PROBLEMS AND EVILS!

I have spoken, during the past 20 years, to many heads of governments over Europe, Asia, Africa, South America. In China, I believe the Communist heads of government believe that communism, once it gains control of the earth, will solve all problems and evils. But many kings, emperors, presidents and prime ministers I have conferred privately with now realize the problems are *beyond* human ability to solve. And this I said plainly to many leaders of the People's Republic of China.

The problems and evils are of a *spiritual* nature. And a carnal mind without God's Spirit cannot come to grips with spiritual problems.

The many decades and centuries of ancient Israel PROVED THAT! Until Israel, God withheld knowledge of the *right ways* of human living from mankind. To Israel God gave his statutes and judgments, as well as his spiritual law. But these perfect laws did not, without God's Holy Spirit, solve the nation's problems!

God *could* say: "I am GOD. Take my word for it." But God gave PROOF, through Israel, that WITHOUT the Holy Spirit, MAN IS HELPLESS! They even had GOD to appeal to. But they did not have his Spirit within them.

Let this point be emphasized. When the first man, Adam, rejected the tree of life, and took to himself the knowledge of good and evil, he limited his power and ability to do good to the level of his human spirit. There is good as well as evil in human nature. Good is a spiritual attribute, not a physical or material action. Had Adam taken of the tree of life, the Holy Spirit of God would have entered him and joined with his spirit, uniting him with God as a son of God. The Holy Spirit meant more than spiritual knowledge of good. Not the hearers of the law (good) but the doers of the law are justified (Rom. 2:43). Love is the fulfilling of the law, but not human love. It requires the "love OF GOD . . . shed abroad in our hearts by the Holy [Spirit]" (Rom. 5:5).

God revealed his law to the nation Israel. One of the purposes of this nation was to prove by human experience that man without the Spirit of God within him cannot be righteous.

So, at this point, let us cover a brief synopsis of the actual history of the nation, and of the gentile nations of the world.

A most important declaration and promise was given to the people of Israel, as recorded in Leviticus 26. Again I quote from my book *The United States and Britain in Prophecy,* starting page 110:

The Pivotal Prophecy

In this central prophecy, God reaffirmed the birthright promise—but with conditions—for those of Moses' day! The birthright tribes of Ephraim and Manasseh were then *with* the other tribes—as one nation. Obedience to God's laws would bring the vast national wealth and blessings of the birthright not only to Ephraim and Manasseh, but the whole NATION would automatically have shared them at that time.

Notice carefully that two of the Ten Commandments are mentioned for emphasis. These were the main *test commandments!* They were the test of obedience, and of faith in and loyalty to God. God said: "Ye shall make you no idols nor graven image . . . to bow down unto it: for *I* am the Lord your God. Ye shall keep MY sabbaths . . ." (verses 1-2).

There was a *condition*—a great big "if "—to their receiving actual fulfillment of this stupendous birthright promise *in their time!* God said: "*If* ye walk in my statutes, and keep my commandments, and do them; *then* I will give you rain in due season, and the land shall yield her increase . . . " (verses 3-4). All wealth comes out of the ground. They would enjoy bumper crops the year round, one harvest on the heels of another. Verse 6: "And I will give PEACE in the land . . . and none shall make you afraid . . . neither shall the sword [of war] go through your land." What a blessing! What nation enjoys continuous peace, without fear of invasion?

Of course, in this world, every nation has enemies. What if enemy nations attacked? Verses 7-8: "And ye shall chase your enemies, and they shall fall before you by the sword. And five of you shall chase an hundred, and an hundred of you shall put ten thousand to flight. . . ."

Since many nations in this world always have been aggressors, Israel would have been attacked. A nation with the military superiority to defeat all attackers would soon become the dominant, most powerful nation on earth—especially with resources and great wealth from the ground. Verse 9: "For I will have respect unto you, and make you fruitful, and multiply you, and establish my covenant with you."

The Great Big If

But here comes the alternative—*IF* the conditions are not met: "... if ye will *not* hearken unto me, and will not do all these commandments ... I also will do this unto you; I will even appoint over you terror, consumption, and the burning ague [fever], that shall consume the eyes, and cause sorrow of heart [RSV: waste the eyes and cause life to pine away]: and ye shall sow your seed in vain, for your enemies shall eat it. And I will set my face against you, and ye shall be slain before your enemies: they that hate you shall reign over you ... " (verses 14-17). They would be invaded, conquered, become once again slaves—as they had been in Egypt before God freed them.

The Seven Prophetic Times

Now continue in Leviticus 26: "And if ye will not yet for all this hearken unto me, then I will punish you *seven times* more for your sins" (verse 18). . . .

Now when we come to the expression "then I will punish you *seven times* more for your sins" in Leviticus 26, it is evident both by its manner of wording in the sentence and by the fact of actual fulfillment that it was speaking of a DURATION of seven prophetic "*times*," or YEARS. And on this "year-for-a-day principle," it becomes seven 360-day years—a total of 2,520 *days*. And when each *day* is a *year* of punishment ... the punishment becomes the withdrawing of and withholding the promised blessings for 2,520 years! For that is precisely what did happen!

That national punishment—the withholding of the birthright promises of national prosperity and dominance, applied only to the house of Israel headed by the tribes of Ephraim and Manasseh.

How these promises were actually fulfilled at the precise time of 1800 to 1804 is one of the most amazing fulfillments of prophecy in the Bible and in the history of mankind. This fulfillment, step by step, is vividly revealed in our free book *The United States and Britain in Prophecy*.

This nation Israel promised to obey God. But they never did. Even while Moses was with the Eternal atop Mount Sinai receiving further instructions, the people melted and fashioned a golden calf to worship instead of the Eternal God. Because of their grumbling, their lack of faith and their disobedience, God did not allow them to enter the Promised Land for 40 years.

At the end of the 40 years Moses died. The Israelites were led across the Jordan River into the Promised Land under Joshua. During Joshua's life they obeyed God more or less but not fully.

After Joshua died, every man did what seemed right in his own mind. These people through disobedience to God would fall captive to surrounding kings. Then they would cry out to the Eternal and he would send a leader to free them. Again and again this process was repeated.

Israel Demanded Human King

After some generations God gave them a prophet to lead and rule them, the prophet Samuel. But in due time the people demanded a human king to rule them, as other nations were ruled. God said to Samuel it was not him that they rejected, but God. Samuel had ruled only as God's servant and actually it had been God's divine rule.

God gave them what they wanted, King Saul, a tall and towering leader. But Saul disobeyed God and the Eternal replaced him with King David. David personally was not without sin, but each time he repented and turned from each sin. David became "a man after God's own heart." He wrote a most important book in the Bible, the book of Psalms. God made an unconditional and unbreakable covenant with David, assuring that his dynasty, ruling over Israelites, would continue unbroken forever. Finally, in God's due time, that throne will be taken over by Jesus Christ, at his Second Coming to earth.

Israel Split into Two Nations

David's son Solomon became the wisest man who ever lived (except Christ). But he taxed the people very heavily, and when he died his son Rehoboam became king. The people sent a delegation with an ultimatum to Rehoboam. If he would reduce their taxes, they would serve him. If not, they would reject him as king. On the advice of the younger men among his councilors, Rehoboam told the people he would lay even heavier taxes on them.

Thereupon the people decided against the royal house of David. They named as king, Jeroboam, who had occupied the office we would today call prime minister, under King Solomon. Since Rehoboam was seated on the throne in Jerusalem, the people of Israel chose a new capital some distance north of Jerusalem. (Under a later king, Omri, they built a new northern capital at Samaria.)

Thereupon the tribes of Judah and Benjamin decided to remain loyal to Rehoboam. This brought about a secession of the rebellious tribes from Israel, and they became the nation of Judah.

Upon ascending the throne, Jeroboam deposed the Levites from the office of priesthood because he feared they might turn the hearts of the people back to Rehoboam and thereby he would lose his new throne. He also changed the holy festivals of the seventh month to the eighth month. There is strong indication that he also changed the seventh day Sabbath to Sunday, the first day of the week. The Sabbath had been made an everlasting covenant by God between him and Israel, by which they would be identified from all other people (Ex. 31:12-18) as God's nation Israel and by which they would be brought into weekly remembrance that the Eternal was their creator. For in six days God renewed or re-created the earth and creation is the proof of God.

The Ten Lost Tribes

Thus the people of Israel became known as the ten lost tribes. They had lost the covenant sign identifying them as Israel. They had lost the knowledge of God their creator. They soon lost even the Hebrew language.

During the time of 19 kings and seven dynasties, the 10-tribed kingdom of Israel continued in sin, rejecting the pleadings of prophets God sent to them. In a siege of war, about 721 to 718 B.C., the House of Israel was conquered by

Assyria. They were moved from their homes, farms and villages and transported as a captive people to Assyria on the southern shores of the Caspian Sea.

From there, within a hundred years, they migrated northwest and became known as the Lost Ten Tribes.

The world has never known what became of them. The world in general, mistakenly, has considered that all Israelites were Jews. But in the Bible, the term Jew applied only to the tribes of Judah, Benjamin and Levi. The Levites had joined the kingdom of Judah when they were expelled by Jeroboam.

The 2,520 Years Punishment

Dating from the captivity of Israel—721 to 718 B.C—that nation entered its 2,520 years of punishment as foretold in Leviticus 26. During this time the promises made to Abraham of national wealth, prosperity and dominance was withheld from them. This duration carried to the years 1800-1804 when national supremacy and economic dominance was to become theirs. This had to be, because God had promised it unconditionally to Abraham.

How they finally, beginning the year A.D. 1800, regained the national dominance and wealth God had unconditionally promised Abraham is recorded in the book *The United States and Britain in Prophecy.*

Meanwhile, the Jews of the kingdom of Judah were conquered and removed from their land by King Nebuchadnezzar of Babylon about 585 B.C.

Among the Jewish captives taken to Babylon was a brilliant young man, Daniel, a prophet who wrote the book under his name in the Bible.

God used the prophet Daniel as a go-between between the Eternal and King Nebuchadnezzar.

This great gentile king had organized the world's first empire uniting several nations under one government. God used Daniel to make known to the Babylonian king that the Creator God ruled over the whole earth, and that Nebuchadnezzar held his throne only by God's will. Actually, God was giving this gentile king opportunity to come under God's rule and have the consequent blessings of God.

The prophecy of Daniel chapter 2 pictured a stupendous image, representing Nebuchadnezzar's Chaldean Empire, to be followed by the Persian Empire, and then, in turn, the Greco-Macedonian Empire, the Roman Empire, and the entire system of human governments to be destroyed and replaced by the kingdom of God headed by Christ as King of kings ruling all the earth.

The Gentile World Government

The prophecies of Daniel 7, and of Revelation 13 and 17 foretell the same thing.

Of course, although Nebuchadnezzar acknowledged the existence of God, he never obeyed. Meanwhile, God kept hands off of the other peoples of the world.

The Persian Empire succeeded Nebuchadnezzar's Chaldean Empire. Seventy years after the captivity of Judah and destruction of Solomon's Temple God put it in the mind of King Cyrus of Persia to send a colony of captive Jews back to Jerusalem to build a second Temple.

This colony was headed by Zerubbabel as governor. The prophets Ezra and Nehemiah also joined this colony in Jerusalem. Zerubbabel built the second Temple, to which Jesus came some 500 years later. The Romans had come into power before the birth of Jesus. Just prior to the birth of Jesus, King Herod, who ruled over Jews and served the Romans, had remodeled and enlarged the Temple.

This colony of Jews sent back to Jerusalem some 500 years before Christ had expanded over the area of Judea. None of the kingdom of Israel had gone back to Jerusalem in this colony. They had migrated west by northwest and lost their Hebrew language, and even the knowledge of their identity. The world has called them the Lost Ten Tribes. More of them later.

It was during this 500 years that God sent so-called minor prophets to the Jews in Judea. Also it was during the latter part of this period that Jewish elders altered points in the religion started through Moses into the Judaism found among Jews in the lifetime of Jesus. The stage was set for his appearing.

Now let us return to the 10-tribed kingdom of Israel. As

stated above, they had, before the captivity of Judah, migrated west by northwest. The Assyrians settled in central Europe, and the Germans, undoubtedly, are, in part, the descendants of the ancient Assyrians.

However, the so-called Lost Ten Tribes—the kingdom of Israel—continued into western Europe and Britain. We cannot be positive in respect to the various tribal identities today, but probably France or at least the northern French are the tribe of Reuben. Ephraim and Manasseh journeyed on into the British Isles. They became a colonizing people, and according to prophecy they were to lose their first colony.

Name "Israel" Given to Joseph's Sons

The dying Jacob, who had been renamed Israel, conferred the birthright blessing on Joseph's two sons, Ephraim and Manasseh. Jacob, now renamed Israel, though blind so he could not see the lads before him, *crossed his hands*, "and Israel stretched out his right hand, and laid it upon Ephraim's head, who was the younger, and his left hand upon Manasseh's head, guiding his hands wittingly; for Manasseh was the firstborn. And he blessed Joseph, and said, God, before whom my fathers Abraham and Isaac did walk, the God which fed me all my life long unto this day, the Angel which redeemed me from all evil, bless the lads; and *let my name be named on them*, and the name of my fathers Abraham and Isaac; and let them grow into a multitude in the midst of the earth" (Gen. 48:14-16).

Continuing from *The United States and Britain in Prophecy*:

Let *who* grow into this promised multitude? Let *whose* descendants become that numerous seed, which shall number into billions? Not Judah, the father of the Jews—note it!—but EPHRAIM AND MANASSEH! Why have the eyes and understanding of church leaders and Bible students been blinded to this plain fact of Scripture?

Notice, Israel did not confer this blessing on just one, but on *both*—"Bless the lads," he said. This blessing went upon them jointly. "Let my name be named on them" was part of this blessing. His name was ISRAEL. Hence, it was the descendants of *these* lads, not the descendants of Judah, or the Jews, who were named ISRAEL. How clear it is that the name ISRAEL was to be indelibly stamped on EPHRAIM and MANASSEH!

A shocking fact—and yet plainly *proved*, right before your eyes! And remember, this scripture needs no "interpretation" or "special meaning" or "hidden symbolism" for you to understand! Here is the plain, simple statement that Jacob's name, which was changed to *Israel*, would become the very POSSESSION and *property*—the label on the peoples of Ephraim and Manasseh!

WHO, then, according to your Bible, is the real Israel (racially and nationally) of today?

Ephraim and Manasseh!

Ephraim and Manasseh *together* received the *right* to the name ISRAEL. It was to become the national name of their descendants. And their descendants were never Jews! Fix this fact firmly in your mind!

Thus it is that many of the prophecies about "Israel" or "Jacob" do not refer to Jews or to any of the nations that are today the descendants of the other tribes of Israel. Mark that well! Few, indeed, are the clergymen, theologians, or professed Bible scholars who know that today. Many *refuse* to know it!

Together the descendants of these two lads, Ephraim and Manasseh, were to grow into the promised multitude—the nation and company of nations. These national blessings are poured upon them jointly. These are the collective blessings which the lads together received—but not the other tribes!

Jacob Crosses Hands

But at this juncture, Joseph noticed that Jacob's right hand was not resting upon the head of the firstborn. He endeavored to remove it.

"Not so, my father," said Joseph, "for this is the firstborn; put thy right hand upon his head. And his father refused, and said, I know it, my son, I know it: he [Manasseh] also shall become a people, and he also shall be great: but truly *his younger brother shall be greater than he*, and his seed shall become a multitude [or, COMPANY] of nations. And he blessed them that day, saying, In thee shall Israel bless, saying, God make thee as Ephraim and as

Manasseh: and he set Ephraim before Manasseh" (Gen. 48:18-20). Here the promises are no longer collective, possessed jointly. Jacob now was prophesying as to the blessings of each, individually.

Promised Blessings to Britain and the United States

Remember, if ancient Israel obeyed God in the land (Sabbath breaking and idolatry were specifically mentioned in Leviticus 26), they would, in the ancient days of Moses, Joshua and up to the time of their captivity about 721-718 B.C., have inherited the national and material blessings of the birthright promise God made to Abraham. But, remember, if they did not obey, these promises would be denied for a duration of 2,520 years—that is, until A.D. 1800.

So it now becomes plain and clear that after the 2,520 years, beginning A.D. 1800 it was the descendants of Joseph, subdivided into two nations descended from Ephraim and Manasseh, who were to become the wealthiest and most powerful nations on earth.

The United States Is Manasseh

From the prophetic blessings passed on by the dying Jacob, it is apparent that Ephraim and Manasseh were in a large measure to inherit the birthright jointly; to remain together for a long time, finally separating.

In Genesis 48 Jacob first passed the birthright on to the two sons of Joseph jointly, speaking of them both together. Then, finally, he spoke of them separately—Manasseh was to become the single GREAT nation; Ephraim, the COMPANY of nations.

And in his prophecy for these latter days Jacob said, "Joseph is a fruitful bough, even a fruitful bough by a well; whose *branches run over the wall*" (Gen. 49:22). In other words, Joseph—Ephraim and Manasseh jointly and together—was to be a *colonizing* people in this latter day, their colonies branching out from the British Isles around the earth.

Together Ephraim and Manasseh grew into a multitude, then separated, according to Jacob's prophetic blessing of Genesis 48. Our people have fulfilled this prophecy.

But how can the U.S.A. be Manasseh when a large part of the population have come from many nations besides England? The answer is this: A large part of Manasseh remained with Ephraim until the separation of NEW England. But our forefathers were to be sifted through many nations, as corn through a sieve, yet not a grain to fall to the earth or be lost (Amos 9:9). The people did filter through many nations. Ephraim and much of Manasseh finally emigrated to England together, but many others of Manasseh who had filtered into and through other nations did not leave them until they came, as immigrants, to the United States AFTER the New England colony had become the separate nation. This does not mean that *all* foreigners who have emigrated to America are of the stock of Manasseh, but undoubtedly many are. Ancient Israel, however, always did absorb gentiles, who became Israelites through living in Israel's land.

The U.S. has become known as the "melting pot" of the world. Instead of refuting a Manasseh ancestry, this fact actually confirms it. The proof that the U.S. is Manasseh is overwhelming. Manasseh was to separate from Ephraim and become the greatest, wealthiest single nation of earth's history. America alone has fulfilled this prophecy. Manasseh was in fact a *thirteenth* tribe. There were twelve original tribes. Joseph was one of these twelve. But when Joseph divided into two tribes and Manasseh separated into an independent nation, it became a *thirteenth* tribe.

Could it be mere coincidence that it *started*, as a nation, with *thirteen* colonies?

But what about the *other* tribes of the so-called Lost Ten Tribes? While the *birthright* was *Joseph's*, and its blessings have come to the British Commonwealth of nations and the United States of America, yet the other eight tribes of Israel were also God's chosen people. They, too, have been blessed with a good measure of material prosperity—but *not* the dominance of the birthright.

We lack space for a detailed explanation of the specific identity of all of these other tribes in the nations of our twentieth century. Suffice it to say here that there is ample evidence that these other eight tribes have descended into such northwestern European nations as Holland, Belgium, Denmark, northern France, Luxembourg, Switzerland, Sweden, Norway. The people of Iceland are also of Viking stock. The political boundaries of Europe, as they exist today, do not necessarily show lines of division between descendants of these original tribes of Israel.

Prophecy for United States and Britain for Now

Just as God has bestowed on us such material blessings as *never before* came to any nations, now to correct us so we may enjoy such blessings, he is going to bring upon our peoples such national disaster as has *never before* struck any nation! Many prophecies describe this!

An important additional proof of modern Israel's identity is found in a fantastic, detailed and *most specific* prophecy found in Micah 5:7-15. It is speaking specifically about the "remnant" of Israel—modern Israel *today*—wherever it is. It describes the *wealth*, the beneficent dominance among nations, and then the coming *downfall* of the American and British Commonwealth peoples in detail!

Notice: "And the *remnant of Jacob* [not Jews] shall be in the midst of many people [nations] as a dew from the Lord, as the showers upon the grass, that tarrieth not for man, nor waiteth for the sons of men" (verse 7). Remember that dew and showers are *absolutely necessary* to agricultural productivity and are a symbol of national BLESSING and WEALTH from God.

Continue: "And the *remnant* of Jacob shall be among the Gentiles in the midst of many people as a lion among the beasts of the forest, as a young lion among the flocks of sheep: who, if he go through, both treadeth down, and teareth in pieces, and none can deliver" (verse 8).

Again, this symbolism describes the *last generation* of Israel as a GREAT POWER—as a lion among the other nations of the earth.

"Thine hand shall be lifted up upon thine adversaries, and all thine enemies shall be cut off" (verse 9) or defeated. They WERE defeated from the beginning of God's birthright blessing on America and Britain starting about 1803, through the First World War, the Second World War, until the turning point of the Korean War at the end of 1950.

Since that time, however, these blessings are surely being *taken away*—and neither America nor Britain has come out on top in any major conflict since that time!

So this prophecy shows that *at the very time* we were receiving God's blessings, we were a tremendous BLESSING to the other nations of the earth—for it is *our peoples* who have rescued the other nations of the world time and again through the Marshall Plan, the Point Four program, the Alliance for Progress, the hundreds of millions of bushels of wheat for starving nations.

The Hoover Program saved up vast food supplies after World War I. It saved millions in *other* nations from starvation!

Anciently Joseph saved up the wheat and food and made it available to others. MODERN Joseph did also. *BUT*—we are stiff-necked and rebellious toward God and his law, while our ancient forefather Joseph served and obeyed God with a whole heart.

It is *our peoples* who have been like a "lion" among the other nations of the earth—*preserving* in two great world wars the peace of the world and stability for all human life on this planet!

Sudden Destruction

Yet, in this detailed prophecy, God says: "And it shall come to pass IN THAT DAY, saith the Lord, that I will cut off thy horses" ["war-horses," Moffatt translation]—tanks, ships, rockets—"out of the midst of thee, and I will destroy thy chariots: and I will *cut off the cities* [by hydrogen bombs?] of thy land, and throw down all thy strong holds" (verses 10-11). (Notice, all the strongholds.)

God says he will do this! GOD determines the outcome of wars (Ps. 33:10-19).

How plain can you get? Here God identifies the GREAT peoples of the earth who are the most wealthy and beneficent, the most POWERFUL—yet *at the very time* their power reaches its zenith, he suddenly "breaks" the pride of their power (see Leviticus 26:19), *cuts off* their implements of war and destroys their cities! Why?

Because, as the prophet continues to explain, we have too

much "witchcraft" and too many "soothsayers" (astrology) and false ministers in our lands who refuse to preach with authority the commandments and ways of the living God!

In America, we print on our money "In God We Trust." But instead we rely on foreign allies and our own human ingenuity, not in God.

Stealing from God

God has a financial law for our nations. He says 10 percent of the increase, or gross income of each one of us, belongs to God for his purposes and his work.

In Malachi 3:8-10: "Will a man rob God? Yet ye have robbed me. But ye say, Wherein have we robbed thee? In tithes and offerings. Ye are cursed with a curse: for ye have robbed me, even this whole nation. Bring ye all the tithes into the storehouse, that there may be meat in mine house, and prove me now herewith, saith the Lord of hosts, if I will not open you the windows of heaven, and pour you out a blessing, that there shall not be room enough to receive it."

After the year 1800 we prospered because of Abraham's obedience and God's unbreakable promises to him. But now having received such individual and national prosperity, we sin by stealing from God. That has brought our nations under a curse. We have won our last war. Nothing but troubles now lie ahead until we repent.

God's tithe is holy to him (Lev. 27:30). God's Sabbath, the seventh day of every week, is holy to him. Yet we have put no difference between the holy and the profane (Ezek. 22:26).

Giving Sin Public Acceptance

We commit individual and national sins and give such sinning wide public acceptance.

Very early in 1927, when I was in my first biblical studies, leading to my conversion, my wife and I often visited various churches. I was searching for the truth. One Sunday morning we attended a church service at a leading downtown Baptist church in Portland, Oregon. They were announcing the conclusion of a contest at which a very handsome new Bible was awarded to the winner. The contest question had been, "What is the most universal sin?" The winning answer was "Ingratitude."

Assuredly that is a very prevalent sin. Another very prevalent sin, and one of the oldest, is the misuse of sexuality. Indeed, prostitution is often spoken of as "the world's oldest profession."

Satan has seized on this sin to make it far more universal than is generally realized. Satan, himself, has no sex. He is resentful of the fact God has endowed humans with sex. Therefore, Satan sways humanity into making sexual sins one of the most universal and destructive.

During most of the so-called "church age" in Roman Catholic teaching, and in England and the United States since the Victorian age, sex was a virtually forbidden topic of conversation, seldom mentioned. Satan made sure sex was considered as "shameful" and so evil it was not talked about. About the turn of the century, Sigmund Freud, founder of psychoanalysis, changed all of that. Up until World War I it was illegal in the U.S. to publish, sell, or even loan a book containing sex knowledge. After World War I the legal barriers on the imparting of sex information toppled. An avalanche of books, pamphlets, newspaper articles descended on the public. Yet in all this the most vitally needed dimension of knowledge was missing.

The Missing Dimension in Sex

The author's book *The Missing Dimension in Sex* is offered, gratis, upon request.

It provides this missing dimension of knowledge.

Beginning the middle of the twentieth century, the catch phrase "the new morality" was completely changing public attitudes. Today sexuality is openly discussed in the public media, especially in television, turning promiscuous sex into public acceptance. Today it may be questioned whether as many as 2 percent of young brides go to the altar as virgins. Marriage for much of society is on the way out. In some areas divorces virtually equal marriages. Family life is being broken down though the family is a basic building block of any stable civilization.

More and more, children are not wanted. Abortion is fast gaining public acceptance.

God created sex, not only to keep humanity alive, but to bring delectable, joyfully pleasurable happiness in pure and wholesome love between husband and wife, and as a means of binding tightly together a happily married couple. But under modern attitudes, the cord supposedly tying a husband and wife tightly together is proving to be the cord that cuts the marriage in two.

It's time you knew the truth about the missing dimension in sex. It is set forth frankly, fearlessly, rationally and spiritually, as well as physically, in our book mentioned above.

God condemns homosexuality. He destroyed the whole populations of Sodom and Gomorrah for this sin. It is condemned in the first chapter of Romans, saying no such person can enter the kingdom of God. Then we try to change the ugly, reproachful name *homosexual*, and call those who practice it "gays." The public media and the public in general are coming to make this perversion acceptable by calling it "sexual preference." We are becoming nations of drunkards and thousands are being killed on our highways by drunken drivers. Yet excessive drinking of alcohol is encouraged through millions of dollars of advertising on TV commercials.

We inflict on ourselves through sin, such diseases as alcoholism, AIDS, herpes and other venereal diseases, and then try to prevent the penalty of those sins by medical and scientific studies to produce cures that will allow the sins to continue.

Now continue the prophecy in Micah 5. Therefore, God will punish and *destroy us—unless we repent—*just before and leading up to the utter destruction to come *"upon the heathen"* (verse 15), which will take place at the very END of this age and at the second return of Jesus Christ as King of kings!

There is no other people that even remotely fulfills this great prophecy! But the American and British peoples fulfill it precisely!

As the "pride of our power" continues to be BROKEN, as

the British gradually lose their foreign sea gates and possessions around the earth, as America signs away ownership of the Panama Canal—control over this vital sea gate—as the gold supply drains away, and weather upsets increase, this focal prophecy alone represents giant PROOF as to where the modern "remnant" of the peoples of Israel resides today!

Punishment on All Nations!

It will now be made plain—from God's own warning prophecies—that this greatest multiplied *intensity* of corrective punishment will fall on Britain and America—including British peoples in Commonwealth countries. And it will strike them down *first!*

But they are not the only nations to suffer corrective disaster. God is Creator of all other nations, too! God is concerned about the people and races we have called "heathen." They, too, are human. They, too, are made in God's own likeness, with the potential of being molded into God's spiritual and character IMAGE! God sent the apostle Paul to gentile nations!

All mankind has rebelled against, rejected, and turned from God and his ways! There can never be peace on earth until all nations will have been turned to God and his ways, ruled by his supreme government!

All mankind, right now, is caught in the vortex of the swiftly accelerating crisis marking the utter destruction of this world's man-built, Satan-inspired civilization.

Through Jeremiah God says: "A noise shall come even to the ends of the earth; for the Lord hath a controversy with the nations, *he will plead with all flesh"*—how? Right now the *World Tomorrow* program carries his *peaceful* pleading worldwide, but the world, except for scattered individuals, does not heed *this* kind of "pleading." The next words tell HOW God is now about to plead: ". . . he will give them that are wicked to the sword, saith the Lord. . . . Behold, EVIL shall go forth *from nation to nation*, and a great whirlwind shall be raised up from the coasts of the earth" (Jer. 25:31-32).

God will use a United Europe to punish Britain-America.

Then he will use the Communist hordes to wipe out the Roman Europe.

We are entering a time of world trouble—utter WORLD chaos! There is war, strife, violence in Asia, Africa, South America, Central America, Ireland, the Middle East—as well as Europe and North America. The population explosion is a worldwide threat to human existence. Crime, violence, sickness, disease, inequality, poverty, filth, squalor, degeneration, suffering—these infest ALL nations!

But, as salvation is given *first* to Israel, so is corrective punishment!

Our Great Tribulation

Notice Jeremiah's prophecy:

"For thus saith the Lord; We have heard a voice of trembling, of fear, and not of peace. Ask ye now, and see whether a man doth travail with child? wherefore do I see every man with his hands on his loins, as a woman in travail, and all faces are turned into paleness? Alas! for that day is great, so that none is like it: it is even the time of Jacob's TROUBLE ..." (Jer. 30:5-7).

Remember—in passing on the birthright to the two sons of Joseph, Ephraim and Manasseh (Gen. 48:16), Jacob said, "Let MY NAME be named on them"—on Ephraim and Manasseh—who today are Britain and America. This tells ON WHOM this most terrible of national calamities is to fall—on Britain and America!

But now when is it to fall? Do not assume this is referring to anything that did happen to ancient Israel. Read right on—see WHEN this prophecy is to be fulfilled!

Continue in Jeremiah 30:7: "... it is even the time of JACOB's trouble; but he shall be saved out of it." (After he has learned his lesson *IN* it!) Continuing from RSV, "And it shall come to pass in that day, says the Lord of hosts, that I will break the YOKE from off their neck [yoke of slavery], and I will burst their bonds, and strangers shall no more make servants of them. But they shall serve the Lord their God *and* David their king, whom I will *raise up* for them." (David, at the time of the RESURRECTION—at the very time of Christ's COMING!)

So *the time* is just prior to Christ's COMING—coming *to liberate* our peoples—even as Moses liberated ancient Israel from Egyptian slavery.

Jesus Foretold It!

Other prophecies speak of this same time of national calamity greater than any before. The pivotal New Testament prophecy is that of Jesus on the Mount of Olives—recorded in Matthew 24, Mark 13 and Luke 21.

The apostles had asked Jesus privately WHEN his Second Coming would occur—and the END of *this* world and the beginning of the happy world tomorrow. Jesus said the SIGN by which we might know when this is very NEAR would be that his original gospel of the kingdom of God would be preached in all the world as a witness to all nations (Matt. 24:14). But what else—just before his coming?

Jesus continued: "For then shall be GREAT TRIBULATION, such as was not since the beginning of the world to this time, no, nor ever shall be. And except those days should be shortened, there should no flesh be saved [alive]: but for the elect's sake those days shall be shortened" (Matt. 24:21-22).

Here is described the greatest time of TROUBLE—TRIBULATION—in all history, or ever to be. Jeremiah described it as "Jacob's trouble," so great "that none is like it."

Daniel described the same most severe trouble of all history. Speaking of a time now in our immediate future, Daniel foretold: "And at that time shall Michael stand up, the great prince [archangel] which standeth for the children of thy people: and there shall be a time of TROUBLE, such as never was since there was a nation even to that same time" (Dan. 12:1).

The same *most intense punishment* on Britain and America. And WHEN? Continue, same verse, " . . . and at that time thy people shall be delivered [from this enslaved trouble], every one that shall be found written in the book. And many of them that sleep [are dead] in the dust of the earth shall awake [RESURRECTION], some to everlasting life . . ." (verses 1-2).

The time is just before the RESURRECTION of the just, at Christ's coming. Christ's Second Coming will end this world's civilization and start the wonderful peaceful, happy world tomorrow.

MYSTERY
OF THE CHURCH

ERHAPS the greatest mystery of all will not seem, at first
glance, to be a mystery to most readers of this volume.
The reason that is true is the fact that the true purpose
and meaning of the Church is as little understood as the Bible
itself. The revelation of that mystery must come as a shocking
truth. The real truth about the Church, the reason for its
origin, and its purpose has remained hidden from even the
professing Christian world.

This is inextricably intertwined with the gospel of Jesus
Christ. It is a fact to stagger the mind of the reader that the
gospel of Jesus Christ was not proclaimed *to the world* from
about A.D. 50 until the year 1953. The apostle Paul foretold
this when he said, "But if our gospel be hid, it is hid to them
that are lost: in whom the god of this world hath blinded the
minds of them which believe not, lest the light of the glorious
gospel of Christ, who is the image of God, should shine unto
them" (II Cor. 4:3-4). Millions have read over this passage
without grasping its real meaning.

Church Exclusive to Christian World

The term *church* is applicable only to the Christian religion.
(The Christian religion, as is generally understood, is the
largest religion in the world in number of professing adherents.) Other religions may have mosques, synagogues and

temples. But is the Church a building? Many assume it is, which assumption reflects their ignorance of the purpose and meaning of the Church. But in this volume we are concerned only with the Church. For when stripped of its mystery, the Church is of paramount concern to all peoples of the earth.

The Church, founded by Jesus Christ, has an all-important meaning to every human life that ever lived. Yet almost no one has ever known that meaning.

Even within the Christian world, apostasy, division and changing times have blotted out the true original meaning and purpose that now is indeed a mystery.

The word *church* is an English-language word translated from the original Greek *ekklesia*. *Ekklesia* means called-out-ones. Old Testament Israel was usually called by the term "congregation." In some respects the word *congregation* is synonymous with the word *church*. Yet there is a distinct difference between the terms church and congregation. The congregation of Israel was separate, as a separate nation. But they were not called-out-ones spiritually in the same sense that characterizes the New Testament Church.

What has been hidden from even the professing Christian world is the real purpose of the Church—the real reason why Jesus Christ, the second Adam, founded the Church.

Real Purpose of Church

To the shocking surprise to nearly every reader of this volume, I will state first what the Church was not and is not. It is not the instrumentality by which God is trying to "save the world." Few may realize it, but Jesus made no attempt to gain converts or to invite people to "give their hearts to him" or to "accept him as their personal savior."

On the contrary, he "called out"—drafted—twelve disciples. The word disciple means student. These twelve were students being taught by Jesus the true gospel of the kingdom of God. This involved the entire purpose of God in creating the human race on this earth. That meaning had been rejected, lost, by the first created man, Adam.

At this point let us recapitulate. God is the Creator and Supreme Ruler over his entire creation. He had placed the archangel Lucifer on earth's throne to administer the government of God. God's government is based on God's law. God's law is a way of life—the way of outgoing love.

God's government was repudiated by Lucifer, who became Satan, and Satan ruled with the opposite way of life—rebellion, self-centeredness and conflict.

Adam, the first created human being, was given opportunity to receive eternal God-life with obedience to God and total submission to the law of God and God's government. He could have replaced Satan on earth's throne. He rejected the government and way of God. Thus Satan was left on the throne where he still rules as of this day. Adam and the human family were kidnapped, deceived into living the self-centered hostile way of Satan. Thereupon God closed off the tree of life and the Holy Spirit of God, until Jesus Christ, the second Adam, should conquer and replace Satan on earth's throne. At his First Coming, appearing on earth as the human Jesus, Christ came, not to seize the throne, but to conquer Satan, qualify to replace him on the throne, and to ransom the kidnapped world with his shed blood.

Now, why the Church? Christ came also to call out selected and chosen ones from Satan's world to turn from Satan's way into the way of God's law and to qualify to reign with Christ when he comes to replace Satan on the throne of the earth. Those called into the Church were called not merely for salvation and eternal life, but to learn the way of God's government and develop the divine character during this mortal life in the Church age.

Seven annual festivals were given to Old Testament Israel and were ordained forever. Their true meaning had long remained a hidden mystery. They picture God's plan of redemption—the divine plan by which God is reproducing himself. The Passover pictures the death of Christ in payment for the penalty of human sin repented of. The seven days of the Festival of Unleavened Bread picture the Church coming out of sin, even as Israel came out of Egypt. The Day of Pentecost, originally called Feast of Firstfruits, pictures the Church as the first to be begotten and born as children of God during the Church age. The Feast of Trumpets pictures the Second Coming of Christ to take over earth's throne and to rule all nations. The Day of Atonement pictures the putting away of Satan. The Feast of Tabernacles pictures the thousand-year reign under the rule of Christ and the born children of God. The Final Great Day pictured the final judgment which will be covered in chapter seven. Let's return now to the subject of this chapter, the Church.

The Institution of the Church

What is the Church? Why is the Church? The institution of the Church, at first mention, may not seem to be a mystery. The modern Western world takes the fact of the existence of churches for granted, as a part of the world's civilized life.

WHY the institution of the Church in the world? —WHY was it started, and for what purpose?

If you ask people in the non-Christian world where other religions are accepted they would probably have no answer. They know little about the Church. Those in the more modernist and liberal areas of traditional Christianity would probably say the Church exists merely as an emotional lift, having a psychological influence on those who have not embraced the evolutionary theory as accepted in modern higher education.

If you ask those who follow one of the evangelical Christian denominations they would probably say that the Church is God's instrument in his effort to save the world from an eternal hell fire. It has been assumed by those people that the Church is a sort of soul-saving station to get people "saved." If the Church came into existence as an instrumentality for "getting people saved," then, I ask, by what means did God try to save people prior to Christ's founding of the Church? Jesus did not appear until 4,000 years after Adam and the original sin. If God is and has been trying to convert the world, what means did he use during that 4,000 years between Adam and Christ? As we have seen in chapter three, God closed the tree of life at the foundation of the world. The Holy Spirit and salvation were shut off from the world during all these years.

But in view of the facts revealed by God Almighty in his Word, covered in the preceding chapters, all these suppositions are wrong. They only give vociferous testimony to the fact expressed in Revelation 12:9 that the whole world has been deceived by Satan the devil. Their minds have been blinded to the truth about God's purpose for humanity as stated in II Corinthians 4:3-4.

The existence of the Church, then, does indeed become a mystery to nearly everyone on the face of this earth.

News concerning some church appears frequently in newspapers and on newscasts. People think of a church on some near corner, or perhaps of some denomination in the news, but the fact of its existence would not occur to the mind to be a mystery. But when we ask, why do churches exist, how did the Church as an institution come into being?—what is its reason or purpose for its existence?—does it make any difference whether, or to which church you belong?—then, indeed, it becomes a mystery. The average person has no answer.

The facts of the Church's origin and its purpose are revealed in that book of mystery—the Holy Bible. To make clear that mystery may well require more pages in this book than any other subject.

My Personal Experience

I am reminded of my own personal experience, probably typical of many others. My parents were members of the Friends Church, commonly known as the Quakers. The family had been Quakers for many generations. I was taken to church from babyhood, taking it for granted as a normal part of life. I was in church every Sunday because my parents took me. As a routine habit I continued until age 18. It never occurred to me to question why we should attend church or how the church came into existence, or what was its real meaning and purpose.

I never went through the experience in those years of being "converted." As I grew into the teens, I was told that I had a birthright membership in the church. I was led to take it for granted that I was an immortal soul and that when I died I would not really die, but rather pass away into heaven where I would have no responsibilities but only a life of idleness and ease in sublime glory forever and ever. But I was not religiously or doctrinally interested. I simply took churchgoing and a religious phase of life for granted. But I had no special or deep religious or spiritual interest, and by age 18 I started in the advertising business, lost all interest in religion or the things of God and gave up regular church attendance. I still believed in God—that is to say, I took the existence of God for granted since I had been taught of God's existence from earliest memory.

Then at age 25 I had met and married that one and only particular young woman. She was more seriously interested in the things of God. We began to feel that we should join a church. My wife's ancestry had been part Quaker and part Methodist. There was no Quaker church in the neighborhood where we lived in a Chicago suburb. We joined a Methodist church because it was located within walking distance, we liked the personality of the minister, and we liked the membership socially. I think our experience was typical of millions of others. But it never occurred to me to ask or even wonder why we ought to go to church, or why the institution of the church had ever come into being. Like millions of others I assumed that the "good people" went to church and so ought we.

The Church in Relation to Past History

And so now I ask, does anyone question the reason or purpose for the church as an institution? I ask, DOES ANYONE KNOW *WHY* there are churches? Is there a REASON for it? The very existence of the church known as "Christianity" is one of the great mysteries of our time. This very subject brings to mind again the fact that, not having lived through and seen events of the past 6,000 years that led up to the present, we do not grasp the real meaning or purpose of the Church. In this chapter we shall view the Church in its TRUE relationship to all the events described in the first five chapters of this book. Again, what is the Church?

Most think of the CHURCH as a building with a sharply sloping roof, a steeple pointing heavenward atop and a cross on its face. Indeed Webster defines the word *church* as a building. It was something altogether different when originally founded.

People suppose a church is a building to which people— some of them—flock on Sunday morning for "worship." They think *people* go to the *church*. As founded in the New

Testament, the *Church* went to a *building,* at first a private home. And the Church assembled on a Saturday, not Sunday.

The churches of today have changed drastically from Christ's pattern! This fact, also, is cloaked in mystery, understood by virtually no one. But for WHAT PURPOSE did Christ found the Church? What has happened to it since?

Some may know Christ started the Church. But who and what is Christ? And if he was the founder of the Church, for what purpose did he start it? But Jesus founded only one Church. Yet in the Western world today there are many different churches—Catholic, Protestant, independents. And within them many denominations, sects and divisions or congregations, each with its differing beliefs, teachings, rituals and programs.

The Church started out as one Church. As it is recorded in I Corinthians 12 the Church consisted of many members, but only the one body—the one Church—of which Jesus Christ was the Head.

At the outset of this chapter we are primarily concerned with four basic questions that constitute a mystery that needs to be revealed with understanding.

1) Who and what is Christ? Why did he appear on earth?

2) What is and why was the Church brought into existence?

3) What is the gospel the Church is commissioned to proclaim?

4) What is the history of the Church? Why is Christianity so different today than at its inception in the first century?

Institutionally the CHURCH is thought of today as a religious organization, association or society. One—if "good"—is supposed to join the "church of his choice." Of course there are the "good guys" and the "bad guys" and the "good" go to church. But does it make any difference which church—which denomination?

A Minister without a Pastorate

I am reminded of an incident of more than 50 years ago. I was still in Eugene, Oregon. An ex-minister came to me who had just recently been married. His wife had money, but he was too proud to let her support him. He had not been employed in the ministry for some time but now needed a job.

"Do you know of any pulpit vacancies in Lane County?" he asked. "I want to support my wife, and she wants to remain here in Lane County."

"Well, yes," I replied. "I do know of one vacancy, but that wouldn't help you because that is a Christian church, and you are a Methodist with different beliefs and practices."

"Oh, that won't make any difference," he assured me. "I'll preach whatever doctrines they want me to preach."

But does it really make any difference what we believe? Let the Word of God answer that question.

The Church seems to be something concerned with worshiping with others. Supposedly it refers to the worship of God.

But if GOD is related to the Church, what is his relationship? How did the Church start? All this is a mystery to today's world.

Back in the early part of 1927 when my intense Bible study was bringing me toward conversion, I asked myself such questions. I supposed questions of that sort never enter the average mind.

In the New Testament Greek, the Church is called the *ekklesia,* a Greek word meaning called-out-ones—an assembly, a congregation, a gathering, a group. There is no sanctity to the word *ekklesia.* The *name* of the Church, however, used 12 times in the New Testament, is "Church of God," which denotes that it is GOD's Church—which NAME attaches sanctity. The Old Testament Church was the "Congregation of Israel," a human man.

Why Jesus Founded the Church

The first place in the New Testament where the word *church* appears is Matthew 16:18, where, speaking to Simon Peter, Jesus said, "I will build my church." As noted above, the inspired Greek word for church was *ekklesia,* meaning called-out-ones. Stated in more clear English language, Jesus said "I will call out of Satan's world disciples, to grow into the altogether new and different world, which will be God's kingdom." And in Ephesians 5:23 it is stated that Christ is the Head of the Church.

So this we know. Whatever the Church is, it belongs to GOD and its name is the CHURCH OF GOD. Jesus Christ is its founder, and he its living HEAD.

But if it is GOD's Church—if Jesus Christ founded it and today heads it—it is something IMPORTANT TO GOD, and therefore VITAL THAT WE COME TO UNDERSTAND! We must bear in mind what *went before*—what led up to it—to understand *WHY* the living Christ created it—*WHAT* it is, and where it fits into the divine PURPOSE being worked out here below.

Church of the Old Testament

Old Testament Israel had a function preparatory to ultimate establishment of the KINGDOM OF GOD. The first mention in the Bible of the Church, in time of existence, is Acts 7:38 where it speaks of "the church in the wilderness" at Mount Sinai, under Moses. So Old Testament Israel was the "Church." Most generally in the Old Testament, Israel, as a Church, is referred to as the "Congregation of Israel."

However, as we shall see, the Church of the New Testament is entirely different and has an entirely different purpose than the Old Testament "Congregation of Israel." Almost no one has understood that the gospel could not be proclaimed to the world, nor could God's called congregation of people have the Holy Spirit *UNTIL* Jesus a) had qualified by overcoming Satan, and b) had been glorified after ascension to heaven (John 7:37-39).

And that is something not even the theologians and church leaders of our day understand. It is, indeed, a mystery, which needs to be revealed and understood. Now let us understand clearly who and what is Christ.

We have already seen in chapter one that Christ, in the eternity before the world came into being, was the "Logos" who also was God, and as Jesus, was born as the Son of God. Now as the Son of God just what was Jesus? He was called the second Adam (I Cor. 15:45). Why should he be called the second Adam? The first Adam had the opportunity of taking of the tree of life, which meant God-life—obeying God and thereby replacing Satan on the throne of the earth. Jesus came to do just that, to qualify to replace Satan on that throne and to start the government of God on the earth through those called out from Satan's world. He came also with a message from God called the gospel. The word *gospel* means good news. And actually, his gospel—the message sent by him from God—was the good news of the kingdom of God. And the kingdom of God, as we shall see, is to be the restoration of the government of God over the earth and the ousting of Satan from that throne.

Jesus came also to build the Church. And he came to pay the ransom price for a kidnapped world and by that price—his death—to pay the penalty incurred by all humans for their sins.

Jesus—Earth Ruler and King

Next, what nearly all "Christians," including theologians, do not realize: Jesus was born to become a KING!

On trial for his life before Pilate, Jesus was asked, "Art thou a king then?" And Jesus answered: "Thou sayest that I am a king. To this end was I born, and for this cause came I into the world . . ." (John 18:37). Jesus also said (verse 36), "My kingdom is not of this world . . . [else] would my servants fight"—showing that this is Satan's world. Jesus came to call people out of this world to be prepared to teach and rule under him when he becomes King and takes over the throne of the earth.

Prior to the begettal and birth of Jesus, God had said to his mother-to-be, Mary, by his angel: "And, behold, thou shalt conceive in thy womb, and bring forth a son, and shalt call his name JESUS. He shall be great, and shall be called the Son of the Highest: and the Lord God shall give unto him the throne of his father David: and he shall reign over the house of Jacob for ever; and of his KINGDOM there shall be no end" (Luke 1:31-33). His gospel was the good news of that kingdom—the kingdom of God.

It is vital that we understand, at this point, that Jesus, during his human life, was both God and man. In Isaiah 7:14, Mary, the mother of Jesus, was prophesied as the virgin who was going to bear a son. That Son's name, in this prophecy, was to be called Immanuel, which means "God with us." In other words, Jesus was God as well as human man. He had no human father. God Almighty was his father who begat him by means of the Holy Spirit. But though Jesus was actually "God with us," he was also human like all other humans. He was subject to being tempted just as all other humans are tempted. Although he was actually God in the human flesh, yet in his ministry he functioned as a human. Remember, he was the second Adam. It was necessary for him that he, as a human, reject the "forbidden tree" and accept the tree of life. It was necessary that he, as the first Adam might have done, choose to rely completely on God the Father. In fact, God was actually in Christ and Jesus obeyed the Father completely. He qualified to wrest the throne of the earth from Satan.

Jesus Was God

Why was it necessary that Jesus be actually God in the human flesh? Why was it necessary that he be God? Why was it necessary that he be human? As God, he was the Maker of all mankind. In Ephesians 3:9 it is revealed that God created all things by Jesus Christ. When Jesus was born as a human, his life as our Maker was greater than the sum total of all human lives. Since it is humans who have sinned and come under the death penalty, God's law required human death as the penalty for human sin. But, as our Maker Jesus was the only human whose death could pay the penalty for the sins of all humans.

In no other way could the Creator God have redeemed a vast humanity condemned to the penalty of death.

Jesus Beaten for Our Healing

We need to bear in mind that though Jesus was God in the human flesh, he was also human even as you and I. He could suffer the same physical pains. He had been condemned to death by the Roman governor Pilate on clamorous demand of shouting Jews.

He was a strong, vigorous, young man of about 33 years of age, in the peak of health. Because he had never broken even a law of health, he suffered the process of dying as no other human ever did. He had been up all night without sleep during the trial before Pilate. Pilate, later that morning, delivered him to be scourged before being put to death.

Scourging consisted of being stripped to the waist, bound over in a bent position, tied to a post. He was beaten by whips made of leather thongs weighted down by pieces of lead, broken shards of bone and sharp jagged pieces of metal attached at intervals of four to five inches, along the leather thongs. They were designed to imbed themselves deeply into the flesh as the thongs wrapped themselves around the body. He was whipped until his flesh was torn open and even his ribs appeared. Scourging was intended to weaken the victims so they would die quickly on the stake of crucifixion. As foretold in Isaiah 52:14: "His visage was so marred more than any man, and his form more than the sons of men."

This indescribable scourging was endured that believers might be healed from physical transgression, sicknesses or disease (Isa. 53:5; I Pet. 2:24). What a terrible price our own very Maker paid that we might, by believing, be healed. Yet nearly all professing believers totally ignore what their Savior provided for them, and instead of relying on him, put their faith in human doctors, drugs, medicines and knives.

Jesus was so weakened by this terrible chastisement that he was unable to carry his cross, as he was required to do, but for a short distance. Another was appointed to carry it for him.

The Most Painful and Despicable Death

Outside the city walls, at the Place of the Skull (Golgotha), Jesus was nailed to the cross. He was humiliated, spat upon, ridiculed, and jeered at.

More than that, because at that moment he had taken on himself our sins, in order to pay the penalty in our stead, he was forsaken by even his Father, God. As he hung on the cross, helpless, a soldier stabbed him with a spear, he screamed in pain (Matt. 27:50, Moffatt) and then died. He did this because you and I have transgressed the law of God. He paid the supreme possible sacrifice for you and for me.

One more supremely vital truth. The resurrection of Jesus from the dead was that of a human being and the only one that could make possible the resurrection of humans, once dead, to immortal life.

Now another vital prophecy. In Isaiah 9:6-7: "For unto us a child is born, unto us a son is given: and the government shall be upon his shoulder: and his name shall be called Wonderful, Counsellor, The mighty God, The everlasting Father, The Prince of Peace. Of the increase of his government and peace there shall be no end, upon the throne of David, and upon his kingdom, to order it, and to establish it with judgment and with justice from henceforth even for ever. The zeal of the Lord of hosts will perform this." Notice the government would be on his shoulder. Jesus is going to be King over all the earth. And one of the purposes of his coming was to announce that kingdom. Jesus' gospel was not only good news—it was an announcement or good news proclamation of the coming kingdom of God. What a tragedy that a "traditional Christianity" has forsaken and lost that vital and glorious gospel message and substituted their own gospel about the person of Christ.

Jesus was born as a human, to become a KING, ultimately to establish the KINGDOM OF GOD, ruling the whole earth with the GOVERNMENT OF GOD! But that RULE required more than the individual JESUS. The king, president, prime minister or ruler over every nation governs with and through a more or less vast organization of others who rule various phases and departments under him. Likewise, Christ must have an organized government with numerous others trained and qualified to rule under him. Jesus said, "I will build my church" (Matt. 16:18). The Church was to consist of many to be called out of Satan's world to be taught and trained for numerous governmental positions under Christ when he comes to rule over all the nations.

Jesus—Spiritual Savior

Jesus came also as spiritual Savior, to save God's people in their due time from their sins, that they might be BORN into the very divine FAMILY OF GOD (Matt. 1:21).

Remember, the tree of life, symbolizing the Holy Spirit, had been cut off from mankind at the foundation of the world after the sin of Adam. What the world does not understand is that the Spirit of God was cut off from humanity as a whole UNTIL the second Adam actually removes Satan and restores the government of God on the earth.

As for humanity as a whole, it was appointed at the time of Adam's sin for humans once to die and after death, by resurrection, shall come the judgment (Heb. 9:27).

The Holy Spirit was not given to the people of ancient Israel. Since God called and raised up prophets for a specific purpose preparatory to the salvation of humanity, it was necessary, in order for them to perform their called function, that an exception be made and they be empowered by the Holy Spirit.

In the same manner since God through Jesus was now calling out his Church for a specific function preparatory to the establishment of his kingdom and government over all nations, it was now necessary that the same exception be made for the Church and that they be empowered by the Holy Spirit.

God emphatically did not empower the prophets with his Spirit merely for the purpose of giving them salvation. Likewise, God did not call saints out of this world merely for their salvation and entrance into his kingdom. Otherwise God would be a respecter of persons to have called the few of his Church at this time, while refusing to call others to salvation.

If God is opening salvation to the few in his Church only to give them salvation, while he excluded the preponderance of the world as a whole until later, then God certainly would be a respecter of persons, discriminating against the world as a whole. Jesus said plainly no man can come unto him except God the Father draws him (John 6:44). A professed Christianity believes precisely the opposite. This false Christianity teaches that God is calling and trying to save everybody in this present time. If that were so, then Satan is certainly winning a great victory over God. For the overwhelming majority of mankind know little or nothing about Christ or salvation through him.

A Time Order for Salvation

God's master plan calls for offering salvation and eternal life to every person ever born, but his plan calls for doing that in a time-order.

Those called out of the world and into the Church at this time are called for a specific purpose and a specific work. This specific work was to make possible the spiritual training to aid in the conversion of humanity as a whole. They are called at a time when they are persecuted and fought against by Satan and by the rest of the world. The rest of the world will be called at a time when Satan is removed and they are aided and helped by Christ and the saints then made immortal in the kingdom of God.

Satan has blinded the minds of the unbelieving world and the professing traditional "Christianity" to this fact (II Cor. 4:4). Satan has deceived the entire world, including a professing traditional "Christianity" (Rev. 12:9).

Neither professing Christians nor their scholarly theologian leaders today comprehend the major PURPOSES for which Jesus Christ came!

Why Jesus Came

Jesus did not come to save Satan's world while Satan sits on the throne deceiving them. Jesus will save the world at his Second Coming, when Satan shall be put away. Why, then, did Jesus come more than 1,900 years ago? Not to rule, not to reign over all nations, not to save the world while Satan still rules over them.

His human birth was the arrival of the "second Adam." He had come 1) to qualify, where the first Adam failed, to replace the former archangel Lucifer on the THRONE OF THE EARTH, ruling with the GOVERNMENT OF GOD. He had come 2) to announce the future establishment of the KINGDOM OF GOD and teach that prophetic good news (gospel) to his chosen future apostles. He had come 3) to take on himself, as our direct Creator, the penalty for our sins by his death on the cross—that we might share in that world. And he had come 4) to be resurrected from the dead by God, making possible ETERNAL GOD-LIFE for the people of God and after his Second Coming for all who are willing, of all humanity, who have ever lived on this earth. And he had come 5) to establish GOD'S CHURCH, to be trained to rule under him.

Meanwhile, Satan's Rule

Meanwhile, for 4,000 years since the first Adam, the wily and evil Satan had been invisibly swaying and ruling a mankind CUT OFF from all contact with and knowledge of GOD! He still sits at that throne of POWER—though not administering God's government, but subtilely swaying all humanity to live under the precise opposite to the law of God's government—that is, the ways of vanity, coveting, competition, strife and violence, instead of God's way of outflowing love, cooperation, peace, happiness and joy.

Immediately after the birth of the Christ-child, Satan sought, through the Roman-appointed King Herod, to physically slay the future KING (Matt. 2:13-15). But God warned Joseph and Mary to flee with the Christ-child into Egypt until King Herod was dead.

When Jesus was about age 30, he was ready to begin choosing his apostles, and proclaiming and teaching them his message from God to man—his gospel. But first, it was imperative that he QUALIFY to replace Satan and set up the KINGDOM OF GOD, by overcoming the devil.

This perhaps was the most important, momentous, decisive confrontation and battle ever fought in all time in the universe. It is described in detail in Matthew, chapter 4.

The Titanic Battle of the Ages

Jesus fasted 40 days and 40 nights—with neither food nor water. But in his physical weakness he was made spiritually strong.

Satan now used his most cunning, subtle, masterful powers of deception. He must have thought he really could outwit and spiritually strike down the Christ. Satan knew well he was now fighting to prevent his dethroning over all the earth.

Satan struck his first blow at what he regarded as the most vulnerable points both physically and spiritually. Surely a man without food or water for 40 full days would be weakened to yield to almost any temptation for food. And the most vulnerable spiritual weakness is VANITY!

"IF," sneered Satan tantalizing—he used that effective little word IF—"IF thou be the Son of God"—a normal human would have been insulted, indignant. He would have defiantly hurled back: "What do you mean, IF I be the Son of God? I'll show you that I am the Son of God!"

But Satan in this first attack, said, "IF thou be the Son of God, command that these stones be made bread." In other words, "The Son of God can produce miracles. PROVE to me you are the Son of God! You are desperately hungry. Perform a miracle. Feed yourself by a miracle!"

But Jesus only answered by quoting and obeying the Word of God: "It is written, Man shall not live by bread alone, but by every word that proceedeth out of the mouth of God."

Satan's first and most effective strike was parried. But Satan never gives up. He took Jesus into Jerusalem and sat him on a high pinnacle of the Temple. He continued to QUESTION that Jesus was the Son of God.

"*IF* thou be the Son of God, cast thyself down: for it is written, He shall give his angels charge concerning thee: and in their hands they shall bear thee up, lest at any time thou dash thy foot against a stone." Now Satan quoted Scripture. But *he misapplied* it, twisted its contextual meaning, just as Satan so frequently influences scholars to do.

Jesus came back to him, "It is written again, Thou shalt not tempt the Lord thy God." This is quoted from Deuteronomy 6:16 and refers to tempting YHWH (Hebrew), who became Christ.

But still Satan did not give up.

Next he took Jesus atop a high mountain, showing him all the kingdoms of the world and their glory. "All these things will I give thee, if thou wilt fall down and worship me."

Jesus did not deny that Satan was now over the nations of this world. This was a temptation for gaining immediate power. Satan well knew Jesus would inherit all these kingdoms more than 1,900 years later. But he tempted Jesus to take Satan's word that he would turn them over and give Christ world power IMMEDIATELY. But Jesus decided it was time to END this titanic battle for the rulership over the earth.

Jesus now snapped out an ORDER—a COMMAND showing that he was MASTER over Satan!

"Get thee hence, Satan!" he commanded with supreme AUTHORITY! Satan slunk away defeated. But Satan did not give up. Nor has he given up yet. He battles against God's CHURCH still today!

Jesus Had Qualified

Jesus Christ, the second Adam, had QUALIFIED! Never until that minute could the GOOD NEWS of the coming KINGDOM OF GOD be announced to the world. Now the Son of God resisted and conquered Satan—had QUALIFIED to reestablish GOD'S

GOVERNMENT and set up the KINGDOM OF GOD on the earth! But now the CHURCH must also qualify to rule with him!

Jesus came, among other purposes, to call out of the world his CHURCH. Those called out had been in—and OF—this world. Each had brought on himself by sin the supreme DEATH PENALTY. But God had created ALL THINGS by the *WORD* who became Jesus Christ. Therefore, Jesus' life was greater in value than that of all humanity collectively!

Picture a human son of the wealthiest, most powerful man on earth. The tycoon's son is his heir—to inherit his immense wealth. He has been allocated a sizable portion of it already while an heir. This young man feels deep affection for another young man. His friend has committed a crime, plunged into debt for millions of dollars, which he cannot pay. He is deeply repentant but unable to save himself from imprisonment for the theft. In compassion for his friend, the son pays the multimillion-dollar debt out of his own money. His guilty friend's debt is PAID IN FULL. His guilt—his tremendous obligation—no longer hangs over him—he is freed from that obligation and its heavy penalties!

All humanity had followed father Adam—had brought over it the supreme DEATH PENALTY. Before Jesus (the "WORD"), now the Son of GOD, could found his CHURCH, those called out of the world *into* that CHURCH must be freed from the supreme DEATH PENALTY, so that they might inherit ETERNAL LIFE!

One of the purposes for which Jesus came as a human to earth was to PAY THAT PENALTY—that supreme DEATH PENALTY—for those called into his Church not only, but ultimately to free ALL HUMANITY each in his due time!

But since that DEATH PENALTY he would pay *for* sinning humanity would END his human life, paying it was reserved as his final human act after all other purposes of his human life had been finished.

Nevertheless this gives the reader a grasp of *HOW GREAT* is the Jesus who came to found the CHURCH OF GOD!

Continually bear in mind that, although his earthly ministry began when he was barely 30 years old (in his HUMAN life) yet he was the EVER-LIVING—the ETERNAL—who had

ALWAYS existed. HOW GREAT was that 30-year-old human life!

And this Jesus, who had grown up in the town of Nazareth, had since human birth resisted and overcome SATAN—had rejected Satan's self-centered way of "GET," and in the final titanic confrontation had QUALIFIED to RESTORE the GOVERNMENT OF GOD and to establish on earth the KINGDOM OF GOD, to rule that government! Where the first Adam had failed to do this, Jesus the second Adam succeeded.

"Peter" a Title Designating Leadership

Immediately after the decisive battle to overcome Satan, two of the disciples of John the Baptist saw, with John, Jesus. Jesus asked them to follow him to his home. One of these was Andrew, son of Jona. He called his brother, Simon bar-Jona.

Jesus looked on Simon, and said to him, "Thou art Simon the son of Jona: thou shalt be called Cephas [in Greek, PETER]," meaning a stone (John 1:42).

In Mark 3:14, 16, we read: "And he [Jesus] ordained twelve, that they should be with him, and that he might send them forth to preach. . . . And Simon he surnamed Peter." A surname is, according to Webster, "an added name derived from occupation."

The surname Peter had for centuries been a surname or TITLE, designating a religious LEADER, HEAD or HEADQUARTERS. Peter was the first and chief apostle. An apostle is "one sent forth to proclaim or preach."

So, at the very beginning of his earthly ministry, preparing the FOUNDATION for the Church, Jesus Christ chose his chief human apostle and the other original 11. They, with the prophets whose writings were preserved from the days of God's first chosen Congregation (and NATION), Israel, were to form the very FOUNDATION of God's CHURCH. Jesus himself was to be not only Founder but HEAD, and chief "corner stone" of the CHURCH (Eph. 2:19-21; 5:23).

Importance of a Firm Foundation

Prior to age 30, Jesus had been a carpenter—also building with stone as well as with wood. He well knew the FOUNDATION should be laid first, before the structure itself.

But Jesus had himself chosen his apostles. He said to them later, "Ye have not chosen me, but I have chosen you" (John 15:16, 19).

Now Jesus began proclaiming the gospel MESSAGE God the Father had sent into the world by him as God's Messenger (Mal. 3:1).

We read of it in Mark, chapter 1: "The beginning of the gospel of Jesus Christ the Son of God. . . . Jesus came into Galilee, preaching [proclaiming, teaching] the gospel of the KINGDOM OF GOD, and saying, The time is fulfilled, and the kingdom of God is at hand: repent ye, and believe the gospel" (Mark 1:1, 14-15).

And, from Matthew, "And Jesus went about all Galilee, teaching in their synagogues, and preaching the gospel of the kingdom" (Matt. 4:23).

This prophetic message (gospel) of the KINGDOM OF GOD will be explained in detail in chapter seven, It was the GOOD NEWS of the future establishment on earth of the GOVERNMENT OF GOD, restored and administered by the divine GOD FAMILY—the KINGDOM OF GOD, to replace the present evil world of Satan.

Jesus' proclaiming of this amazing future NEWS—combined with his miracles of healing, turning water into wine and others, caused great excitement. Immense crowds followed him and his disciples. He was teaching his disciples to become the future apostles, while he preached this message to the public.

Why Pharisees Opposed Jesus

The news proclamation had spread to Jerusalem. There the Pharisees, scribes and Sadducees became alarmed by it. The Pharisees were a Jewish religious sect some of whom occupied minor—yet to them important—government offices. The Roman Empire then ruled over Palestine. The Romans sent a district king and a limited occupation army to supervise rule in Judea. But the Romans set some of the Jewish Pharisees in offices of lower civil rule, under the Roman king. These were well-paying political jobs, and these Pharisees did not want to lose their jobs or their power over the people. These Jewish rulers and their chief priests completely MIsunderstood Jesus' gospel message. They knew he proclaimed a government that would take over and rule ALL NATIONS of the earth. What they MISunderstood was the TIME and NATURE of that kingdom of God. And a professing "Christianity" still misunderstands it today. They assumed Jesus was a subversive, intending himself, immediately in his human lifetime, to overthrow the Roman Empire and set up his own kingdom.

Immediately they feared being accused of sedition and disloyalty, losing their jobs and probably being executed as subversives. So they opposed and denounced Jesus.

Traditional Christianity has really never understood this basic reason for Pharisaical opposition and persecution of Jesus. The Pharisees included unscrupulous politicians.

At the time of the first Passover to occur during Jesus' ministry, the spring of A.D. 28 (almost exactly 100 time cycles—1,900 years—before I kept my first Passover), Jesus went up to Jerusalem for the Passover.

While there, a notable Pharisee named Nicodemus came to see Jesus secretly by night. He feared having fellow Pharisees know he had talked personally with Jesus.

Nicodemus said, "Rabbi, we know [we Pharisees know] that thou art a teacher come from God."

The Pharisees KNEW JESUS WAS THE MESSIAH! They were familiar with Isaiah 7:14, Isaiah 9:6-7, Isaiah 53. The Pharisees KNEW Jesus was the prophesied Messiah. But they understood only one Messianic appearance. So they supposed he was planning to overthrow the Roman Empire *then!*

Of course Jesus knew what they were thinking. So he launched immediately into the fact that the KINGDOM OF GOD, ruling all nations, could not be set up *UNTIL* the time of the NEW SPIRIT BIRTH—the time of the RESURRECTION!

The "Born Again" Question

Jesus answered immediately, "Verily, verily, I say unto thee, Except a man be born again, he cannot see the kingdom of God."

But Nicodemus did not understand this. He knew that being born was an actual BIRTH—parturition from the womb of the mother. Today's theologians do not know even that! They deny a real second birth as a spirit being. They spiritualize away the real truth by assuming that merely saying that one accepts Christ as his Savior constitutes being born again. In this, Satan has deceived them and in turn they have deceived millions of others.

Nicodemus said, "How can a man be born when he is old? can he enter the second time into his mother's womb and be born?"

Jesus now made the meaning PLAIN—but Nicodemus did not receive his PLAINNESS of speech, nor do theologians or religious leaders today.

"Verily, verily," replied Jesus, ". . . except a man be born of water and of the Spirit, he cannot enter into the kingdom of God. That which is born of the flesh *IS FLESH;* and that which is born of the Spirit *IS SPIRIT*" (emphasis mine— John 3:5-6).

The Pharisees knew about water baptism. They had used it for years in converting gentile proselytes to Judaism. They knew of John the Baptist's baptism—a baptism of repentance "for the remission of sins" (Mark 1:4). Jesus' meaning should have been PLAIN to Nicodemus—that water baptism was an initiatory rite preparatory to the start of being BORN of the Spirit.

Jesus made it doubly PLAIN when he said, "That which is born of the flesh *IS* flesh." That which is born of humans IS mortal HUMAN—composed of flesh and blood—composed of MATTER from the ground. "That which is born of the Spirit *IS* SPIRIT"—no longer human but composed of SPIRIT, immortal! No longer composed of matter or flesh.

Jesus explained even further.

"Marvel not that I said unto thee, Ye must be born again." Then he compared one born again to INVISIBLE WIND—invisible to human eyes. "The wind blows where it wills, and you hear the sound of it, but you do not know whence it comes or whither it goes; so it is with every one who is born of the Spirit" (John 3:8, RSV).

But Nicodemus did not understand such plainness of speech, nor do religious leaders today!

Our free booklet *What Do You Mean—Born Again?* should be read by every reader of this book.

To this representative of the Pharisees Jesus referred to

the "salvation" or "spiritual" phase of the kingdom of God. *That kingdom will NOT be composed of mortal humans!* It is NOT composed of mortal flesh-and-blood persons who have "accepted Christ" and joined a church of their choice! Yet millions of church members are deceived about that today.

These millions of church members do not understand WHAT the Church *IS*, nor WHY—its PURPOSE—the REASON for it!

Compare Jesus' explanation to Nicodemus with the "resurrection chapter" of the Bible, I Corinthians 15: "And so it is written, The first man Adam was made a living [mortal] soul; the last Adam was made a quickening spirit. Howbeit that was not first which is spiritual, but that which is natural; and afterward that which is spiritual. The first man is of the earth, earthy: the second man is the Lord from heaven. As is the earthy, such are they also that are earthy: and as is the heavenly, such are they also that are heavenly. And as we have borne the image of the earthy, we shall also bear the image of the heavenly. Now this I say, brethren, that flesh and blood cannot inherit the kingdom of God . . ." (I Cor. 15:45-50).

I repeat again and again, GOD IS REPRODUCING HIMSELF!

The popular teaching in churches today is that THE CHURCH is the kingdom of God. But "flesh and blood [mortal humans] cannot inherit the kingdom of God" (I Cor. 15:50).

Once Again: Why the Church?

But *WHAT*, then, *IS* the Church? And *WHY* is the CHURCH! Why should there be the Church of God?

To many—and probably most—the Church plays no part in their lives. Indeed God plays no part in their lives. God is not consciously in their world. Just people, material things and interests. Of course, far back in the subconscious recesses of many minds may lie the dormant supposition that God exists. But he does not seem REAL to them.

That means also that the average person has no conception of what he is, why he is, or of any purpose or meaning for his being alive.

Yet the CHURCH, too, does exist. But, again, WHY? WHAT is it, really? What PURPOSE does it serve?

We have seen that there is indeed a PURPOSE being

worked out here below. Winston Churchill stated that before the United States Congress. There is a REASON for the presence of humanity on the earth. And for the working out of that PURPOSE there is a MASTER PLAN. The CHURCH is an important part of that plan.

Never lose sight of the setting that led up to the raising up of the Church. Keep in mind WHO and WHAT God is—the divine creating *family,* now reproducing himself in man.

Bear in mind further: In order for Christ to RESTORE God's government over the earth, he would need with and under him a qualified and organized personnel of GOD BEINGS—all having rejected Satan's false way and having proved their loyalty to the government and righteous ways of GOD!

God's CHURCH was designed in his supreme master plan to prepare that dedicated and organized personnel of GOD BEINGS. The Church, then, became God's instrumentality for aiding him in bringing about the salvation to humanity.

Remember God has set out a 7,000-year master plan for accomplishing his purpose. We have stated that his purpose is to reproduce himself. But actually reproducing himself means converting the world from sin into God's righteousness. It means instilling within God's potential children the perfect spiritual character of God. They would become finally born sons in the God family.

And just as God has not created all at once, but in successive stages, so he is bringing salvation to the world in successive stages. The Church is a necessary instrumentality preparatory to, and in order to, bring salvation to humanity. Therefore, once again, let it be emphasized that the purpose of the Church is not merely to give salvation to those called into the Church, but to teach and train those predestined and called into the Church as instruments God shall use in bringing the world to salvation.

Church a "Teachers' College"

Let us illustrate by an analogy. Many states in America have state teachers' colleges. The states could not start or conduct schools until they had first trained teachers for those schools. The Church may be called God's teachers' college to prepare rulers and teachers for the kingdom of God when God does offer redemption and eternal life to the world as a whole.

The CHURCH was planned to be God's instrumentality for calling predestinated human beings out of this world to be trained for positions of leadership in the world tomorrow, when they shall teach and train others. That is why in the New Testament, the Church is called the firstfruits of God's salvation.

All this necessitated certain vital steps—one at a time—in the procedure of God's supreme master plan!

Now we remind the reader that the Holy Spirit was closed to humanity at the time of Adam's sin at the very foundation of the world. It was closed to humanity as a whole UNTIL Christ the second Adam should restore the government of God and unseat Satan from the throne of the earth. That fact is made clear by Jesus' statement in John 6:44, applying to this Church age, that no person could come to him except the Father that sent him draws them. That is why repeatedly in the New Testament those in the Church are referred to as having been called or chosen. That is why the Church is called a chosen generation. That is why predestination is mentioned twice in the New Testament—that the called were predestinated to be called. Indeed, they have been drafted. They are not volunteers.

True Christians: Draftees—Not Volunteers

It is only through Christ that sinning humanity may be reconciled to God the Father. They must first come to Christ. But no person can come to Christ except God the Father selects and, through his Holy Spirit, draws them.

That may come as an astonishing new truth, but the more you study the New Testament, and how this truth is constantly borne out throughout the New Testament, the more clear this will become to you.

No wonder the Church and its purpose has been a mystery. Satan has blinded the minds of a deceived and counterfeit Christianity.

Anyone who "joins the church of his choice" has not come into God's true Church. One cannot just "join" the TRUE

Church of God. One is first selected and drawn by God the Father through his Spirit, brought to a complete heartrending repentance, and changed in his total life-style, and has also not only believed in and accepted Jesus Christ as personal Savior, but also has believed Christ. Remember Christ is the Word of God. Jesus was the Word of God in Person. The Bible is the same Word of God in writing. To believe Christ is to believe what he says—in other words, to believe God's Word the Holy Bible.

So, once again, WHAT and WHY is the CHURCH? The Church is the called out (from this world) begotten children of God. It is the Body of Christ (I Cor. 12:27; Eph. 1:23). It is the spiritual organism that shall be the "Bride of Christ"—after its resurrection to immortality. Then it shall be married to Christ! It is the spiritual TEMPLE to which Christ shall come at his second appearing (Eph. 2:21).

The Church could not be actually founded *UNTIL* Jesus had ascended and been glorified (John 7:37-39). But in a sense God began calling out some to form the foundation of the Church with Abraham and the prophets of the Old Testament— even, perhaps, with Abel, Enoch and Noah (Eph. 2:20).

And Jesus, immediately after qualifying by overcoming Satan, began calling out his future apostles. They were to form, with the prophets, the very FOUNDATION of the Church, under Christ who himself is the real foundation and HEAD of the Church (I Cor. 3:11; Eph. 5:23).

The average person has no conception whatever of the *tremendous, supreme* supernatural achievement Almighty God has undertaken in REPRODUCING HIMSELF—ultimately into billions of spiritual GOD BEINGS! Or of the many-faceted stages of development necessitated in this pinnacle of all divine accomplishments!

God's Plan: A Step at a Time

God could not hurry. It required a master plan, which must proceed a step at a time. It required PATIENCE and never-deviating determination on the part of the divine Creator!

Few UNDERSTAND this!

God put it in my mind and heart when I was a child only 5 years old to desire—to literally crave—UNDERSTANDING!

Solomon desired wisdom and God gave him wisdom above all who ever lived.

What, then, is the necessary prerequisite to receiving UNDERSTANDING? "A good understanding have all they that do his commandments" (Ps. 111:10). The one *test commandment* is the fourth—keeping God's Sabbath. My conversion resulted from a struggle to resist that commandment! But when a merciful God conquered me—brought me to surrender to him *on that point*—he revealed also the necessity of observing his ANNUAL Sabbaths and festivals. These picture the seven major spiritual steps in the great master plan. (This truth is explained in our free booklet *Pagan Holidays or God's Holy Days—Which?*) Through this and other revealed knowledge of the Holy Bible, God gave me UNDERSTANDING of the working out of his great PURPOSE! And also the necessary part of his CHURCH in fulfillment of that glorious purpose!

After Adam's rebellion, with Satan still on earth's throne, only God could have known how gradually, cautiously, a step at a time, must be the procedure.

Such righteous men as Abel, Enoch and Noah undoubtedly were used to play some part in the ultimate creation of the KINGDOM OF GOD. But the Eternal began laying the actual foundation of that ultimate GOD FAMILY through the patriarch Abraham. Isaac, Jacob and Joseph formed part of that prefoundation.

Then through Moses, God raised up the nation Israel— God's first Congregation or Church. That Old Covenant Church was given God's government, but NOT his Holy Spirit! Israelites were not begotten to become future GOD BEINGS. Yet ancient Israel fulfilled a necessary part in God's supreme program.

Nevertheless, during those years, God continued to call and prepare individual PROPHETS to become part of the FOUNDATION for his CHURCH.

The Church—First Harvest

And *WHAT*, then, was to be the *CHURCH*? As pictured by the third of God's annual Holy Days (festivals) it was to provide the FIRST ACTUAL HARVEST of mortal humans being translated into Spirit-composed GOD BEINGS! Again, the Church is the instrumentality prepared to be used with and under Christ in completing God's wonderful purpose of saving humanity and reproducing himself. However, the CHURCH is the BEGOTTEN (not yet born) children of GOD. But the CHURCH shall be the firstBORN harvest (Heb. 12:23) (Christ being the foregoing Pioneer) at Christ's coming in POWER and GLORY!

Through the years from Abraham until Christ, God had called out of Satan's world begotten and prepared PROPHETS, as the preliminary co-foundation of God's CHURCH! Jesus himself is the main foundation.

During Jesus' 3½-year earthly ministry, he called out, chose and trained, to begin with, the second co-foundation, his original 12 apostles.

During his human earthly ministry, Jesus announced publicly the future KINGDOM OF GOD. He taught and trained his apostles as he proceeded.

But he DID NOT CALL to salvation the public to whom he preached. He spoke to them frequently in parables. And WHY in parables? To cloud, to hide from them the meaning (Matt. 13:10-17) that was given to his chosen apostles to understand. There was an all important reason why God's plan, a step at a time, did not, as yet, call for saving the world. God first called out the Church to be converted and changed to become kings and priests (Rev. 5:10) under Jesus *WHEN* Jesus comes to save the world. Consequently, much of the truth was revealed to the Church, which was being trained to assist Christ in saving the world. But the time had not yet come to reveal these truths to the world. Yet this world's churches are teaching doctrines diametrically contrary to this truth.

Completion of Jesus' Earthly Ministry

By the end of his earthly ministry, Jesus had completed preparations for founding his Church. He had finished the work he, as a human had come to do. Then he gave his life on the cross. He took on himself our human guilt for our sins.

Understand, however, Christ did NOT take on himself Satan's primary share in all human sins. Satan will continue to pay his own penalty throughout all eternity!

The FOUNDATION for the Church of God had been laid. Christ himself is the Head and chief cornerstone—the main foundation. His apostles, with the prophets, formed the remainder of the foundation.

The apostles were chafing at the bit to GET STARTED—to go forth proclaiming the gospel message. But God has wisely used restraint, with patience, taking a proper step at a time. So Jesus cautioned his apostles to WAIT! "Tarry ye," he commanded (Luke 24:49), "in the city of Jerusalem, *UNTIL* ye be endued with power from on high."

Ten days later came the annual Day of Pentecost, originally named the Feast of Firstfruits (Num. 28:26).

On that day the Holy Spirit came! On that day THE CHURCH WAS FOUNDED!

That day symbolized the very firstfruits for God's kingdom. God's feast days picture God's spiritual harvest. The very first portion of God's spiritual harvest of humans finally to be born of God—made GOD BEINGS—is THE CHURCH! That's why even those who shall be born into the kingdom of God at Christ's return starting with ancient prophets are part of the CHURCH OF GOD. Even prophets of Old Testament times are part of the FOUNDATION OF THE CHURCH (Eph. 2:19-21).

All—prophets, apostles and Church brethren in whom resides the Holy Spirit—shall be resurrected and/or changed to immortality at Christ's coming in GLORY and POWER!

Thus the WHOLE CHURCH constitutes the very *FIRST* of all humans who shall be finally BORN AGAIN into the kingdom of GOD. They shall be GOD BEINGS!

How DECEIVED (Rev. 12:9) have been all those who think they already have been "born again." The reader should request our free booklet *Just What Do You Mean—Born Again?*

Salvation Now Only for Minute Few

Now before proceeding further, UNDERSTAND WHY only the minute FEW have so far been called to salvation—WHY the world as a whole has been CUT OFF from God—WHY the world has not been yet judged—WHY neither "saved" nor "lost"!

Unless or *UNTIL* a son of Adam could qualify where Adam failed—could overcome and conquer SATAN—could pay the penalty of human sin and ransom the world from Satan—none could restore GOD's GOVERNMENT—none could be given eternal GOD-life!

The supreme master plan for working out GOD's PURPOSE—reproducing himself—called for the self-existing "WORD" to be born of human flesh as a son of Adam. But *ALSO* that plan called for him to be born as the only begotten Son of GOD!

The Messiah, and he alone, would be able to overcome and conquer Satan—to QUALIFY to replace Satan ON THE THRONE OF THE EARTH! Only through him could the sons of Adam be reconciled to GOD, receive God's Spirit, become GOD's sons—become the GOD BEINGS by whom God should have finally reproduced himself!

What a superb incredible master plan for such a SUPREME PURPOSE!

HOW GREAT IS THE ETERNAL GOD WHO DESIGNED IT!

This wonderful plan of God therefore of necessity called for the sons of Adam in general to be NOT YET JUDGED! God left them to their own devices—knowing full well they would willingly and willfully follow automatically Satan's *"GET"* way.

But meanwhile they would not be finally judged, but "reaping what they sowed." They would live this sinful life, die, and God would RESURRECT them in a special resurrection to JUDGMENT in the end of the 7,000 years of the master plan. Christ already having atoned for their sins—Satan having been removed—Christ and the kingdom of God having restored the government of God over the earth—then they could be CALLED to repentance, to reconciliation to GOD, to becoming, on their then free choice, GOD BEINGS!

And THAT'S WHY God has kept the world as a whole CUT OFF from him, even as their progenitor Adam had cut off himself and his human family.

Why a Mystery to the World

As the apostle Paul was inspired to write, in Romans 11: "I would not, brethren, that ye should be ignorant of this mystery" (and it is a mystery to the world) "that blindness" to these mysteries has happened to this world—even to its "Christian theologians"—*UNTIL* the kingdom of God has been established in rule of the earth!

"For," continues Paul, "as ye [Christians] in times past have not believed God, yet have now obtained mercy through their unbelief: even so have these also now not believed, that through your mercy they also may obtain mercy. For GOD hath concluded them all in unbelief, that he might have mercy UPON ALL"!

And at this point Paul shouted out in writing: "O the depth of the riches both of the wisdom and knowledge of God! how unsearchable are his judgments, and his ways past finding out!" (Rom. 11:25, 30-32).

True, the apostle wrote the above concerning ISRAEL, and I have applied it to all uncalled humanity—but it is truly applicable.

God called and prepared the Old Testament prophets. He has called and still calls and prepares the CHURCH to overcome Satan—whereas those now blinded, uncalled and cut off from God have NOT had to overcome Satan. WHY?

WHY the CHURCH?

That we may QUALIFY to rule WITH and UNDER CHRIST in the kingdom of God—that *we* may prepare the way for the ULTIMATE CALL AND SALVATION OF THE WORLD!

At this point let me quote two passages from the direct word of Jesus, which apply ONLY to the CHURCH:

To the CHURCH of this twentieth century Jesus says, "To him that overcometh will I grant to sit with me in my throne, even as I also overcame, and am set down with my Father in his throne" (Rev. 3:21).

Then again to the CHURCH Jesus says, "He that overcometh, and keepeth my works unto the end, to him will I give power over the nations: and he shall rule them with a rod of iron . . ." (Rev. 2:26-27).

In that passage of Scripture Jesus showed plainly why some are called out of this world into the Church at this present time. Not because he is trying to save the world, and we are part of the world. Not just that we may be saved and make it into his kingdom, but, as Jesus also said in

Revelation 5:10, to be kings and priests and reign with and under Christ when he sets his hand to bring salvation to the world.

Thorough Conversion Necessary for Church

I cannot repeat too emphatically that those being called into the Church now are not being called merely and only for salvation. Nevertheless, in order that they may be kings and priests, as actual God Beings aiding Christ in the salvation of the world, those in the Church themselves must be genuinely converted.

I cannot make this truth too plain. I fear many, even in the Church, do not fully comprehend just what is a real conversion.

Conversion takes place in the mind, and that faculty of mind we call the heart. This could never be fully understood without an understanding of the actual makeup of the human mind, as explained in chapter three of this work. It could never be understood, until the knowledge was revealed through the Bible, of the human spirit in man and the actual composition of the human mind.

As the human mind differs from the animal brain by the addition of the human spirit, so the converted person differs from the unconverted person by the addition of the Holy Spirit.

How much greater is the capacity and output of the human mind than that of the animal brain? The realization of that difference should make clear to us the vast difference between a converted mind being led by the Holy Spirit, and mind of the unconverted.

One does not receive the Holy Spirit until he has first of all repented. God grants repentance (Acts 11:18). The second condition to receiving the Holy Spirit is faith. That means not only believing in God and in Christ, but since Christ is the Word or Spokesman of the God family, it means believing what he says.

Repentance means a change of mind. Godly sorrow is a much deeper sorrow than remorse. And godly sorrow leads to repentance. It involves not only heartfelt sorrow for past sins, but a total change of attitude, of mind and direction and purpose of life. Actually, repentance is more concerned with future conduct than the past. The blood of Christ has atoned for the past. Repentance is not penance. Nothing you can do can make up for past guilt. The blood of Christ has paid the price of past guilt. It has washed the slate clean.

A converted person is a person with a totally changed, or converted mind. A converted mind in which the very mind of God is joined with the human mind. As God says through the apostle Paul, "Let this mind be in you, which was also in Christ Jesus" (Phil. 2:5). The Holy Spirit is the spirit of a sound mind, which is a completely changed mind. It has made an about-face in its desires, purposes and intentions.

Error of Traditional Christianity

The "salvation" in what is called traditional Christianity does not actually change one into a new and different person. Too often ministers and evangelists tell people that if they have just "received Christ," "accepted Christ," or "given their heart to the Lord," they are saved. They are already "born again." It is as if some mystic switch has been flipped and the person will be shot instantly up to heaven upon death, which so many believe is not really a death after all. God, in the Bible, teaches no such thing. God reveals that as in Adam all die, even so the same "all" in Christ shall be made alive by a resurrection from the dead. Meanwhile, God reveals the dead are totally unconscious.

In ancient Israel God gave them knowledge of his law, but not his Spirit. Their minds were not converted or changed. They were still carnal. And the natural mind is hostile against God (Rom. 8:7). There was no conversion in ancient Israel—no salvation. The 37th chapter of Ezekiel reveals how those of ancient Israel will receive the Spirit of God, if willing, in the Great White Throne Judgment.

One receiving and led by the Holy Spirit is a changed person. He has undergone a renewing of the mind. Until the knowledge of the human spirit in man was revealed, and that God's Spirit can unite with human spirit, true salvation could not be fully understood. A Christian must grow and develop in grace, spiritual knowledge and godly character.

Why Church Called First

At this juncture let me explain further why the Church is called the firstfruits of God's salvation. Far from being a discrimination against the overwhelming majority of the world not yet called to salvation, it is for the very purpose of calling the rest of the world to salvation. Once again let me remind you there is a definite order in sequence in God's plan for saving the world—for reproducing himself.

Jesus Christ is the first of the firstfruits. He is the firstborn of many brethren (I Cor. 15:23; Rom. 8:29). The Church is being called to be changed, developed in character, and finally born at Christ's Second Coming as God Beings, to be kings and priests under Christ when he will set his hand to save the world.

In a sense, then, the Church shall become co-saviors with Christ. Two things basically were required of Christ to save the world. First it was necessary for him, who was the Maker of us all, to die for all, thus paying the death penalty in our stead. No one could do this but Jesus Christ alone.

But many have not realized that we are not saved by the blood of Christ. You will read in Romans 5:10 that we are reconciled to God the Father by the death of Christ, but we shall be saved by his life—by the resurrection. I am writing this particular passage on what the world calls "Easter Sunday." Today, the churches and the evangelists have said much about the resurrection of Christ, but virtually nothing about the resurrection of all who shall be saved, and of the resurrection by which people may be saved.

Jesus alone could make the sacrifice in payment of our past sins. But the world must look for salvation through his life after his resurrection. The Church is the affianced Bride of Christ to be married to the Son of God on his return, after the resurrection of those in the Church. After we have attained to the resurrection of the dead, as the wife of the Son of God, and members of the God family, we shall be not only heirs and coheirs with Christ, but in a sense, co-saviors.

The family of God will grow. As kings and priests, the

Church in the resurrection will be co-rulers under Christ in restoring the government of God over all nations. But we shall also be, as priests, co-saviors with him in saving the world.

Why Firstfruits Necessary

Now why was it absolutely necessary that the Church be called out of the world to receive salvation during this Church age, while the rest of the world was left in spiritual darkness and deception?

Before Jesus could qualify to become our Savior and future King, it was necessary for him, as the second Adam, to do what the first Adam failed to do—to overcome Satan and to choose the mind and government of God instead. If the Church is to rule with and under him—if the Church is to be priests as well as kings, aiding, under Christ in saving the world, it was also necessary that those in the Church must also qualify by resisting and overcoming Satan.

That will not be required of the overwhelming majority of others when salvation comes to them. Salvation will not come to them until after Satan has been put away. So, you see, it was far from discriminating against the rest of the world, when Jesus said, "No man can come to me, except the Father which hath sent me draw him" (John 6:44). It was necessary that the Church be called at a time when each member had to turn from, resist and overcome Satan. Otherwise we of the Church could not qualify for the wonderful position of becoming kings and priests in the kingdom of God during the 1,000 years.

This explains the *WHY* of the Church—its great PURPOSE.

Is the Church Organized?—if So, How?

But *WHAT* is the CHURCH—HOW ORGANIZED—HOW does it function?

When I came among the brethren of the Church of God, there were questions among the leaders respecting the nature of Church organization. At that time, 1927, the Church was organized on the pattern of a biannual general conference. Each local congregation could send one member to the biannual general conference and thus had one vote in election of officers, questions of Church doctrine and Church policy. A local congregation could consist of as few as five members.

But division over Church organization and government began about 1930. By 1933 the Church was divided right down the middle. Two leaders organized a new Church, departing from its headquarters at Stanberry, Missouri, setting up its new headquarters at Salem, West Virginia. They adopted a system of organization that they erroneously called "Bible organization."

This new organization consisted of twelve men named as *apostles*—designated as "the twelve." Seven men were appointed to the office of deacon, the chairman of whom was the treasurer handling the money. Then there were "the seventy"—or seventy leading elders. This was copied from the ancient Sanhedrin in Judaism. However, there were not enough ordained ministers within the church to make up more than half of "the seventy."

The Roman Catholic Church is organized on the hierarchical system with the pope in supreme authority, a college of cardinals next in authority, a curia at headquarters in the Vatican with archbishops, bishops and priests.

The Presbyterian Church is organized with the presbyters or ministers in control. The Congregational Church delegates top authority to the congregation—"government by the consent of the governed."

And so it goes. The churches of this world of Satan are organized according to humanly devised patterns. But the Bible gives explicit directions in regard to Church government. Jesus Christ is the Head of the Church. God's form of government is, indeed, hierarchical. God the Father is head over Christ—the sole Lawgiver and supreme authority.

God explains in I Corinthians 12 functions, offices, administrations and their officers as GOD set them in his Church.

"Now concerning spiritual gifts, brethren, I would not have you ignorant. . . . Now there are diversities of gifts, but the same Spirit. And there are differences of administrations, but the same Lord. And there are diversities of operations, but it is the same God which worketh all in all. . . . But all these worketh that one and selfsame Spirit, dividing to every man severally as he will. For as the body is one, and hath many members, and all the members of that one body, being many, ARE ONE BODY: so also is Christ. For by one Spirit are we all baptized into one body, whether we [in the Church] be Jews or Gentiles, whether we be bond or free . . ." (I Cor. 12:1, 4-6, 11-13).

One Church with One Government

Notice especially, there is only the ONE CHURCH. Not MANY churches. The CHURCH is not divided. There is only one Church. Not a parent church and many little daughter churches that have split off in disagreement. Divisions splintering off are NOT STILL IN THE CHURCH. It is the CHURCH that is to marry Christ in the resurrection at his coming—not disagreeing churches—not groups who have broken off! Not a parent church and apostate daughters. That will become more obvious as we continue.

So notice, too, the Church conducts VARIOUS OPERATIONS. For these in the ONE Church there are also various ADMINIS-TRATIONS or executive departments, with an executive manager over each department or operation (verses 4-6). Remember, an executive administrator DOES NOT SET POLICY OR PROCEDURES OR DOCTRINES. He administers—he carries out and directs—what has been already set from above.

Even in this world, in the United States the President does NOT MAKE THE LAWS. He administers the policies as functions authorized by Congress—enforces the laws made by Congress. Administrators are set in the Church merely to supervise, direct, execute the policies, procedures, doctrines assigned to them from above.

The ONE Church, undivided, is emphasized again in verse 20: "But now are they many members, yet BUT ONE BODY"—ONE UNDIVIDED CHURCH! Even GOD is composed of more than one Personage, yet but the ONE GOD! GOD, remember, is the divine GOD FAMILY. Those in the Church are already begotten sons—begotten members of that GOD FAMILY. But not yet BORN as GOD BEINGS!

Notice verse 25: "That there should be no schism in the body; but that the members should have the same care one for another."

To administer these many operations, God—not a vote of the members—"hath set some in the church, first apostles, secondarily prophets, thirdly teachers." Or, as stated in more detail in Ephesians 4:11 (RSV): "And his gifts were that some should be apostles, some prophets, some evangelists, some pastors and teachers."

An apostle is "one sent forth" with Christ's gospel message, including the supervision of proclaiming that message to the world by means and persons other than himself. Also an apostle was given supervision over all the local congregations or churches (I Cor. 16:1). The apostle Paul had oversight over the churches of the Gentile world (II Cor. 11:28).

The prophets set in the foundation of the Church are those of the Old Testament, whose writings were used to form a considerable part of New Testament and gospel teaching and functioning. No prophets are mentioned as having either administrative, executive or preaching functions in the New Testament Church.

Evangelists were leading ministers, proclaiming the gospel to the public, even raising up local churches and having supervision over some churches under the apostle. Therefore an evangelist may hold executive functions under the apostle in the Church headquarters or work today. An evangelist is not necessarily stationary. Pastors are stationary pastors over a local church or contingent group of local churches. Then there were placed in the Church teachers—not necessarily preachers. Yet all ministers and teachers are called elders in other New Testament texts. Therefore, in God's Church today there are both preaching and non-preaching elders. Preaching elders pastor local churches. Then some elders, not preaching, are called local elders in the Church today.

Temple to Which Christ Shall Come

Now further about CHURCH ORGANIZATION.

The CHURCH is the spiritual Body of Christ—not a secular or worldly organization, club or institution. Yet it is HIGHLY ORGANIZED.

Notice how thoroughly organized: "Now therefore ye are

no more strangers and foreigners, but fellowcitizens with the saints, and of the household of God." Notice the Church is a FAMILY, even as GOD is a divine FAMILY—"the household of God."

Continue: "And are built upon the foundation of the apostles and prophets, Jesus Christ himself being the chief corner stone; in whom all the building"—the Church is a building "fitly framed together" (WELL ORGANIZED—all parts joined and functioning together in harmony and teamwork)—"groweth unto an holy temple in the Lord: in whom ye also are builded together for an habitation of God through the Spirit" (Eph. 2:19-22). This scripture plainly reveals the temple to which the glorified world-ruling Christ shall come at his soon Second Coming. There is no scripture foretelling the construction of a material temple in Jerusalem before Christ's appearing. The 40th chapter of Ezekiel, however, describes the building of a temple after the return of Christ.

The Church, then, is to grow into a HOLY TEMPLE—the spiritual TEMPLE to which Christ shall come—even as he came to a material temple of stone and metals and wood the first time.

Notice further: ". . . the head, even Christ: from whom the whole body fitly joined together"—ORGANIZED—"and compacted by that which every joint supplieth, according to the effectual working in the measure of every part, maketh increase of the body . . ." (Eph. 4:15-16). Compacted means knit together, compressed together, as closely together as if welded together. This shows ORGANIZED UNITY, HARMONY! It is commanded that those in the Church be so united that they "all speak the same thing" (I Cor. 1:10).

Old Testament Israel, the Church of the Old Testament, was also a nation in the world—though not OF the world as God organized it. Its GOVERNMENT was HIERARCHICAL. It was theocratic government—government from the top down—the very opposite of "democracy."

The CHURCH is organized under theocratic government, hierarchical in form. The members do not set officials in the Church. God sets EVEN THE LAY MEMBERS in the Church (I Cor. 12:18).

Jesus said explicitly, "No MAN CAN come to me, except the Father which hath sent me draw him" (John 6:44). The world, except for the specially called, is CUT OFF from God!

We have just covered the truth that GOD set officials to serve on the human level under Christ, in the Church. Members do not elect them. Yet in the churches of this world some believe in government by the entire congregation— "democracy"—and call themselves "Congregational." Others have organized themselves into government by ministers or presbytery and call themselves "Presbyterian." Some follow Luther and call themselves "Lutheran." Some follow Wesley, who was strong on "method," and call themselves "Method- ist." Some learned God's truth about baptizing and call their church after the name of "John the Baptist," who first taught baptism. One wanted complete universal world dominion, and called itself "Catholic," which means "universal." What is the name of the Church Jesus founded?

True Name of Church

Jesus prayed for his Church: ". . . Holy Father, keep through *thine own name* those whom thou hast given me, that they may be ONE, as we are. While I was with them in the world, I kept them *in thy name*. . . . And now come I to thee. . . . I have given them thy word; and the world hath hated them, because *they are not OF* the world, even as I am not OF the world. I pray not that thou shouldest take them out of the world, but that thou shouldest keep them from the evil [one]. *They are not OF the world*, even as I am not OF the world. Sanctify them through THY TRUTH: THY WORD IS TRUTH" (John 17:11-17).

Jesus said his true Church was to be KEPT *in the name* of the Father—GOD. *Twelve times* in the New Testament, the NAME of this one *true* Church is the CHURCH OF GOD! It is GOD's Church, and Jesus Christ is its guiding, sustaining, directing HEAD!

In five passages where the true NAME of the Church appears, the entire body of Christ—the Church as a whole—is indicated. Thus when speaking of the entire Church, includ- ing all its individual members on earth, the name is "The CHURCH OF GOD." Here are these five passages:

1) Acts 20:28: The admonition to the elders is to "feed THE CHURCH OF GOD."

2) I Corinthians 10:32: "Give none offence, neither to the Jews, nor to the Gentiles, nor to THE CHURCH OF GOD."

3) I Corinthians 11:22: ". . . Despise ye THE CHURCH OF GOD, and shame them that have not?"

4) I Corinthians 15:9: Paul wrote: "For . . . I persecuted THE CHURCH OF GOD."

5) Galatians 1:13: This verse repeats the one last given—"I persecuted THE CHURCH OF GOD."

Where one specific local congregation is mentioned, the true Church is called "The Church of God," often in connection with the *place* or location. Here are four more passages:

6) I Corinthians 1:2: "THE CHURCH OF GOD which is at Corinth."

7) II Corinthians 1:1: "THE CHURCH OF GOD which is at Corinth."

8) I Timothy 3:5: In speaking of a local elder in a local congregation, Paul wrote Timothy: "For if a man know not how to rule his own house, how shall he take care of THE CHURCH OF GOD?"

9) I Timothy 3:15: ". . . behave thyself in the house of God, which is THE CHURCH OF THE LIVING GOD." Here it is the Church of the *living* God.

In speaking of the local congregation collectively, not as one general body, but as the total of all local congregations, the Bible name is "The CHURCHES OF GOD." Here are the final three verses of the 12 which name the Church:

10) I Corinthians 11:16: " . . . We have no such custom, neither THE CHURCHES OF GOD."

11) I Thessalonians 2:14: "For ye, brethren, became followers of THE CHURCHES OF GOD which in Judaea are in Christ Jesus."

12) II Thessalonians 1:4: "So that we ourselves glory in you in THE CHURCHES OF GOD."

Yet none is truly the Church OF GOD, unless it is GOD'S CHURCH, continuing in doctrine, practice, organization, in all ways on the original biblical pattern, headed by Jesus Christ, yet belonging to God the Father, empowered by the Holy

Spirit, having GOD'S TRUTH, fulfilling Christ's commission of proclaiming his GOOD NEWS of the KINGDOM OF GOD to the world as a whole.

And there is only ONE such Church!

And it CANNOT BE DIVIDED. It remains ONE.

In I Corinthians 1, the apostle Paul was inspired to command that all in the Church "SPEAK THE SAME THING." There must be no division in what is believed, taught or preached.

Traditional Christianity

But what about all the many organized churches labeled under the category "Christianity"—some with millions of members? They are all described in Revelation 17:5: "Mystery, Babylon the great, the mother of harlots and abominations of the earth."

Are they, then, evil?

Not consciously or knowingly, necessarily. The world of humanity has been CUT OFF from God. Satan is still on earth's throne, next in power to GOD himself! And the whole world is DECEIVED by Satan (Rev. 12:9). Those deceived are not aware that they are deceived. If so they would not *be* deceived! They may be ever so sincere in believing they are right!

Are they condemned? By no means! They are simply NOT YET JUDGED—neither "condemned" nor "saved." Few indeed realize the magnitude of Satan's power and the extent of his DECEPTION!

It is SATAN who is evil and diabolical. But he is an INVISIBLE being and force—unseen and unrecognized by mortal humans.

Satan is a great COUNTERFEITER! He appears as "an angel of light" (II Cor. 11:13-15). And he has his counterfeit CHURCHES! His ministers are deceived by him into believing they are "ministers of righteousness" and of Christ (II Cor. 11:15; Matt. 24:5).

"But I fear, lest by any means, as the serpent beguiled Eve through his subtilty, so your minds should be corrupted from the simplicity that is in Christ. For if he that cometh preacheth another Jesus, whom we have not preached, or if ye receive another spirit, which ye have not received, or another gospel, which ye have not accepted, ye might well bear with him.... For such are false apostles, deceitful workers, transforming themselves into the apostles of Christ. And no marvel; for Satan himself is transformed into an angel of light. Therefore it is no great thing if his ministers also be transformed as the ministers of righteousness; whose end shall be according to their works" (II Cor. 11:3-4, 13-15).

Notice these deceived but false churches believe they are the true church, and their ministers "are transformed as the ministers of righteousness"—in other words, appear to be the true ministers of Jesus Christ. And indeed, many of them may be entirely sincere, being themselves deceived. Yet they have neither known nor preached Jesus' true Gospel of THE KINGDOM OF GOD (Matt. 24:14). Nor do they comprehend what is written in this book about the CHURCH OF GOD!

Partial Truth

Many Protestant denominations, and some personal "ministries," quote certain scriptures, especially concerning Christian living, faith, love, etc., correctly. But they ignore numerous basic scriptures, cited in this book. Satan seems willing to let the deceived have parts of the truth.

But these run afoul on pivotal truths. Usually they do not have the proper name, The Church of God. Neither do they know or proclaim the kingdom of God or what it is—that is to say, they do not have or proclaim the true gospel of Christ. They do not have God's government headed by Jesus Christ, with apostles, evangelists, pastors and other elders. They do not know what salvation is. They do not understand God's purpose or plan.

One original Church, much persecuted and opposed, but still in existence, has these evidences proving it to be the original true Church. And even this Church, until after the year of 1933, had lost many of these vital truths. At least 18 basic and essential truths have been restored to the true Church since that year.

Human Mind Alone Can't Know

Until now, I have not been able to give a clear concise explanation of precisely WHAT and WHY is the CHURCH.

And WHY NOT?

People naturally and normally think only of and about physical and material things. People do not realize it, but they have been CUT OFF from God! The human mind, unless and until it receives the Holy Spirit of GOD, cannot think spiritually—cannot know spiritual knowledge—cannot understand human problems, troubles, evils or purposes of human existence.

But the CHURCH is GOD's Church. And the things of GOD are a mystery—not understandable to the natural carnal mind. So people may have some kind of human idea of what and why the Church is, but it is not GOD's concept.

God has communicated to man in our day through his printed Word, the Holy Bible. But the real central meaning in the Bible is spiritual. And natural minds without God's Spirit cannot think spiritually or comprehend revealed spiritual knowledge. To make it still more a MYSTERY, I repeat once again, the Bible is like a jigsaw puzzle, made up of thousands of parts that, for understanding, must be put together "precept upon precept; line upon line ... here a little, and there a little" (Isa. 28:9-10, 13). And it requires the addition of the Holy Spirit to the human mind to put this spiritual "jigsaw puzzle" properly together. Even then it requires time, diligence, patience. I have not been able to give this "what and why" of the Church to the reader all at once briefly. I want fully to reveal the MYSTERY!

WHAT, then, IS THE CHURCH?

Why "Firstfruits"

It is that body God has specially called out of Satan's world. It is a body called for a very special purpose—to be trained to become rulers and teachers when God does set his hand to convert the world. To be enabled to rule and teach the world with and under Christ. It is also necessary that they be first converted from human into actual God Beings, members of the divine God family. That explains why they are repeatedly called the "first-fruits" of God's salvation (Eph. 1:11; Rom. 11:16; Rev. 14:4). The day of Pentecost was originally called the Feast of Firstfruits, picturing the Church being called and trained for their special mission prior to the time when God will open salvation to the world. Let it be clearly understood that the time has not yet come when God has opened the tree of life to Satan's world. Rather than open the tree of life to Satan's world, God has selected those predestined to be specially called that they might be prepared as kings and teachers, being actual God Beings under Christ when God does open the tree of life to the whole world. That will be the time when, as in Joel 2:28, God shall at last pour out his Spirit upon all flesh.

The New Testament passage that incorrectly reads "Now is *the* day of salvation" (II Cor. 6:2) is quoted from Isaiah 49:8 where it is "a day of salvation," not *the* day of salvation. The Greek text also does not have the word *the*. It was inserted by translators who were deceived into believing this is the only day of salvation for everyone.

The very truth that the Church is not called merely and only for salvation—not merely to "make it into the kingdom" as so many have expressed it—is plainly affirmed in the parables of the pounds and of the talents.

Parable of the Pounds

In the parable of the pounds (Luke 19:11-27), Jesus is pictured as the rich young ruler going to God's throne in heaven to receive the kingdom of God. He gave to each in the Church a pound, representing a portion of God's Holy Spirit. This illustrates that we must grow in the Spirit, or in grace and knowledge, during the Christian life. When Christ returns to earth, having received the kingdom and being already crowned, he shall call those of the Church to an accounting. The one who has multiplied the portion of the Holy Spirit received (has grown and developed in grace and knowledge) by ten times over, shall be rewarded by being given rule over ten cities. He who qualified by spiritual growth and develop-ment only half as much shall reign over five cities as his reward. Remember we shall be rewarded according to our works or spiritual growth, but salvation is a free gift. But what of the person who thought he "had it made into the kingdom" without spiritual growth and development? He shall have taken away from him that first portion of the Holy Spirit—he shall lose the salvation he mistakenly thought he had. HE

SHALL NOT MAKE IT INTO THE KINGDOM! He WAS NOT CALLED
MERELY FOR SALVATION, BUT TO QUALIFY to rule and teach under
Christ in the kingdom, when God does open salvation to all on
earth. It is well to note that it will not be opening salvation to
those in Satan's world. It shall then be GOD's world—the
world tomorrow.

The parable of the talents (Matt. 25) emphasizes the
same truth.

Parable of the Sower

Also the parable of the sower and the seed in Matthew 13:1-9.
But Jesus' disciples did not understand the parable. They
questioned Jesus (verse 10), asking why he spoke to the
multitudes in parables. To his disciples, called out of the world
to a special commission, Jesus replied, "It is given unto you to
know the mysteries of the kingdom of heaven, but to them it is
not given." Here is another example showing God is not now
calling the world to understanding and salvation. Jesus spoke
to the uncalled world in parables to hide the meaning (verse
13). He explained the parable to his called disciples (verses
18-23). Some who are called in this Church age hear the Word
of God when preached, but do not understand, and Satan
catches away that which was sown in their hearts. Some receive
the truth when preached with joy, but lack the depth of mind
and character; when persecution comes, they are offended and
turn away. Others hear and initially respond, but are so
encumbered with earning a living and pleasures of the world
they produce no fruit—like the one who received the one pound
but did not grow in spiritual character and knowledge. But, of
the others called out of the world and into God's Church, some
produced spiritual fruit 100 fold, some 60 and some 30. They
are saved by God's free grace, but in the next life in God's
kingdom, shall be rewarded or given positions of responsibility
and power according to their works.

That means according to fruit borne. And fruit borne
means more than regular Bible reading, prayer, church
attendance or volunteer church duties. It means "the fruits of
the Spirit" as explained in Galatians 5:22-23—showing more
love or outgoing concern toward others, growing in joy, which
is happiness running over, in peace with your own family, with

neighbors, with all others. Growing in patience, being more kind and gentle toward others, goodness and faith, as well as meekness and temperance.

The CHURCH, then, is that body called out from Satan's world *being prepared* to restore, with and under Christ, the GOVERNMENT of God. That shall be a time when Satan shall have been REMOVED. It shall be a time when all living shall be called to repentance and salvation with eternal life through the Holy Spirit of GOD! The CHURCH, immortal, shall be RULING with Christ—replacing the present rule of Satan!

The CHURCH, then, is that body of called-out-ones, who at the resurrection shall form the FIRSTFRUITS of God's harvest. That harvest is the reaping of physical flesh-and-blood, matter-composed humans converted into divine immortal GOD BEINGS—those in whom God actually *has* reproduced himself!

Church Still Carnal

WHY has God in wisdom gone slow—a step at a time? Few realize HOW GREAT is God's PURPOSE!

After all these years of sinning, human life CUT OFF from God, even with God's own Holy Spirit given to those *changed* by initial conversion, those in the Church are initially "babes in Christ"—still far more carnal than spiritual.

UNDERSTAND THIS!

The CHURCH, as initially called in this life, is NOT YET capable of RULING the earth—of sitting with Christ in the THRONE where God originally placed Lucifer—of administering THE GOVERNMENT OF GOD.

And THAT IS *WHY* God has placed HIS GOVERNMENT in his Church. That is *WHY* God's Church government is theocratic instead of democratic. That is why God has set ranks of government in his Church, apostles, evangelists, pastors, elders, both preaching and non-preaching, "till we [in the Church] all come in the unity of the faith, and of the knowledge of the Son of God, unto a perfect man, unto the measure of the stature of the fulness of Christ" (Eph. 4:13). It is not a matter of having "made it into the kingdom" upon being baptized, but a matter of spiritual growth and development in knowledge and in righteous character. That is *WHY* it is hierarchical in form—government from GOD at the top on down, not from the bottom up. Otherwise those at the bottom would be ruling GOD!

It is the SAME government by which Christ shall rule all nations beginning with the millennium!

And that is *WHY* Satan has subtilely influenced dissidents in God's Church to become resentful and bitter over God's government—why some have gone out of the Church!

The churches of this world—"traditional Christianity"— DO NOT speak of the government of GOD. They do not picture Jesus as coming world RULER. They do not preach Jesus as coming KING—but only as Savior. They overlook—reject— scriptures speaking of Christ as King and coming Ruler, and *government* rule in the kingdom of God. And that is to say, they deliberately REJECT and OMIT the gospel MESSAGE of Christ in their teaching and preaching! They teach that one is *already saved* on "receiving" (GETTING) Christ!

I repeat, the individual whom God calls and adds to his Church is not, at initial conversion, remotely capable of being given POWER of rule over nations!

He is called a "babe in Christ." He has, if repentant and really converted in this preliminary human state, actually received a portion of the Holy Spirit of God. Indeed in Romans 8:16 we read: "The Spirit itself beareth witness with our spirit, that we are the children of God."

But we need to grow spiritually before we are qualified to rule over cities and nations and teach those being converted.

As the apostle Paul said to those in the first century Church who were not growing spiritually: "That ye be not slothful, but followers of them who through faith and patience inherit the promises. For when God made promise to Abraham, because he could swear by no greater, he sware by himself, saying, Surely blessing I will bless thee, and multiplying I will multiply thee" (Heb. 6:12-14).

We are already, though yet unborn, the begotten children of God. By direct comparison the impregnated embryo or fetus in a mother-to-be's womb is *already* the child of its parents, though not yet born. Therefore I remark, in passing, *abortion is MURDER!*

But this brings us to a most important PURPOSE and FUNCTION of the Church!

Beginning verse 22 of Galatians 4 is an allegory about the two covenants—the Covenant made with national Israel at Mount Sinai and the New Covenant to be made at Christ's return. However, ministers in the Church are "able ministers of the new testament" (II Cor. 3:6).

The CHURCH is a part of, and preliminary to the final making of, the NEW TESTAMENT.

In this allegory of the two covenants, the Church is called "THE MOTHER OF US ALL"—that is, of those in the Church.

So notice the direct comparison. God is reproducing himself through humans. He endowed us with power to reproduce *our*selves. And human reproduction is the exact type of God's SPIRITUAL REPRODUCTION!

How Human Reproduction Pictures
Spiritual Salvation

Now see and UNDERSTAND how human reproduction pictures spiritual SALVATION!

All human life comes from a tiny egg, called an ovum. It is produced inside the human mother. This ovum is about the size of a pin point. Inside it, when highly magnified, can be seen a small nucleus. But this ovum has a very limited life, *of itself!* Some doctors and scientists believe it has a life of only some 24 hours, unless fertilized by a sperm from a male.

But human life may be imparted *to* it by a sperm cell, produced in the body of the human father. The sperm cell is the smallest cell in the human body—about one fiftieth the size of the ovum. The sperm—technically named a spermatozoon (plural, spermatozoa)—on entering an ovum, finds its way to and joins with the *nucleus*. This imparts *life*—physical *human* life—to the ovum.

But it is not yet a born human being. Human life has merely been *begotten*. For the first four months it is called an *embryo*. After that, until birth it is called a *fetus*. This human life starts very small—the size of a tiny pin point—and the sperm that generates it is the *smallest* cell in a human body!

Once begotten, it must *be fed* and nourished by physical food from the ground, through the mother. From this physical nourishment it must grow, and *grow* and GROW—until physically large enough to be born —after nine months. As it grows, the *physical* organs and characteristics gradually are formed. Soon a spinal column forms. A heart forms and begins to beat. Other internal organs form. Then, gradually, a body, a head, legs, arms. Finally hair begins to grow on the head, fingernails and toenails develop—facial features gradually shape up. By nine months the average normal fetus has grown to a weight of approximately six to nine pounds, and is ready to be born.

A human has to be BEGOTTEN by his human father. To be born *again* of the Spirit—of GOD—one must first be begotten by the SPIRITUAL FATHER—Almighty God.

The Amazing Comparison

Now see how HUMAN begettal, period of gestation, and birth is the astounding identical TYPE of spiritual salvation—being BORN of God—being given ETERNAL LIFE in the kingdom of God—the God FAMILY into which we may be BORN!

Each adult human is, spiritually, an "egg" or "ovum." In this spiritual ovum is a nucleus, the human mind with its human spirit. This spiritual "ovum" has a very limited life span, of itself—compared to ETERNAL LIFE—an average of some 70 years. But spiritual, *divine immortal* life may be imparted *to* it by the entrance into it of the HOLY SPIRIT, which comes from the very Person of GOD the Father. This divine Spirit of GOD joins with the nucleus of the human ovum, which is the human spirit and mind, and imparts to us also the *divine nature* (II Pet. 1:4). Heretofore we have had only human, fleshly or carnal nature.

As the human sperm cell is the very *smallest* of all human cells, even so, many newly begotten Christians start out with a very *small* measure of God's Holy Spirit and character. Many may still be, at first, about 99.44 percent carnal! Apparently those in the Church of God at Corinth were (I Cor. 3:1-3). The apostle Paul said he still had to feed them on the spiritual *milk*—not yet adult spiritual "food." They certainly were not yet "BORN AGAIN."

Now, as the physical male sperm finds its way to, and unites with the *nucleus* in the ovum, so God's Spirit enters and combines with the human spirit and MIND! There is, as explained before, a *spirit* IN *man*. This human spirit has combined with the brain to form human MIND. God's Spirit unites with, and witnesses with *our* spirit that we are, now, the children of GOD (Rom. 8:16). And God's Holy Spirit, now combined with our human spirit in our MIND, imparts to our mind power to comprehend SPIRITUAL KNOWLEDGE (I Cor. 2:11)—which the carnal mind cannot grasp.

Now we have the presence of ETERNAL LIFE—God-life—through God's Spirit. In like manner the human embryo was an actual human life as yet undeveloped. But we are not yet immortal spirit beings—not yet BORN of God—just as the human ovum was not yet born of its human parents—not yet inheritors, and possessors, but physical HEIRS (Rom. 8:17). But *IF* God's Holy Spirit dwells in us, God will, at the resurrection, "quicken" to immortality our mortal bodies *BY* his Spirit that "dwelleth in us" (Rom. 8:11; I Cor. 15:49-53).

Now we see how the astonishing analogy continues!

As yet we are not *born* divine beings. We are not yet *composed* of spirit, but of physical matter. The divine life has merely been begotten. This divine CHARACTER starts so very small it is doubtful if much of it is in evidence—except for the glow of that ecstasy of spiritual "romance" that we may radiate in that "first love" of conversion—spiritually speaking. But so far as spiritual KNOWLEDGE and developed spiritual CHARACTER goes, there is not much, as yet.

The Spiritual Embryo

So now, once spiritually begotten, we are merely a spiritual embryo. Now we must be fed and nourished on SPIRITUAL food! Jesus said man shall not live by bread (physical food) *alone,* but by EVERY WORD OF GOD (spiritual food)! This we drink in from the Bible! But we drink in this spiritual knowledge and character, also, through personal, intimate, continuous contact with God through PRAYER, and through Christian fellowship with God's children in his Church. And also by the continual teaching imparted by the Church.

Now the *physical* embryo and fetus is fed physically through the mother. God's CHURCH is called Jerusalem *above* "which is the MOTHER OF US ALL" (Gal. 4:26).

Notice the exact parallel! The CHURCH is the spiritual MOTHER OF ITS MEMBERS. God has set his called and chosen ministers in his Church to FEED THE FLOCK—"for *the perfecting* of the saints, for the work of the ministry, for the edifying of the body [CHURCH] of Christ: TILL WE all come in the unity of the faith, and of *the knowledge* of the Son of God, unto a perfect man, unto the measure of the stature of the fulness of Christ" (Eph. 4:11-13).

It is the duty of Christ's TRUE ministers (and *how scarce today*) to PROTECT the begotten but yet unborn saints from false doctrines, from false ministers.

The HUMAN mother carries her unborn baby in that part of her body where she can best PROTECT it from *physical* harm; and that protection is part of her function, as well as to nourish the unborn child! Even so, the CHURCH, through Christ's ministers, instructs, teaches, counsels with, advises, and PROTECTS from *spiritual* harm the unborn members! What a WONDERFUL picture is human reproduction of spiritual SALVATION!

Continue further! As the physical fetus must grow *physically* large enough to be born, so the begotten Christian must *grow* in grace, and in the knowledge of Christ (II Pet. 3:18)—must overcome, must develop in spiritual CHARACTER during this life, in order to be BORN into the kingdom of GOD! And as the physical fetus gradually, one by one, develops the physical organs, features and characteristics, even so the begotten Christian must gradually, continually, develop the SPIRITUAL character—love, faith, patience, gentleness, temperance. He (or she) must live by, and be a DOER of the Word of God. He must develop the divine CHARACTER!

Finally—Immortality!

Then in God's due time—though the person may die meanwhile—by a resurrection, or by instantaneous CHANGE to immortality at Christ's coming, he shall be BORN of God—into the KINGDOM OF GOD—because GOD *is* that kingdom! He is no longer material flesh from the ground, but composed of spirit, even as God is a Spirit (John 4:24).

How WONDERFUL is the TRUTH OF GOD!

Yet, by his dastardly deceptions Satan has DECEIVED THE

WORLD—has blinded humanity to the fact that God *IS* this KINGDOM Jesus proclaimed—and that WE may be *born* as spiritual individuals—as part of that divine FAMILY—as part of the GOD KINGDOM!

How precious is GOD'S TRUTH! God designed reproduction to picture his truth in physical manner and to KEEP US CONSTANTLY IN THE KNOWLEDGE OF HIS WONDERFUL PLAN OF SALVATION!

It is the function of the CHURCH—as the spiritual MOTHER of Christians in it—to develop holy, righteous and perfect godly CHARACTER in those God has called—those God has added to the Church.

Remember, none CAN COME to Christ, except called and drawn by God the Father (John 6:44). Newly converted members are not brought to spiritual conversion by "salesmanship" of human evangelists—are not "talked into" being "converted"—are not emotionally high pressured by high-powered evangelistic oratory or fervor—or by emotion-packed "altar calls" in evangelistic crusades to the moanful strains of a choir singing, "Just as I am, I come, I come."

You cannot find that sort of *MODERN* "Old-Fashioned Gospel" crusading either taught or used to set us an example in the New Testament! Yet people today suppose falsely that is the way Christ intended—the way Jesus initiated.

Jesus *DID NOT* come on a "soul-saving crusade!" to try to save at that time all those in SATAN'S world. He came to call out of Satan's world a people predestinated and specially called and drawn by God. Jesus said it was impossible for others of SATAN'S WORLD to come to him for salvation unless specially called by God to become kings and teachers when God's WORLD TOMORROW has replaced SATAN'S WORLD. NEVER did Jesus beg or plead with anyone to "give one's heart to him." At Jacob's well in Samaria Jesus spoke to a woman about the Holy Spirit in terms of "living water."

The woman said to Jesus, "Sir, give me this water, that I thirst not." Here was a direct request from an unconverted woman for salvation and the gift of the Holy Spirit. BUT JESUS ONLY TOLD HER OF HER SINS—OF WHAT SHE HAD TO REPENT OF! He did NOT say, "Come to me, just as you are, in your sins."

None CAN COME to Jesus except God the Father draws him! All have sinned. Sin is against GOD the Father. Sin must first be repented of—turned from! It is much more than remorse for guilt. It is a matter of being sufficiently SORRY to TURN FROM the sin, overcome the sin. This reconciles one to God on faith in Christ. It is GOD the Father who adds to the Church such as he calls to be saved (Acts 2:47). It is GOD who sets members in the Church (I Cor. 12:18)—not the emotional oratory of the evangelist in the emotional altar call!

God sets individual members in his Church in order that his holy, righteous perfect CHARACTER may be developed in them. And WHY? To prepare them to become GOD BEINGS in the KINGDOM (family) OF GOD, to GOVERN and RULE the whole earth with the government of God!

But HOW does the CHURCH as the spiritual MOTHER of its members DEVELOP THAT SPIRITUAL CHARACTER?

This brings us to the real PURPOSE of the Church. This brings us to an UNDERSTANDING of WHY one cannot be BORN AGAIN outside the CHURCH.

Real Purpose of the Church

Now MOST IMPORTANT OF ALL—what is the REAL PURPOSE for the Church? WHY did God have Christ raise it up?

The CHURCH is the spiritual MOTHER of human converts. They are the spiritual embryos and fetuses as yet UNBORN, although begotten by God's Holy Spirit—already children of GOD.

The CHURCH is God's spiritual ORGANISM, well organized, for feeding on spiritual food, training and developing in spiritual righteous CHARACTER the future GOD BEINGS—sons of God the Father!

For that training—that spiritual development of God's CHARACTER, God has given his Church a DUAL responsibility:

1) "Go ye into all the world" and proclaim the GOOD NEWS—announcement—of the coming kingdom of God.

2) "Feed my sheep."

But in FEEDING the "sheep," developing in them God's spiritual CHARACTER, God has given them THEIR PART in supporting, backing up, the great commission: "Go ye into all the world."

This first and great commission was given to the apostles. To a lesser extent evangelists were used in carrying forth the message. Other leaders—ordained ministers—were stationary, yet even the local pastor of a church may hold evangelistic services in his area—not the "soul-saving crusade" type, but lectures ANNOUNCING and PROCLAIMING as a witness the coming KINGDOM OF GOD (the true gospel)!

This ENTIRE GREAT COMMISSION—proclaiming the GOOD NEWS of the coming kingdom, and "feeding the sheep"—is a COMBINED administration and function of the Church.

The individual lay member HAS HIS VITAL PART in proclaiming the GOOD NEWS (gospel) to the world. How? Not by going out and himself proclaiming Christ's message to the neighborhood or to the world. That is done primarily by the apostles, to some extent by evangelists, and to even a lesser extent in local areas by local pastors. (The chief responsibility of local pastors is supervision of and preaching to the local church.)

But the ENTIRE CHURCH OPERATION is one WHOLE, organized into various operations and administrations (I Cor. 12:5-6).

Part of the Lay Member

For example, what part does the individual local member have in taking the gospel message to ALL THE WORLD? This is done primarily and directly by the APOSTLE. In this latter half of the twentieth century it is done also by radio, television and in PRINT!

In the first century it was done by personal proclamation. Then WHAT PART did the individual lay member have in it?

MUCH! Without this larger body of lay members the apostle could do nothing!

Notice a scriptural example: Peter and John had been proclaiming the message at the Temple in Jerusalem. A miracle had been performed by Peter and a large crowd had gathered. As a result Peter and John were thrown in prison overnight, and severely threatened. Their lives were in danger. They were unnerved.

They went immediately upon release to the lay brethren (Acts 4:23). They needed the backing, support, encouragement of the brethren. They fervently PRAYED! Peter and John sorely NEEDED this loyalty, backing and the prayers of the lay members. THEY WERE ALL A TEAM TOGETHER!

Take a recent modern example.

The office of the attorney general of America's most populous state—California—had made a sudden, unexpected massive armed assault on the headquarters of the Worldwide Church of God at Pasadena, California. They claimed, in violation of the U.S. Constitution, that all church property and assets belong to the State, and a court had secretly appointed a receiver to TAKE OVER, RUN AND OPERATE the Church of the living GOD!

But when the receiver was about to enter with his staff and deputy sheriffs the Hall of Administration and other headquarters buildings, some 5,000 lay members, with children and babies, crowded these buildings in extended and continuous prayer services. The doors were locked. The armed officials did not quite dare to break down the doors and disturb these massive and orderly prayer services. After three days they gave up. The receiver, an ex-judge of a non-Christian faith, resigned. The civil lawsuit went on "the back burner." And the OPERATION OF THE CHURCH CONTINUED! The higher appellate court later ruled that this lawsuit was without foundation and never should have been started.

The author, Christ's apostle, can say emphatically that the apostles, evangelists, pastors and elders could not carry on the work of God without the loyal backing and continual encouragement of the lay members.

Neither can the individual lay member develop and build within him God's holy, righteous and perfect CHARACTER without the operations of the apostle, evangelists, pastors and elders. All these various members GOD HAS SET in his Church are interdependent—mutually dependent on one another. They form a TEAM—an ORGANIZED SPIRITUAL ORGANISM—utterly different from any secular and worldly organization!

How, more specifically, does this mutual dependency operate?

God Has Provided Modern Methods

In general, the whole operation of the Church costs money in this late twentieth century world. Facilities and methods are available to the Church for performance of its commission that did not exist in the first-century world. Without the tithes and generous freewill offerings of lay members the Church commission could not be performed in today's world.

Without the fervent and prevailing continual prayers of all members the work could not be accomplished. Without the continual ENCOURAGEMENT of lay members and those over them locally, those of us operating from headquarters could not bear up under the persecutions, oppositions, trials and frustrations.

Also in reverse, the lay members need just as urgently the encouragement, teaching, counseling and leadership from headquarters and local pastors.

An example of the former: I frequently receive large cards—often beautifully illustrated or decorated—signed by the hundreds of local members of churches, giving encouragement and assurances of loyalty, backing and support. Lay members scattered over the world simply cannot conceive fully how much encouragement and inspiration this gives the one Christ has chosen to lead this tremendous worldwide activity, God's CHURCH! The assurance of the earnest PRAYERS crying out to God continually from these thousands from all parts of the earth inspire the confidence of FAITH to persevere in the direction and oversight in this great work!

Specifically, HOW is God's Church organized today—HOW does it operate in this modern late twentieth century?

Christ's gospel message—the kingdom of God—goes out worldwide in dynamic POWER by radio, by television, and by the mass-circulation magazine, *The Plain Truth.* This unique magazine of more than seven million copies monthly, in seven languages, is full color, effectively and interestingly carrying Christ's gospel. Then, sent free on request are millions of copies of attractive booklets and even full books. A campaign of dynamic full-page messages appeared as advertisements in leading newspapers, *The New York Times, The Wall Street Journal, Los Angeles Times, San Francisco Chronicle,* and other daily newspapers. Large space has been used in the London *Times.*

Then to encourage local church members and the ministry, a 14-to-20-page mimeographed *Pastor General's Report* is mailed from headquarters weekly to all ministers. Twice monthly a tabloid newspaper *The Worldwide News* goes out to all members. Monthly a handsome full-color magazine *The Good News* is sent to all lay members, ministers and near-member co-workers. And finally, Christ's apostle sends out monthly a mimeographed Co-Worker letter to all members and co-workers reporting on progress in the work, current activities and needs.

And we must not overlook a very important department, the Bible Correspondence Course, sent free on enrollment to lay members, and the public, giving monthly lessons in-depth of basic subjects covered by the Bible.

The author's personal travels to all parts of the world representing Christ's message personally before kings, emperors, presidents, prime ministers and leaders under them in numerous nations perhaps ought to be mentioned.

All this is a well-organized operation carrying out the PURPOSE of the Church, 1) proclaiming the coming kingdom of God to the world and 2) feeding the flock.

The "loner"—the "individual Christian," who wants to climb up into the kingdom of God some other way than by CHRIST and HIS WAY through his CHURCH—is not being trained in CHRIST'S MANNER OF TRAINING, to rule and reign with Christ in his kingdom!

"Individual Christians"—Ex-Members

Now what about the "private," or "individual Christian," who says, "I don't want to be a part of the Church—I want to seek my salvation direct and alone with Jesus Christ."

The answer is this: God himself laid out the plan and the method by which humans may be, after begettal, trained and prepared to become part of the divine personnel of born GOD BEINGS that shall form the KINGDOM OF GOD!

The kingdom of God will be the GOD FAMILY—a superbly and highly trained and organized family of GOD BEINGS. The Church is God's special school for training those he has selected and called to be trained in his Church—to be kings and priests, to rule and to teach—for their part in that kingdom. Only those so trained in the Church will be kings and priests in the kingdom of God.

The person who says "I will get my salvation alone, outside of the Church" is totally deceived. This is not the time when salvation is opened to those in Satan's world. Those called now, I repeat emphatically, are NOT CALLED just for salvation. They are called for a special training provided only in God's Church.

Those in Satan's world cannot train themselves outside of the Church for the special calling of being rulers and teachers in God's kingdom when Satan is removed and the world has become God's world.

The Church is ORGANIZED on GOD's pattern of mutual teamwork and cooperation to function perfectly together. They shall become the GOD FAMILY as it shall exist at the time of Christ's Second Coming. Remember God *IS* that divine FAMILY!

Take an analogy from Satan's world. A football player says: "I want to play in all of the games, but I'll train *alone*. I don't want to be part of the TEAM until the games start." Would the coach let him be part of the team in the games, without having learned TEAMWORK during practice season? Neither will God let one INTO his family at the resurrection any who refused to be part of it now—in the CHURCH—in the spiritual "training season."

To those chosen to be apostles in the start of the CHURCH, Jesus said, speaking of the CHURCH:

"I am the vine, ye are the branches." Those not joined with others of the branches, all joined to the main vine, were NO PART OF THE CHURCH, and God the Father will cast them away as DEAD branches. The LIFE (spirit life impregnated now) is received along with all other "branches" from the main vine—Christ, the Head of the CHURCH!

What about one who has been IN Christ's "spiritual BODY"—the Church—and is PUT OUT for cause (causing division or rebellion or opposition to Church government)? The CHURCH is like a human mother who is pregnant. If there is an abortion, the HUMAN LIFE departs totally from the fetus. There is, however, perhaps one difference in this analogy. A human who goes out, or is put out of God's Church, could, on repentance and renewed belief, be admitted back into the body again.

What About the World's Churches?

What about the millions of members of other churches or religions?

SATAN is the great counterfeiter. Satan has his churches, his religions, and his ministers in those religions and churches (II Cor. 11:13-15). What about the millions of people in traditional established "Christian" churches? In the book of Revelation, the TRUE Church is pictured in the 12th chapter as the persecuted "little flock," many martyred—put to death for their faith—having to FLEE for safety from persecution, torture and death. In chapter 17 is pictured the big, politically and worldly powerful churches, headed by "mother" "Babylon the great, the mother of harlots and abominations of the earth" (verse 5). In other words, the ancient "Babylonian Mystery" religion, out of whom have gone daughter churches in protest. This politically great church was the persecutor of "the saints" (verse 6). This false church, politically great, sits astride a "beast" pictured in chapter 13 as a government ruling by power of "the dragon" who (Rev. 12:9) is Satan the devil.

This is shocking, but plainly revealed in God's Word!

What about those, in such churches, who profess being "born-again Christians"? They are DECEIVED! They may be ever so sincere. They do not know they are deceived and wrong in their beliefs. But they are not now being judged! They are neither condemned to the lake of fire nor "saved." They are among the WHOLE WORLD, swayed by the deceptions of Satan, CUT OFF from God!

It must be repeated—they shall have their eyes opened to God's TRUTH if still living after Christ comes and Satan is removed—or, if dead before then, resurrected and called to truth and salvation in the Great White Throne Judgment resurrection (Rev. 20:11-12).

Again, the reader is urged to read the free booklet *Just What Do You Mean—Born Again?*

Yes, the whole world is DECEIVED. But praise GOD! Satan soon shall be removed from earth, eyes shall be opened to

Can You Prove It?

Holy Bible

FREE literature offer—see inside!

ASTONISHING TRUTH, and ultimately EVERYBODY who ever lived shall have been called to salvation and eternal life! But when called, each must make his own decision. Sorrowfully as I say it, some will not repent, believe, and be saved. This book emphatically is not teaching a universal salvation. Some are going to finally perish in the lake of fire.

Meanwhile God's GLORIOUS PURPOSE must be worked out here below according to God's wonderful MASTER PLAN—a step at a time!

Teachings and Beliefs

Now we must summarize the teaching and beliefs of God's true Church.

This, naturally, is related directly to the purpose of the Church—to call out of Satan's present world disciples (students, learners) to be trained to become kings and priests (teachers) in God's world tomorrow when God will open the tree of life (salvation, immortality) to all flesh.

But doctrinally, remember what the Church is called to help restore—the kingdom, government and character of God. What was taken away? God's law, the foundation of his government and the very essence of God's character and divine life.

In other words, the pivotal point is the SIN question. Sin is the transgression of God's spiritual law (I John 3:4).

Satan has deceived this world's churches into the belief that God's law was done away—that Jesus, rather than paying the price in human stead for transgressing the law, did away with it—"nailing it to his cross."

The expression used by Protestants "nailing the law to his cross" can mean only one thing. This is Satan's teaching that by being nailed to the cross, Christ abolished the law, making it possible for humans to sin with impunity. What actually was nailed to the cross was Christ our sin bearer, who took on himself our sins, paying the death penalty in our stead, so that we are freed from the ultimate penalty of sinning, not made free to sin with impunity.

The very basic teaching, belief AND DOCTRINE OF God's true Church therefore is based on the righteousness of and obedience to the law of God. That law is LOVE. But it is not human love. Human love cannot rise above the level of human self-centeredness. It must be "the love of God . . . shed abroad in our hearts by the Holy [Spirit]" (Rom. 5:5). Ancient Israel could not really obey God's law—they could have kept it according to the strict letter of the law. But since love is the fulfilling of the law and they had only human self-centered love, they could not have kept the law according to the spirit—because the Holy Spirit had not yet been given.

This basic teaching includes, therefore, all the "fruits of the Holy Spirit"—love, joy, peace, patience, gentleness, goodness, faith, meekness, temperance, etc.

The teachings of God's true Church are simply those of "living by every word" of the Holy Bible.

The first man, Adam, chose to decide for himself right from wrong—to decide his own teachings, beliefs and ways of life. The world has followed that same course for 6,000 years. The Church is called out of the world to live the way God, through the Bible, teaches.

Synoptic History of the Church

Finally, we come to a brief history of the Church from its foundation in A.D. 31 to the present.

The Church started on the day of Firstfruits called Pentecost, in June of A.D 31. The Holy Spirit came from heaven upon the 120 disciples assembled in Jerusalem with a miraculous display such as has never before nor since occurred.

The 120 were all of "one accord." Suddenly "there came a sound from heaven, as of a rushing mighty wind" (Acts 2:2). Have you ever been in a tornado or a hurricane? I have. Wind can make a very loud sound. This sound filled "all the house where they were sitting." Next "there appeared unto them cloven tongues like as of fire, and it sat upon each of them. And they were all filled with the Holy [Spirit], and began to speak with other tongues [languages], as the Spirit gave them utterance."

Never has such a supernatural display occurred before or since. Yet the modern sects calling themselves "Pentecostal" claim to repeat this experience.

But in their meetings no such sound comes from heaven.

No supernatural divided tongues of flaming fire sit on their heads. Some do break out in a kind of gibberish supposed to be some foreign language, but emphatically not anything like that that happened on this one day of Pentecost in A.D 31. Notice what kind of languages were spoken at the Church's inception. Many besides the 120 were present from many countries speaking different languages. Notice particularly, of these strangers, "every man heard them [the 120] speak in his own language. And they were all amazed and marvelled, saying to one another, Behold, are not all these which speak Galilaeans? And how hear we every man in our own tongue, wherein we were born?"

Now notice carefully. Every man—that is, each individual—heard them, the 120, all speaking in his own native language. The Greek heard the 120 speaking the Greek language. The Parthian heard the same 120 speaking in the Parthian language. The Mede heard the 120 speaking the language of the Medes. They understood what was being said. They got the message!

Today, in "Pentecostal" meetings one person may break out in a kind of gibberish that others in the meeting do not understand (I Cor. 14:28). It says if one speaks in a foreign language there must be an interpreter so the others can understand. "But if there be no interpreter, let him keep silence in the church; and let him speak to himself, and to God." In verse 33 it says God is not the author of confusion. In verse 19, God shows the relative unimportance of "tongues" by saying: "Yet in the church I had rather speak five words with my understanding, that by my voice I might teach others also, than ten thousand words in an unknown tongue."

When I speak to an audience in Japan or some other country, I always have an interpreter who will interpret into the language of that country, every few words, my message in their language. When I speak in this kind of "tongues" I speak with understanding, and the people get the message.

Baptism of the Holy Spirit

This entire modern "Pentecostal" movement is based on a total misunderstanding and a deception of Satan in relation to the true meaning of the baptism of—or, more correctly, by—the Holy Spirit. Christ said through the apostle Paul that by one Spirit are we all baptized into the one body—the Church (I Cor. 12:13). The word *baptize* means "immerse" or "plunge into."

"Pentecostal" people have been deceived into thinking that one is what they called "saved" when one receives Jesus Christ as his personal Savior. They consider "the baptism of the Holy Spirit" evidenced by speaking in "tongues" as a subsequent imbuement of power. I have had a great deal of experience with these people. This "baptism" as they call it seems to loosen their tongues in what they call an "imbuement with power," which, in practice, means power to speak emotionally, often braggingly.

The above explanation will not change those already hooked on this deception, but hopefully it will prevent others from becoming misled by this counterfeit emotional "spirituality."

Today's customary gospel *about* Christ contends that simply "believing on Christ," which is professing Christ as personal Savior, means that one is already saved. Yet Mark 7:7-9 shows that many even go so far as to worship Christ, and all in vain because they do not obey God's commandments—especially the Sabbath—but follow the traditions of men by which Satan has deceived the whole world.

In John 8:30-44 the Jews who "believed on Christ" but who did not believe Christ or keep his commandments were called, by Jesus, the children of their father the devil. In I John 2:4 it shows that he who claims to know Christ as Savior, but does not keep his commandments is a liar and the truth is not in him.

On the original day of Pentecost, of these Jews from other countries, some three thousand were baptized after a real repentance and belief in Christ and in his Word, on that same day. A day or two later, after Peter had healed the lifelong cripple at the gate of the Temple, 2,000 more were baptized. The new fledgling Church grew, not merely by addition, which God added to his Church, but by multiplication.

But this phenomenal growth was not to continue long at such an amazing rate of growth.

Remember, these in the Church were being specially called by God out of Satan's world. Satan was sitting on the throne of this earth. He fought fiendishly to protect his reign and upset God's purpose to redeem mankind. Satan had sought to kill the Christ-child. Satan tried desperately to tempt and disqualify Jesus at age 30. Satan did not give up, nor has he to this very day. He now sought to destroy the Church and if he could not destroy it, at least counterfeit it and deceive his world into a false Christianity.

At the very outset Satan moved on Jews to fight the Church by denying Jesus as the prophesied Messiah. At the first the Church was almost wholly Jewish. The unconverted Jews fought to retain the physical rituals and animal sacrifices of the law of Moses.

Very soon, while the membership in God's Church was being multiplied (Acts 6:1), there was a great persecution against the Church (Acts 8:1). Members were all scattered abroad throughout Judea and Samaria, except the apostles.

False Gospel Proclaimed

Soon a violent controversy arose over whether the gospel to be proclaimed was the gospel of Christ (which was Jesus' gospel or good news about the kingdom of God) or whether they should preach a gospel ABOUT Christ, merely preaching the acceptance of Christ as Savior. As apostasy from Christ's truth gained momentum, much of the Church was turning to a different and counterfeit gospel, proclaiming Christ as Savior, but omitting entirely that sin is the transgression of God's spiritual law, and the good news of the kingdom of God, removal of Satan, and restoration of the government of God over the earth and the final opening of salvation to all of humanity, who, when judged, would repent, believe and receive eternal life as sons of God—as actual God beings.

The apostle Paul wrote in II Corinthians 11:3: "But I fear, lest by any means, as the serpent beguiled Eve through his subtilty, so your minds [those in the early Church] should be corrupted from the simplicity that is in Christ. For if he that cometh preacheth another Jesus, whom we have not preached, or if ye receive another spirit, which ye have not received, or another gospel, which ye have not accepted, ye might well bear with him."

Then Paul goes on and describes the false preachers as stated previously, that were coming in and changing the gospel of Christ right at that time.

Then we turn next to Galatians 1:6-7. Paul wrote: "I marvel that ye are so soon removed from him that called you [you had to be called to become a member of the Church—no one can come to Christ, except those that are called] into the grace of Christ unto another gospel: which is not another; but there be some that trouble you, and would pervert the gospel of Christ." The gospel of Christ was the message about the coming kingdom of God. They were already turning to a different gospel.

Counterfeit Called "Christianity"

Already the curtain was rung down on the history of the true Church. You read of it in the book of Acts, but it doesn't go much beyond that. But the curtain seems to lift, and we begin to get a little bit of the history in about A.D. 150. There we see a church calling itself Christian, but it's a totally different church, as different as night is from day, down from up, or black from white. But it called itself Christian.

Now we quote from a book of history, *The Decline and Fall of the Roman Empire*, Volume I and chapter 15: "The scanty and suspicious materials on ecclesiastical history seldom enable us to dispel the dark cloud that hangs over the first age of the Church." I have often called it "the lost century," because the history of that Church was lost at that time.

Scholars and church historians recognize that events in the early Christian Church between A.D. 50 and 150 can only be seen in vague outline—as if obscured by a thick mist.

The noted English scholar Samuel G. Green in *A Handbook of Church History* wrote: "The thirty years which followed the close of the New Testament Canon and the destruction of Jerusalem are in truth the most obscure in the history of the Church. When we emerge in the second century we are, to a great extent, in a changed world."

In *Lectures on Ecclesiastical History* William Fitzgerald wrote: "Over this period of transition, which immediately succeeds upon the era properly called apostolic, great obscurity hangs. . . ."

In *The Course of Christian History* William J. McGlothlin wrote: "But Christianity itself had been in [the] process of transformation as it progressed and at the close of the period was in many respects quite different from the apostolic Christianity."

In *History of the Christian Church* Philip Schaff wrote: "The remaining thirty years of the first century are involved in mysterious darkness, illuminated only by the writings of John. This is a period of church history about which we know least and would like to know most."

But if we look closely through this mist, we can begin to see what was happening.

The world in which Christ founded his Church was the world of the Roman Empire—the greatest and most powerful empire that had ever existed. It stretched from Britain to the far reaches of modern-day Turkey, encompassing peoples from many different backgrounds and cultures under one system of government.

Rome's ruling hand was firm but the subject peoples enjoyed considerable freedom, within the compass of Roman law. Providing all citizens and conquered peoples paid due homage to the Roman emperor, they were also allowed to practice their religious beliefs and worship the gods of their ancestors.

After the day of Pentecost, the apostles began to follow Christ's instruction to go to all the world preaching the gospel of the kingdom. Once Christianity spread from Judea to the gentile lands to the north it began to encounter those who practiced the pagan religions of Babylon, Persia and Greece.

The apostles came in contact with Simon Magus, a self-proclaimed leader in a cult that was deeply rooted in the mystery religion of ancient Babylon.

Simon Magus' plot to buy himself a position of influence in the early Church was foiled by Peter (Acts 8). But other false teachers soon followed.

In his early epistles, Paul warned the fledgling churches of Greece and Galatia that they were in danger of turning aside after another gospel—a false concept of Christ and his message. The gospel of Christ was being diluted as false ministers with their teaching, heavily influenced by the beliefs of Babylon and Persia, steadily infiltrated the congregations.

As the first century wore on, the original apostles encouraged the members to stay faithful.

Jude, the brother of Jesus, urges the membership to strive for the faith that was once delivered (Jude 3). The apostle John warns the brethren to have nothing to do with those who are bringing in false doctrines (II John 10).

Many who called themselves Christian had not been truly converted. But throughout this period, all who called themselves Christian suffered greatly from the Roman authorities, because they refused to worship the emperor.

The mad Nero in A.D. 64 blamed the burning of Rome on the Christians and persecuted them savagely. Thousands suffered martyrdom.

Shortly afterward, the Jews of Palestine rose in rebellion against the Roman authorities. The rebellion was suppressed and Jerusalem destroyed in A.D. 70.

A small number of true Christians in Jerusalem fled over the mountains to the safety of Pella.

Seven Church Eras

The book of Revelation records seven messages to seven churches that existed in Asia Minor toward the end of the first century A.D.

These churches—Ephesus, Smyrna, Pergamos, Thyatira, Sardis, Philadelphia and Laodicea—were located along one of the mail routes of the old Roman Empire.

Riders would follow the route—carrying messages from town to town.

The messages to the seven churches have words of both encouragement and correction and they clearly show the dominant characteristics of each of the congregations at that time.

But these messages were intended for a wider audience than the Christians in these small towns.

They are a series of remarkable prophecies, by which the future of the true Church was foretold in outline form, from the day it began on Pentecost, A.D. 31, until the Second Coming of Christ.

The history of the Church would fall into seven distinct eras—each with its own strengths and weaknesses and its own special trials and problems.

Just as a message could pass along the mail route from Ephesus to Laodicea, so would the truth of God be passed from era to era.

It was like a relay race—in which the baton is passed from runner to runner, each one doing his part, until the finish line is reached.

Some time during the early decades of the second century, the baton was passed from the Ephesian era to the people that God had called to the Smyrna era of his Church.

Powerless, often persecuted, and rejected as heretics, the world lost sight of them. Instead, there emerged from the lost century a church that was steadily growing in popularity but growing further away from the gospel that Jesus taught.

Persecution continued at various times under the Romans until the fourth century, when Constantine recognized the degenerate Church of that period as an official religion of the empire.

But the Church that he recognized was by now very different from the Church that Jesus founded. The doctrines and teachings that he had taught his apostles were now buried amid the trappings, ceremonies, mysteries and rituals of a church that called itself by the name of Christ. It was essentially the Babylonian Mystery religion, now being called Christian, accepting the doctrine of grace but turning it into license. In other words, it was the old pagan Babylonian Mystery religion wearing a new cloak: "Christianity."

Once Constantine recognized them, this Church threw renewed energy into taking its message to the world. Teachers and preachers went to all parts of the Roman Empire with a message about Christ. Thousands—maybe millions—heard this gospel and believed it. But it was not the gospel Christ preached—his prophetic message of the coming kingdom of God.

Emperor Decreed Doctrine of False Church

What happened to the true Church during those centuries in which the gospel was suppressed?

Emperor Constantine died in A.D. 337, just over 300 years after Christ was crucified. He had given his blessing to a church that claimed to be the one that Christ founded.

Now that they were free from fear of oppression—the persecuted became persecutors. Those of the true Church who dared to disagree with their doctrine were branded as heretics, worthy of punishment.

In about A.D. 365 the Catholic Council of Laodicea wrote in one of its most famous canons: "Christians must not judaize by resting on the Sabbath, but must work on that day, rather, honouring the Lord's Day. But if any shall be found to be judaizers, let them be anathema from Christ." This was a virtual sentence to torture and/or death. The false church did not herself put true believers to death, but caused them to be put to death (Rev. 13:15). This decree of A.D. 365 definitely shows that there were true Christians observing the Sabbath.

The small remnant of Christians of the Smyrna era fled once more—to seek the religious freedom they needed to practice their beliefs.

They left few records. Occasionally they appear as a footnote of history, rejected as heretics, ridiculed, and hounded by their enemies. But their strongest testimony comes from Jesus himself, in his words of encouragement to the Church that was at Smyrna. "I know your works, tribulation, and poverty.... Do not fear any of those things which you are about to suffer.... Be faithful until death, and I will give you the crown of life" (Rev. 2:9-10, Revised Authorized Version).

And so the baton passed from the Smyrna Christians to those of the Pergamos era.

These had been called to carry the truth through one of history's most difficult periods—the Dark Ages.

The power and influence of the great universal church

spread far and wide, driving those who clung to the truth of God ever further into the wilderness.

But they were never far from threat of persecution and martyrdom.

And so very few of the Pergamos Christians remained faithful.

One thousand years after Jesus had founded his Church, the exhausted remnant of the Pergamos era handed over the baton.

The Thyatiran era got off to a vigorous start, preaching repentance throughout the Alpine Valleys of Southern France and Northern Italy. Many heard and were converted.

The religious authorities quickly reacted to this challenge.

Leaders of the true Church were arrested. Some were martyred.

After the death of its first leaders, the Church went into a temporary decline—but emerged once more under the dynamic leadership of Peter Waldo. For several years in the 12th century, these Waldensians flourished in the Alpine Valleys, preaching what truth they had. Booklets and articles were written and copied by hand. This was still before the days of printing.

As Jesus prophesied of the Thyatiran era, they had faith and they worked hard. Their latter works were greater than the first.

But once again, persecution followed, as the full force of the Inquisition was felt in the peaceful valleys that had once provided a safe haven for the work of God.

Many that remained began to adopt the customs and traditions of the world around them.

Europe now had many scattered groups of people calling themselves Christians.

Meanwhile, the world was changing. Printing had been invented—and knowledge began to be increased. The Protestant Reformation broke the monopoly of the Church of Rome.

As religious wars swept across the European continent during the Middle Ages, many refugees fled to the relative safety and tolerance of England. Among them were members of the true Church. They brought with them their doctrines and beliefs, especially the knowledge of the Sabbath.

The strict Sunday-observing Puritans resisted, but in spite of a rising tide of opposition, in the early 17th century, there were several small Sabbath-keeping congregations in England. Jesus was raising up the fifth era of his Church—Sardis.

Protestant England became increasingly intolerant of dissenters, including Sabbath keepers.

The true Church in England withered. But across the ocean, men were beginning to discover a New World.

Stephen Mumford, a member of a Sabbath-keeping church in London, left England for Newport, Rhode Island, in 1664. Rhode Island was the smallest of the American colonies, and had been founded by Roger Williams, a Baptist fleeing persecution from the Puritans of Massachusetts.

Rhode Island was the first place in the world to guarantee freedom of religion as a basic tenet of its constitution. Finding none who kept the Sabbath, Mumford and his wife began to fellowship with the Baptist church in Newport. He did not proselytize, but quietly maintained his own belief. Several members of the Sunday-keeping congregation became convinced that they, too, should observe the Sabbath.

They became the first Sabbath-keeping congregation in America.

At first they met in private homes. In the historical museum at Newport, their record book is preserved—containing names—their contributions—even records of their ordination services.

Also preserved is the simple, but elegant, meeting hall that they built in Newport in the early years of the 18th century. Others joined them in their belief, as God began to call more to his work in the New World.

A second congregation was established at Hopkinton. This soon became a thriving church of several hundred. A bridge today marks the spot where their meeting house once stood. Several thousand were baptized here on the banks of the Pawcatuck River. Then spiritual decline set in.

By the mid-1800s, vigorous new Sabbath-keeping congregations, raised up as a result of the preaching of William Miller, 1831-1849, could be found throughout the American Midwest.

At Battle Creek, Michigan, in 1860, many thousands were persuaded to accept the beliefs of the followers of Ellen G. White.

They departed from the true name—the Church of God. Instead of the true gospel, the kingdom of God, they substituted doctrines of Ellen G. White, called "the shut-door policy," "the investigative judgment," a "2,300 day" doctrine and "the spirit of prophecy," identifying Mrs. White as the church's prophet who actually set the church's doctrine.

They adopted the name Seventh-day Adventists, by which name they are known to this day. But those who remained of the true Church of God refused to accept these teachings and doctrines and restored certain truths that had fallen into neglect in the previous century.

They moved their headquarters to Marion, Iowa, and then to Stanberry, Missouri. A magazine, *The Bible Advocate*, was published. Their efforts bore some fruit—small congregations sprang up across the nation.

And so it was that some time in the 19th century, a small congregation of the true Church of God was established in the peaceful Willamette Valley in Oregon.

They were farmers, without formal education. They lacked trained ministers to teach and guide them. But they had the name, Church of God, and they faithfully kept the Sabbath day.

God's Church had come a long way across the turbulent centuries since the day of Pentecost.

It was weak, and lacked influence. Years of persecution and compromise had taken their toll. Much truth had been lost. But they had stayed the course.

In the Willamette Valley, they waited. It was nearly time for the baton to change again—into the hands of those God would call to do his end-time work.

Restoration of God's Truth to Church

From the year 1931, exactly 1,900 years (a century of time cycles) from the foundation of the Church, this small remnant of the original true Church of God began to take on new life as the Philadelphia era. It had come to the "time of the end." A new spiritual vitality was infused into it. The time had come for Jesus' prophecy of Matthew 24:14 to be fulfilled—"this gospel of the kingdom shall be [proclaimed] in all the world for a witness unto all nations; and then shall the end come." Such vital truth that had been lost was gradually revealed and proclaimed.

This Philadelphia era is described in verses 7 to 13 of Revelation 3. The Sardis era (Rev. 3:1-6) was by this time spiritually dying and had become impotent in spreading the true gospel of Christ. Indeed they had by this time lost knowledge of the true meaning of that gospel. They knew they were approaching the Second Coming of Christ, but they had no knowledge of what would happen during the thousand years millennium, further than the fact Christ would rule.

Of the Philadelphia era of God's true Church we read: "To the angel of the church. . . ." This word *angel* translated from the Greek *aggelos* means messenger or agent. This is not necessarily always referring to a spirit angel but can refer as well to a human agent. It is possible that God's principle of duality may apply here. It may apply to an actual spirit-composed angel that has been assigned as an overall agent or helper of this particular era of the Church. Or it may also apply to the human messenger or agent God has raised up to lead this era of his Church.

At the same time another principle of duality may apply to verses 7-13. It may apply to the Church of this era as a whole, and also it could apply to the human leader God had raised up to this era of his Church.

Continue with verse 8: "I know thy works: behold, I have set before thee an open door, and no man can shut it: for thou hast a little strength, and hast kept my word, and hast not denied my name."

This era of the Church was to produce fruit. To this era—or to its human leader—God had set before it an open door. It is recorded in II Corinthians 2:12 and also Acts 14:27 how Christ opened the door for Paul to go into other countries to preach the gospel. This Church and/or its leader had but little strength. Neither were of great and powerful stature in

Satan's world but those of this era were faithful to the Word of God. Though much of the original gospel truth, imparted to the original apostles by Jesus in person, had been lost, it was restored through the Bible to this era of God's Church who were faithful in keeping it.

It is revealed in Malachi 3:1-5 and 4:5-6 that God would raise up one in the power and spirit of Elijah, shortly prior to the Second Coming of Christ. In Matthew 17:11 Jesus said, even after John the Baptist had completed his mission, that this prophesied Elijah "truly shall first come, and restore all things." Although it is plainly revealed that John the Baptist had come in the power and spirit of Elijah, he did not restore anything. The human leader to be raised up somewhat shortly prior to Christ's Second Coming was to prepare the way—prepare the Church—for Christ's coming, and restore the truth that had been lost through the preceding eras of the Church. Also a door was to be opened for this leader and/or the Philadelphia era of the Church to fulfill Matthew 24:14: "And this gospel of the kingdom shall be preached in all the world for a witness unto all nations; and then shall the end come."

It was to be at a time when, for the first time in the history of mankind, the weapons of mass destruction were produced that could erase all humanity from the earth (Matt. 24:21-22). This also was to occur just before the Second Coming of Christ (verses 29-30).

These prophecies have now definitely been fulfilled. The true gospel has been restored and has now gone in power into every nation on the face of the earth.

The Church has taken on a new Spirit-empowered life.

All the technological advances and facilities are being employed.

First radio was used, beginning on one of the smallest-powered stations in Eugene, Oregon. Then the printed word. This started with an old secondhand Neostyle, ancestor to the mimeograph. In due time the printing press was used. The advent of television came in 1945—immediately after the end of World War II. The Church began using television in the summer of 1955. The true gospel, for the first time in 1,900 years, has finally been proclaimed and published into all nations of the earth. The Church has grown. For the first 25 years it grew at an average rate of 30 percent per year.

The first apostles would be astonished to see the size and scope of the work now. The means of communications, the technology and the modern resources that God has given to his end-time work would indeed be strange to those men who first received the commission to take the gospel to the world nearly 2,000 years ago.

But some things would not be strange—the Sabbath and Holy Days, the name, the Church of God, and the gospel of the kingdom—these they would recognize—handed down through the ages from the time of Christ to the time of the end.

MYSTERY OF THE KINGDOM OF GOD

JUST what do you mean, "the kingdom of God"? That, too, is an unsolved mystery, not only to all in the world but to the world's churches, theologians and "Bible scholars" as well.

Actually that mystery is connected with its associated mystery, the gospel of Jesus Christ.

Why do the churches disagree on what actually is "the gospel of Jesus Christ"? During the first twenty or thirty years after the founding of the Church in A.D. 31 a violent controversy arose over the very question of what is "the gospel of Jesus Christ." There ensued a hundred years in which all history of the New Testament Church was destroyed. It has been called "the lost century of Church history." When the curtain lifted, about the middle of the second century, there appeared an entirely different type of church calling itself Christian, but in the main preaching its own gospel ABOUT Christ, not the gospel OF Christ. The gospel OF Christ was the gospel Christ proclaimed. Jesus was a Messenger sent from God with a message, and that message was THE KINGDOM OF GOD. Christ's message was Christ's gospel—the gospel OF Christ. It had not been proclaimed to the world until the first week in 1953, when for the first time in about 1,900 years—a century of time cycles—it went out on the world's most powerful radio station, Radio Luxembourg in Europe.

It seems that today all churches have lost the gospel of Jesus Christ. They preach primarily their gospel ABOUT Jesus Christ.

Jesus Christ came preaching the gospel of the kingdom of God. Yet *few* preach about the kingdom of God today, for they have lost all knowledge of what it is! But does any, except God's true Church, proclaim the true gospel of the kingdom of God today?

A prominent evangelist said to a worldwide radio audience that the gospel of the kingdom of God is not for us today. Some denominations proclaim a "gospel of grace", some what they call a "gospel of salvation"; most a gospel *about* Christ; some a social gospel; some the "Science of Mind" or "Religious Science."

Not One Is Right!

Some churches claim either that their particular denomination, or "Christianity" as a whole, constitutes the kingdom of God. A prominent television evangelist said, "The kingdom of God is within you." Some have even quoted Luke 17:21: "The kingdom of God is within you." The marginal correction as well as the Revised Standard, the Moffatt and other translations all show it should read, "in the midst of you"—that is, Jesus Christ was in the midst of them. He is the King of the future kingdom of God, and the Bible in Daniel 7 and other places uses the terms king and kingdom interchangeably, that is, the king is, or represents, the kingdom he rules.

Not one is right! Could anything seem more incredible? Yes, to the mind reared in this world's concepts, one thing is, indeed, still *more* incredible! And that is the PLAIN TRUTH about what the kingdom of God really is!

The truth is not merely surprising—it is shocking —staggering! It is a Great Mystery! Yet it is truly GOOD NEWS—the most glorious GOOD NEWS ever to enter human consciousness!

CHRIST'S Gospel

What is the one and *only* gospel of Jesus Christ? THE WORLD DOES NOT KNOW! It has not been preached for 19 centuries, strange as that may seem. Look into your BIBLE. Look at it from the very beginning!

"The beginning of the gospel of Jesus Christ" you'll read in Mark 1:1. "Now after that John was put in prison, Jesus came into Galilee, preaching the GOSPEL OF THE KINGDOM OF GOD, and saying, The time is fulfilled, and the kingdom of God is at hand: repent ye, and believe the gospel" (Mark 1:14-15).

It is necessary to *believe that* GOSPEL to be saved! And how can you *believe* it, unless you know what it is? And for 1,900 years, the world did not know. That gospel was suppressed and replaced by man's gospel about Christ.

Jesus went everywhere preaching the GOOD NEWS of the KINGDOM OF GOD. He taught in parables about the KINGDOM OF GOD. He sent out seventy men preaching, and commanded them to preach THE KINGDOM OF GOD (Luke 10:9). He sent the apostles, on whom the Church of God was founded, to preach only THE KINGDOM OF GOD (Luke 9:1-2). After the resurrection, before ascending to heaven, Jesus taught his disciples about the kingdom of God (Acts 1:3).

Isn't it amazing that the world has LOST the knowledge of what it is?

The apostle Paul preached THE KINGDOM OF GOD (Acts 19:8; 20:25; 28:23, 31). And God Almighty, through Paul, pronounced *a double curse* on man or angel that would DARE preach any other gospel! (Gal. 1:8-9.)

Why, then, do so *many* DARE to preach so many *other* gospels? The good news of THE KINGDOM OF GOD is something you must *understand,* and BELIEVE, in order to be saved! Jesus Christ said so! YOU had better be finding out *what it is!*

That gospel—the kingdom of God—is the subject of this chapter. It follows the chapter on the mystery of the Church, because the kingdom of God follows the Church. The purpose of the Church, remember, is to prepare "called-out-ones" to teach and to rule in the kingdom of God.

Daniel Knew!

Haven't you heard men speak of the kingdom of God something like this: "By Christians everywhere working together to bring about world peace, tolerance and brotherly love, the kingdom of God may at last be established in the hearts of men."

Because they *rejected* Christ's gospel 1,900 years ago, the world had to supplant something else in its place. They had to invent a *counterfeit!* So we have heard the kingdom of God spoken of as merely a pretty platitude—a nice sentiment in human hearts—reducing it to an ethereal, unreal NOTHING! Others have misrepresented that the "CHURCH" is the kingdom. Others confuse it with the millennium. Still others have, earlier in our century, claimed the British Empire is the kingdom of God. But no one makes that claim any longer. HOW DECEIVED CAN THIS WORLD GET?

The prophet Daniel, who lived 600 years before Christ, knew that the kingdom of God was a real kingdom—a *government* ruling over literal PEOPLE on the earth.

Jesus Christ brought additional knowledge about it that the prophet Daniel might not have known. Still, Daniel knew there was going to be a real, literal kingdom of God on the earth.

Daniel was one of four extraordinary, intelligent and brilliant Jewish lads in the Judean captivity. These four men were stationed in the palace of King Nebuchadnezzar of the Chaldean Empire, in training for special responsibilities in the Babylonian government. Daniel was a prophet who had been given special understanding in visions and dreams (Dan. 1:17).

Nebuchadnezzar was the first real world ruler. He had conquered a vast empire, including the nation Judah. This king had a dream so impressive it troubled him—moved him to tremendous concern. He demanded that his magicians, astrologers and sorcerers tell him both *what* he had dreamed, and what it meant. They could not. They were baffled. Then Daniel was brought before the king.

Daniel disclaimed any more human ability to interpret dreams than the Chaldean magicians, "BUT," he said, "there is a GOD in heaven that revealeth secrets, and maketh known to the king Nebuchadnezzar what shall be in the latter days" (Dan. 2:28).

First, God's purpose was to reveal to this world-ruling human king that there is a GOD in heaven—that GOD IS SUPREME RULER over all nations, governments and kings—

that God RULES THE UNIVERSE! It was God who placed the cherub Lucifer on the throne of the earth and Lucifer, who has become Satan the Devil, remains on earth's throne only because God allows it, and only until God sends Jesus Christ to sit on that throne when he removes Satan. This Chaldean king knew only about the many pagan demon gods. He knew nothing of the true *living* ALMIGHTY God. Like people and rulers, even today, he did not know that GOD is the living, REAL, active, RULING and GOVERNING PERSONAGE who actually and literally *governs* not only what is on earth, but the UNIVERSE ENTIRELY!

The whole purpose of this DREAM was to *reveal* GOD's GOVERNMENT—the *fact* that God RULES—the truth of THE KINGDOM OF GOD—the very thing that is the one and *only* true GOSPEL OF JESUS CHRIST! And, secondly, to reveal—preserved in writing for us TODAY—what is to happen *"in the latter days"*—actually within the next two decades—THIS LAST HALF OF THE TWENTIETH CENTURY!

For US, Today!

This is no dry, dull, dead writing for a people of 2,500 years ago. This is LIVING, TREMENDOUS, *BIG NEWS* for *OUR DAY!* It is *advance news* for us, *NOW*. News *before it happens*—of the most colossal event of all earth's history certain to occur *in your lifetime*—during the very next few years!

This is THE TRUE GOSPEL! It is the very gospel Christ preached! It is intended for you and me TODAY! It is vital that you UNDERSTAND!

Read, in your own Bible, Daniel 2, verses 28 through 35. In his dream, this king had seen a vast statue—larger than any image or statue ever built by man—so tremendous it was terrifying, even in a dream. Its head was of fine gold, its breast and arms of silver, the belly and thighs of brass, legs of solid iron, feet a mixture of iron and clay.

There was a time element. Nebuchadnezzar had viewed it *until* a supernatural STONE came from heaven, smashing the statue on its feet. Then the whole of the statue broke into small pieces, and was actually blown away by the wind—it disappeared! Then this STONE expanded miraculously and quickly became a great MOUNTAIN—so great it filled the whole earth!

What did it mean? *Did* it have meaning? Yes, because this was God's doing. Unlike ordinary dreams, this one was caused by God to convey the message of God's sovereignty to Nebuchadnezzar—and, because it is part of the written Word of God, to us today—to reveal important facts of the TRUE GOSPEL!

"This is the dream," said Daniel (verse 36), "and we will tell the interpretation thereof before the king."

This, then, is GOD's interpretation. It is decidedly *not* Herbert W. Armstrong's interpretation. Men ought never to *interpret* the Bible. The Bible gives us GOD's OWN INTERPRETATION! Here it is:

"Thou, O king, art a king of kings"—he was the first real WORLD RULER over a world empire! ". . . for the God of heaven hath given thee a kingdom, power, and strength, and glory." God was revealing himself to this human world-dictator as the MOST HIGH *Ruler over all.*

People today, like this Chaldean king, seem not to think of God as a RULER—as the Supreme One who GOVERNS—as the Head of GOVERNMENT. The Eternal was revealing himself through Daniel to Nebuchadnezzar—and through the Bible *to you and to me* TODAY—as a SOVEREIGN, ALL POWERFUL, *GOVERNING* GOD who *is to be obeyed!*

"Thou," continued Daniel to this human emperor, "art this head of gold. And after thee shall arise another KINGDOM inferior to thee, and another third KINGDOM of brass, which shall bear rule over all the earth" (verses 37-39).

What IS a Kingdom?

Notice! This is speaking of KINGDOMS. It is referring to kingdoms *that bear rule over the people on earth.* It is speaking of GOVERNMENTS! It is not speaking of ethereal sentiments "set up in the hearts of men." It is not speaking of churches. It is speaking of the kind of GOVERNMENTS that bear RULE and AUTHORITY over nations of PEOPLE here on earth. It is literal. It is specific. There is no misunderstanding, here, as to what is meant by the word *kingdom.*

There is no misunderstanding the interpretation. GOD gives his own interpretation through the prophet Daniel. The great metallic image represented national and international GOVERNMENTS—real, literal KINGDOMS.

It represented a *succession* of world-ruling governments. First was the head of gold. That represented Nebuchadnezzar and his kingdom—the Chaldean Empire. *After* him—later, in time sequence—was to come a second, then a third KINGDOM "which shall bear RULE over all the earth"—*world empire!*

Then, verse 40, the legs of iron represent a *fourth* world empire. It was to be *strong,* even as iron is strong —stronger militarily than its predecessors. Yet, as silver is less valuable than gold, brass than silver, iron than brass, though each metal was harder and stronger, the succession would deteriorate morally and spiritually. The two legs meant the fourth empire would be divided.

After the Chaldean Empire came the still larger Persian Empire, then the Greco-Macedonian, and fourth, the Roman Empire. It was divided, with capitals at Rome and Constantinople.

Now—verse 44! Read it! Get your Bible. See it with your own eyes in your own Bible. Here, in PLAIN LANGUAGE, is God's explanation of what the KINGDOM OF GOD IS:

"And in the days of these kings . . ."—it is here speaking of the ten toes, part of iron and part of brittle clay. This, by connecting the prophecy with Daniel 7, and Revelation 13 and 17, is referring to the new UNITED STATES OF EUROPE that is *now forming,* out of the European Common Market, before your very eyes! Revelation 17:12 makes plain the detail that it shall be a union of TEN KINGS OR KINGDOMS that (Rev. 17:8) shall resurrect the old ROMAN EMPIRE.

So, mark carefully the *time element!* "In the days of these kings"—in the days of these ten nations or groups of nations that shall, *IN OUR TIME,* resurrect briefly the Roman Empire—notice what shall happen:

". . . shall the God of heaven set up a kingdom, which shall never be destroyed . . . but it shall break in pieces and consume all these kingdoms, and it shall stand for ever"!

Yes, in OUR TIME!

Now here we have described FOUR universal world empires— the *only* four that ever existed! Revelation 13 and 17 show that, after the fall of the original Roman Empire, there would be ten revivals—SEVEN of which would be ruled over by a gentile CHURCH—the "daughter" of ancient BABYLON—a church claiming to be Christian, but actually named by God "MYSTERY, BABYLON the great"—or, more plainly, BABYLONIAN MYSTERIES!

Six of those have come and gone. The seventh is now forming—the last, final, *brief* resurrection of the Roman Empire by ten European groups or nations. These are revealed in Daniel 2 as the ten toes of iron and clay mixed.

In their days—and they shall last but a *very* short space, possibly no more than two to three-and-a-half years—shall the GOD OF HEAVEN SET UP *A KINGDOM* that shall never be destroyed.

This, then, shall be THE KINGDOM OF GOD!

Compare with Revelation 17. Here is pictured a church. Not a small church—a GREAT church. She rules over "many waters" (verse 1), which are described in verse 15 as different nations speaking different languages. She posed as the Church of GOD—which Scripture says (Eph. 5:23; Rev. 19:7; Matt. 25:1-10; etc.) is the affianced "bride" of CHRIST, to be spiritually MARRIED to him at his Second Coming.

But she has committed fornication. How? By having direct *political* union with HUMAN GOVERNMENTS of THIS WORLD! She "sat on" (Rev. 17:3) all seven of these resurrections of the Roman Empire—called the "Holy Roman Empire." She RULED OVER the human kingdoms—as a common-law and unmarried "wife" ruling her paramour "husband"—a totally unnatural and ungodly relationship.

She is, therefore, to "sit on" this last "head of the Beast"—this final resurrection of the Roman Empire. It will be a *union* of church and state. It is to endure but a *very* short time. It is to FIGHT AGAINST CHRIST at HIS SECOND COMING! That will be its END.

We see it in process of rising, now. (The members of the European Common Market are probably not the same ten that will resurrect the Holy Roman Empire.) Therefore we are CLOSE to the coming of Christ! We are now *very near* the END of this world!

Christ to Rule All Nations

When Christ comes, he is coming as KING of kings, ruling the whole earth (Rev. 19:11-16); and HIS KINGDOM—*the KING-DOM OF GOD*—said Daniel, is to CONSUME all these worldly kingdoms.

Revelation 11:15 states it in these words: "The kingdoms of this world *are become* THE KINGDOMS OF OUR LORD, AND OF HIS CHRIST; and he shall reign for ever and ever"!

This is THE KINGDOM OF GOD. It is the END of present governments—yes, and even the United States and the British nations. They then shall *become* the kingdoms—the GOVERNMENTS—of the Lord JESUS CHRIST, then KING of kings over the entire earth.

This makes completely PLAIN the fact that the KINGDOM OF GOD is a literal GOVERNMENT. Even as the Chaldean Empire was a KINGDOM—even as the Roman Empire was a KINGDOM—so the KINGDOM OF GOD is a government. It is to *take over* the GOVERNMENT of the NATIONS of the world.

Jesus Christ was BORN to be a KING—a RULER!

When he stood, on trial for his life, before Pilate, "Pilate therefore said unto him, Art thou a king then? Jesus answered, Thou sayest that I am a king. To this end was I born, and for this cause came I into the world." But Jesus also said to Pilate: "My kingdom is not of this world"—(John 18:37, 36). How amazing—what a tragedy—that in church services and gospel preaching today, one seldom, if ever, hears of Christ as a coming king and world ruler. Spiritual principalities and powers of evil (Eph. 6:12) are ruling the world today. It is these earthly governments of Satan that will be destroyed and replaced by Christ at his Second Coming. Christ's kingdom is of THE WORLD TOMORROW!

Have you not read what the angel proclaimed to Mary, the mother of Jesus, prior to his birth? Jesus told Pilate he was *born* to become a KING. The angel of God said to Mary: ". . . thou shalt conceive in thy womb, and bring forth a son, and shalt call his name JESUS. He shall be great, and shall be called the Son of the Highest: and the Lord God shall give unto him the THRONE of his father David: and *he shall reign* over the house of Jacob for ever; and of his kingdom there shall be NO END" (Luke 1:31-33).

Why do the churches of this world never mention any of these scriptures? Millions have attended churches all their lives and never heard any of these scriptures about Christ becoming a king or about the coming kingdom of God.

These scriptures tell you PLAINLY *that* GOD is supreme RULER. They tell you in plainest language that Jesus was born to be a KING—that he is going to RULE ALL NATIONS—that his kingdom shall rule eternally.

But all this is only *part* of the fantastic, amazing, actually SHOCKING TRUTH about the KINGDOM OF GOD.

The KINGDOM OF GOD will rule *over* the peoples and nations of the earth. Yet these mortal peoples and nations will *NOT* be the kingdom, not even *in* the kingdom of God. They shall be merely RULED OVER BY IT!

How Utopia Will Come!

But now let's be specific.

Let's see just how tomorrow's utopia is to be ushered in. Remember, this wonderful world-state will not be achieved all at once.

Every major step of these soon-coming events is laid bare before our eyes in biblical prophecy.

The same Jesus Christ who walked over the hills and valleys of the Holy Land and the streets of Jerusalem more than 1,900 years ago is coming again. He said he would come again. After he was crucified, God raised him from the dead after three days and three nights (Matt. 12:40; Acts 2:32; I Cor. 15:3-4). He ascended to the Throne of God, Headquarters of the Government of the Universe (Acts 1:9-11; Heb. 1:3; 8:1; 10:12; Rev. 3:21).

He is the "nobleman" of the parable, who went to the Throne of God—the "far country"—to be coronated as King of kings over all nations, and then to return to earth (Luke 19:12-27).

Again, he is in heaven until the "times of restitution of all things" (Acts 3:19-21). *Restitution* means restoring to a former state or condition. In this case, the restoring of God's government on earth, and thus, the restoring of world peace, and utopian conditions.

Present world turmoil, escalating wars and contentions will climax in world trouble so great that, unless God intervenes, no human flesh would be saved alive (Matt. 24:22).

At its very climax when delay would result in blasting all life from off this planet, Jesus Christ will return. This time he is coming as divine God. He is coming in all the power and glory of the universe-ruling Creator. (Matt. 24:30; 25:31.) He is coming as "King of kings, and Lord of lords" (Rev. 19:16), to establish world super-government and rule all nations "with a rod of iron" (Rev. 19:15; 12:5). Why do the professing Christian churches omit all these scriptures about Christ coming and of his ruling the earth? Jesus' very gospel was that of the kingdom of God he shall then establish on earth. The millions of church members have never heard these scriptures or the actual gospel of Jesus Christ.

Think of it. The glorified Christ—coming in all the splendor, the supernatural power and the glory of God Almighty—coming to save mankind alive—coming to stop escalating wars, nuclear mass destruction, human pain and suffering—coming to usher in peace, abundant well-being, happiness and joy for all mankind. But will he be welcomed by the nations?

World famous scientists now say frankly that the *only* hope for survival on earth is a supreme world-ruling government, controlling all military power. They admit that is impossible for man to accomplish. Christ is coming to give us just that.

But will he be welcome?

A leading American newsweekly gave the following surprising appraisal of man's *only hope:* The once optimistic hope of Americans, the article said, for a well-ordered and stable world, is fading. Expenditures close to a trillion dollars have failed to provide stability. Rather conditions have worsened. This appraisal indicated that among officials, the prevailing view is gaining acceptance that tensions and world problems are becoming too deep-seated to be solved "except by a strong hand from someplace."

"A strong hand from someplace." God Almighty is going to send a very strong Hand from "someplace" to save humanity!

Christ Unwelcome?

But will humanity shout with joy, and welcome him in

frenzied ecstasy and enthusiasm? Will even the churches of traditional Christianity?

They will not! They will believe, because the false ministers of Satan (II Cor. 11:13-15) have deceived them, that he is the Antichrist. The churches and the nations will be angry at his coming (Rev. 11:15 with 11:18), and the military forces will actually attempt to fight him to destroy him (Rev. 17:14)!

The nations will be engaged in the climactic battle of the coming World War III, with the battlefront at Jerusalem (Zech. 14:1-2) and then Christ will return. In supernatural power he will "fight against those nations" that fight against him (verse 3). He will totally defeat them (Rev. 17:14)! "His feet shall stand in that day upon the mount of Olives," a very short distance to the east of Jerusalem (Zech. 14:4).

How Nations Will Submit

When the glorified all-powerful Christ first comes again to earth, the nations will be angry. The military forces gathered at Jerusalem will try to fight him! I said "try." But far more powerful armies follow Christ from heaven—all the holy angels (Rev. 19:14, identified in Matt. 25:31).

Want to see a description of that battle—and what will happen to those hostile human armies?

In Revelation 17, the armies of the now-rising United States of Europe—the resurrected Roman Empire—are referred to in verse 14: "These shall make war with the Lamb [Christ], and the Lamb shall overcome them: for he is Lord of lords, and King of kings. . . ."

But how will he overcome them? We find that in the 14th chapter of Zechariah:

"And this shall be the plague wherewith the Lord will smite all the people [armies] that have fought against Jerusalem; their flesh shall consume away while they stand upon their feet, and their eyes shall consume away in their holes, and their tongue shall consume away in their mouth" (Zech. 14:12).

Perhaps it is even plainer in the Revised Standard Version: "And this shall be the plague with which the Lord will smite all the peoples that wage war against Jerusalem: their flesh shall rot while they are still on their feet, their eyes shall rot in their sockets, and their tongues shall rot in their mouths."

This rotting of their flesh off their bones will happen almost instantaneously—*while they are still on their feet.*

What a divine retribution against armies that will fight against Christ. What a demonstration of the divine power with which the glorified Christ will rule all nations. Rebellion against God's law and God's rule must, and speedily will be, put down.

Can you realize that every unhappiness, every evil that has come to humanity, has been the result of transgressing God's law?

If no one ever had any other god before the true God; if all children were reared to honor, respect and obey their parents, and all parents reared their children in God's ways; if no one ever allowed the spirit of murder to enter his heart, if there were no wars, no killing of humans by humans; if all marriages were kept happy and there were no transgressions of chastity before or after marriage; if all had so much concern for the good and welfare of others that no one would steal—and we could throw away all locks, keys and safes; if everyone told the truth—everyone's word were good—everyone were honest; if no one ever coveted what was not rightfully his, but had so much outgoing concern for the welfare of others that he really believed it is more blessed to *give* than to receive—what a happy world we would have!

In such a world, with all loving and worshiping God with all their minds, hearts and strength—with all having concern for the welfare of all others equal to concern for self—there would be no divorce—no broken homes or families, no juvenile delinquency, no crime, no jails or prisons, no police except for peaceful direction and supervision as a public service for all, no wars, no military establishments.

But, further, God has set in motion physical laws that operate in our bodies and minds, as well as the spiritual law. There would be no sickness, ill health, pain or suffering. There would be, on the contrary, vigorous, vibrant good health, filled with dynamic interest in life, enthusiastic interest in constructive activities bringing happiness and joy. There would be cleanliness, vigorous activity, real progress, no slums, no degenerate backward races or areas of earth.

Resurrected Saints

As the resurrected Christ ascended to heaven in clouds, so he shall return to earth in clouds (Acts 1:9-11; Matt. 24:30). Just *as* he is returning (I Thess. 4:14-17), the dead in Christ—those who have received and been led by God's Holy Spirit (Rom. 8:11, 14)—will rise in a gigantic resurrection, made immortal—including all the prophets of old (Luke 13:28). Those who have the Spirit of God, then living, shall be instantaneously changed from mortal to immortal (I Cor. 15:50-54) and, together with those resurrected, shall rise to meet the descending glorified Jesus Christ (I Thess. 4:17) in the clouds in the air.

They shall be with him, where he is, forever (John 14:3). They shall—with him—come down out of the clouds, and stand with him, therefore, that very same day, on the Mount of Olives (Zech. 14:4-5).

These changed, converted saints, now made immortal, will then rule the nations—nations of mortals—under Christ (Dan. 7:22; Rev. 2:26-27; 3:21).

Satan Removed at Last!

This most glorious event in all earth's history—the supernatural majestic descent to earth, in the clouds, of the glorified all-powerful Christ—will at long last put an end to the subtle, deceitful, invisible rule of Satan.

The coming of Christ in supreme glory as King of kings and Lord of lords is recorded in Revelation 19. But what other great event will have to take place before there can be peace, HAPPINESS and JOY on the earth? SATAN the devil will have to be removed from the throne of the earth.

But in Revelation 20:1-3, the advance news is recorded: "And I saw an angel come down from heaven, having the key of the bottomless pit and a great chain in his hand. And he laid hold on . . . that old serpent, which is the Devil, and Satan, and bound him a thousand years, and cast him into the bottomless pit, and shut him up, and set a seal upon him, that he should deceive the nations no more, till the thousand years should be fulfilled: and after that he must be loosed a little season."

The day of man, swayed, deceived, misled by Satan for 6,000 years, will be over.

No longer will Satan be able to broadcast through the air into the spirit in man. No longer shall he be able to inject into unsuspecting humans his satanic nature—which we have been misled into calling "human nature."

Human Nature Not to Disappear at Once

But that does not mean that the acquired satanic attitude will disappear from human minds immediately. The multiplied millions shall have acquired it. And even though Satan will then be restrained from continuing to broadcast it, what has been acquired as habit will not be automatically removed.

Yet God has made us humans free moral agents. He has given us control over our own minds, except as we may be blinded by Satan's pull of evil by deception.

But no longer will earth's mortal humans be deceived! Now the all-powerful Christ, and the immortal saints ruling under him, will begin removing the scales that have blinded human minds.

That is why I say complete utopia cannot be ushered in all at once. Multiple millions will still hold to the attitude of rebellion—of vanity, lust and greed. But with Christ's coming shall begin the process of re-education—of opening deceived minds—of undeceiving minds, and bringing them to a voluntary repentance.

From the time of Christ's supernatural takeover, and Satan's banishment, God's law and the word of the Eternal shall go forth from Zion, spreading over the whole earth (Isa. 2:3).

The 6,000-year sentence God placed on Adam's world, of being cut off from God, will be ended. Christ will begin calling all mortals on earth to repentance and spiritual salvation!

God's Holy Spirit shall flow out from Jerusalem (Zech. 14:8).

What glory! A new day shall have dawned. Peace shall soon come. Men shall turn from the way of "get" to the way of "give"—God's way of love.

A NEW CIVILIZATION shall now grip the earth!

But what kind of a new world tomorrow will from then be developed? In Isaiah 2:2-4 and in Micah 4:1-3 it says: "And it shall come to pass in the last days, that the mountain of the Lord's house shall be established in the top of the mountains, and shall be exalted above the hills; and all nations shall flow unto it. And many people shall go and say, Come ye, and let us go up to the mountain of the Lord, to the house of the God of Jacob; and he will teach us of his ways, and we shall walk in his paths; for out of Zion shall go forth the law, and the word of the Lord from Jerusalem. And he shall judge among the nations, and shall rebuke many people: and they shall beat their swords into plowshares, and their spears into pruning-hooks: nation shall not lift up sword against nation, neither shall they learn war any more."

Think of it! No more wars. No fear of man or beast. World peace at last. Something will have to cause that peace. The law of God, which a professed "Christianity" teaches was done away, shall go out from Jerusalem and the earth will be as full of the knowledge of God's way of life as the ocean beds are full of water.

Even the wild animals will be tamed and at peace: "The wolf also shall dwell with the lamb, and the leopard shall lie down with the kid; and the calf and the young lion and the fatling together; and a little child shall lead them. And the cow and the bear shall feed; their young ones shall lie down together: and the lion shall eat straw like the ox. And the sucking child shall play on the hole of the asp, and the weaned child shall put his hand on the cockatrice' den. They shall not hurt nor destroy in all my holy mountain: for the earth shall be full of the knowledge of the Lord, as the waters cover the sea" (Isa. 11:6-9).

Now picture the changed conditions!

Look now at the solved problems!

See, now, a glimpse into a world of no illiteracy, no

poverty, no famine and starvation, into a world where crime decreases rapidly, people learn honesty, chastity, human kindness and happiness—a world of peace, prosperity, abundant well-being.

The Population Explosion Solved

God predicts vast reforms everywhere in the wonderful utopian era he says will soon break out on this earth.

Can you imagine it? A world of great strides in solving the most crucial problems facing mankind.

Today—the greatest and most awesome problem of all is the population explosion. Growing populations in all nations are rapidly outstripping the ability of the world to sustain them.

And the areas of the greatest rise in population are the underdeveloped parts of the world—the "have-not" nations of poverty, illiteracy, disease and superstition. Remember, not more than 10 percent of the earth's surface is tillable, or arable, land. And now the latest UN figures indicate the world will double in population in about 34 short years.

The daily, ominous pressure of people is one of the truly incomprehensible problems today.

But God has the solution, and how simple it is. Simply make most of the earth cultivatable. Reduce the bare, snow-swept and craggy mountains, raise up some of the deep, arid desert valleys, change the world weather patterns. Make all the deserts green and fertile. Open up huge slices of the earth, like the Kalahari Desert, the Lake Chad basin and the Sahara in Africa, the Gobi Desert in Asia, and the great American deserts. Make green and verdant the vast wastes of Mongolia, Siberia, Saudi Arabia and much of the Western U.S.

Thaw out the deep ice packs and snowdrifts, the permafrost and tundra from the vast, almost limitless expanses of Antarctica, North America, Greenland, Northern Europe and Siberia. Make level the awesome Pamir Knot, the huge giants of the Himalayas, the Atlas, Taurus, Pyrenees, Rockies, Sierras and Hindu Kush—level the immense sweep of the Andes, and all the other forbidding, towering, virtually uninhabitable mountains of earth.

Then, provide good, gentle rainfall, in right balance, just at the right season.

And what happens?

Multiple millions of acres of unbelievably fertile, productive, wonderful farmland suddenly become available—just waiting to be discovered, and pioneered.

Impossible?

In the hands of man—certainly.

But look what God promises. "Fear not, thou worm Jacob, and ye men of Israel; I will help thee, saith the Lord, and thy redeemer, the Holy One of Israel.

"Behold, I will make thee a new sharp threshing instrument having teeth: thou shalt thresh the mountains, and beat them small, and shalt make the hills as chaff. Thou shalt fan them, and the wind shall carry them away, and the whirlwind shall scatter them: and thou shalt rejoice in the Lord, and shalt glory in the Holy One of Israel.

"When the poor and needy seek water, and there is none, and their tongue faileth for thirst, I the Lord will hear them, I the God of Israel will NOT forsake them. I will open rivers in high places, and fountains [artesian wells] in the midst of the valleys: I will make the wilderness a pool of water, and the dry land springs of water.

"I will plant in the wilderness the cedar, the shittah [acacia] tree, and the myrtle, and the oil tree; I will set in the desert the fir tree, and the pine, and the box tree [cypress] together: that they may see, and know, and consider, and understand together, that the hand of the Lord hath done this, and the Holy One of Israel hath created it" (Isa. 41:14-20).

Pure Water—Fertile Deserts

Can you imagine such a fabulous scene? Deserts becoming green, fertile, garden lands of trees, shrubs, bubbling springs and brooks; mountains brought low, and made inhabitable.

Notice how God describes these conditions in many parts of the Bible.

"Then shall the lame man leap as an hart, and the tongue of the dumb sing: for in the wilderness shall waters break out, and streams in the desert. And the parched ground shall become a pool, and the thirsty land springs of water: in the habitation of dragons [jackals], where each lay, shall be grass with reeds and rushes" (Isa. 35:6-7).

Read the whole 35th chapter of Isaiah.

God says: "The wilderness and the solitary place shall be glad for them; and the desert shall rejoice, and blossom as the rose. It shall blossom abundantly, and rejoice even with joy and singing . . ." (verses 1-2).

Some years ago, in a dry, dusty canyon deep in the profusion of hills between Bakersfield and Los Angeles, California, a minor earthquake struck. The proprietors of a small resort, now almost totally ignored, and nearly always deserted because of the parched conditions of the area, were considering closing up and moving elsewhere.

Suddenly, a groaning, jolting earthquake rippled through the arid hills. Not long after the earth rocked and groaned beneath their feet, they heard a faint gurgling sound. They ran to the dry, dusty creek bed that coursed through their property—and were utterly amazed to see *water* flowing swiftly along. As the creek gradually cleared up, they found the water to be crystal clear and pure—sweet and refreshing to drink.

Needless to say, their business picked up again.

Somehow, the earthquake had broken open an underground water source, sending it cascading through their property.

Think about the vast wastes of this earth. Does it sound incredible, unbelievable that God could make them blossom like a rose? Why should it?

The mountains were *formed*. Great forces caused gigantic upheavals, or huge cracks and slippages in the crust of the earth. Massive blocks of granite lunged up into the sky—the earth rocking and reeling in the throes of the greatest earthquakes in its history. Mountains were made—they didn't just happen.

The God of all power, who formed the hills and mountains (Amos 4:13; Ps. 90:2), will reform them—will reshape the surface of this earth.

Read of the huge earthquakes yet to come that will directly accomplish much of the rehabilitation of the land surfaces. (See Revelation 16:18; Zechariah 14:4.) God says,

"The mountains quake at him, and the hills melt . . ." (Nah. 1:15).

Land Beneath Sea Reclaimed

Man recognizes much of the wealth of the world lies beneath the seas. Oil, gold, silver, and dozens of minerals—these all remain unobtainable today, lying untapped deep under the vast oceans. Also, seawater contains a great deal of gold and most of the world's gold supplies are under the oceans.

Many areas of the earth are ravaged by tidal action—by the ceaseless pounding of the surf that gradually wears away additional land. The lowlands of Europe, Holland in particular, consist to quite an extent of land reclaimed from the sea.

Think of the multiple millions of additional acres available to mankind if some of the world's oceans were reduced in size. And God says they shall be! Notice it, "And the Lord shall utterly destroy the tongue of the Egyptian sea; and with his mighty wind shall he shake his hand over the river, and shall smite it in the seven streams, and make men go over dryshod" (Isa. 11:15).

Sounds incredible—but it's true!

When Jesus Christ becomes the great Ruler of this earth, he will use that great power. In vision, John saw the angels praising Christ at his coming to rule this earth.

They said: "We give thee thanks, O Lord God Almighty, which art, and wast, and art to come; because thou hast taken to thee thy great power, and hast reigned" (Rev. 11:17).

The combined force of right education about true health, and healing of all sickness, when it is repented of, will mean perfect, utopian health.

Notice how God describes it.

"But there the glorious Lord will be unto us a place of broad rivers and streams; wherein shall go no galley with oars, neither shall gallant ship pass thereby. For the Lord is our judge, the Lord is our lawgiver, the Lord is our king; he will save us.

"And the inhabitant shall not say, I am sick: the people that dwell therein shall be forgiven their iniquity" (Isa. 33:21-22, 24).

Listen to this wonderful promise: "Strengthen ye the

weak hands, and confirm the feeble knees. Say to them that are of a fearful heart, Be strong, fear not: behold, your God will come with vengeance, even God with a recompence; he will come and save you. Then the eyes of the blind shall be opened, and the ears of the deaf shall be unstopped. Then shall the lame man leap as an hart, and the tongue of the dumb sing . . ." (Isa. 35:3-6).

God describes the rewards for obedience to his laws of mercy and love. Notice Isaiah 58:8: "Then shall thy light break forth as the morning, and thine health shall spring forth speedily. . . ."

Happiness in Health

In describing the conditions of good health and plenty to be ushered in upon the earth, God says, "For I will restore health unto thee, and I will heal thee of thy wounds . . ." (Jer. 30:17).

"Therefore they shall come and sing in the height of Zion, and shall flow together to the goodness of the Lord, for wheat, and for wine, and for oil, and for the young of the flock and of the herd: and their soul shall be as a watered garden; and they shall not sorrow any more at all.

"Then shall the virgin rejoice in the dance, both young men and old together: for I will turn their mourning into joy, and will comfort them, and make them rejoice from their sorrow. And I will satiate the soul of the priests with fatness, and my people shall be satisfied with my goodness, saith the [Eternal]" (Jer. 31:12-14).

And why not have good health?

Why should we be so willing to believe such a perfect state of health and joy is impossible? Why are all these scriptures ignored by professing Christian preaching? Instead they picture going to heaven with idleness and ease and no accomplishment.

There are blessings for observing the laws of health—absolute guarantees good health will result—and that sickness and disease will become in the third and fourth generations a thing of the past.

Notice what God promised his people: ". . . if thou shalt hearken diligently unto the voice of the Lord thy God, to observe and to do all his commandments which I command thee this day . . . all these blessings shall come on thee, and overtake thee, if thou shalt hearken unto the voice of the Lord thy God.

"Blessed shalt thou be in the city, and blessed shalt thou be in the field. Blessed shall be the fruit of thy body, and the fruit of thy ground, and the fruit of thy cattle, the increase of thy kine, and the flocks of thy sheep. Blessed shall be thy basket and thy store" (Deut. 28:1-5).

Also, God shows individual races returning to their own lands, repopulating them. "He shall cause them that come of Jacob to take root: Israel shall blossom and bud, and fill the face of the world with fruit" (Isa. 27:6).

God says the wastes will be rebuilt.

"For, behold, I am for you, and I will turn unto you, and ye shall be tilled and sown: and I will multiply men upon you, all the house of Israel, even all of it: and the cities shall be inhabited, and the wastes shall be builded: and I will multiply upon you man and beast; and they shall increase and bring fruit: and I will settle you after your old estates . . ." (Ezek. 36:9-11).

Read the whole chapter of Ezekiel 36. God says: ". . . I will also cause you to dwell in the cities, and the wastes shall be builded. . . . This land that was desolate is become like the garden of Eden; and the waste and desolate and ruined cities are become fenced, and are inhabited" (verses 33, 35).

And what about all other nations?

Notice: "In that day shall there be a highway out of Egypt [Egypt still exists as a nation] to Assyria [many of whose people migrated centuries ago to northcentral Europe—modern Germany], and the Assyrian shall come into Egypt, and the Egyptian into Assyria, and the Egyptians shall serve with the Assyrians. In that day shall Israel be the third with Egypt and with Assyria, even a blessing in the midst of the land: whom the Lord of hosts shall bless, saying, Blessed be Egypt my people, and Assyria the work of my hands, and Israel mine inheritance" (Isa. 19:23-25).

Total Literacy

Think what an almost unbelievable step forward it would be,

if all nations and peoples everywhere spoke, and read, and wrote the same language.

But today, vast areas of the earth do not even possess a written language. Millions upon millions are illiterate— cannot read or write, even their own names.

Once the returning Christ conquers this earth, he will usher in an era of total literacy, total education—and give the world one, new, pure language.

This subject by itself needs a book to describe. The whole literary processes of the whole earth changed. Today, all languages are corrupt. They are literally filled with pagan, heathen terms—superstition—misnomers—exceptions to rules—peculiar idioms.

God says: "For then will I turn to the people a pure language, that they may all call upon the name of the Lord, to serve him with one consent" (Zeph. 3:9).

Think of the new era of good literature, good music, and of the avoiding of duplicated effort, misunderstandings through linguistic difficulties and thousands of painstaking hours of translations. What an age it will be, when all the world becomes truly educated—and speaks the same language.

What about the Economic Structure?

God shows Jerusalem will become the financial capital, as well as the spiritual capital, of earth.

The Creator says, of the newly built city: "Then thou shalt see, and flow together, and thine heart shall fear, and be enlarged; because the abundance of the sea [the world's gold and silver reserves are mostly under the seas] shall be converted unto thee, the forces [wealth, margin] of the Gentiles shall come unto thee" (Isa. 60:5).

But, as we've read, God Almighty says he'll raise many places now covered by waters of the oceans; that he'll make much more land available. Scientists know most of the earth's raw materials lie in the strata beneath the depths of the seas. God says this vast wealth will become available for use during the reign of Jesus Christ on this earth.

God says the wealth of the world will be centered in Jerusalem, and that the vast rebuilding programs, rehabilitation processes and new-age pioneering that begin will be backed by that wealth.

"... Yet once, it is a little while, and I will shake the heavens, and the earth, and the sea, and the dry land; and I will shake all nations, and the desire [desirable things, margin] of all nations shall come: and I will fill this house with glory, saith the Lord of hosts. The silver is mine, and the gold is mine, saith the Lord of hosts" (Hag. 2:6-8). But God's great treasury will be for public display. No gold bricks, reposing in deep, subterranean vaults—utterly useless except for their meaning—no fear of thievery, or robbery. But breathtakingly beautiful decorations for the capital building, the Temple in which Christ will dwell.

A fixed standard will be set up, and values will never change.

No more speculating or gambling on other people's ability.

Never again will any person become rich from investing in the labors and creative ability of another person. No more stock markets, world banks, financing centers, insurance companies, mortgage companies, loan agencies, or time payments.

In God's abundant government people will buy only what they need, when they can afford it, when they have the cash to pay for it. No more interest. And no more taxes.

The Tithing System

But the tithing system will be universal.

Today's governments demand up to 40, 50, and even 90 percent in inheritance taxes, income taxes, hidden taxes; federal, state, county, school board and city taxes.

But God requires only ten percent. And out of that ten percent will be financed the entire governmental, educational and spiritual leadership of the whole earth.

"Will a man rob God? Yet ye have robbed me. But ye say, Wherein have we robbed thee? [And God answers] In tithes and offerings. Ye are cursed with a curse: for ye have robbed me, even this whole nation. Bring ye all the tithes into the storehouse, that there may be meat in mine house, and prove me now herewith, saith the Lord of hosts, if I will not open you the windows of heaven, and pour you out a blessing, that there shall not be room enough to receive it" (Mal. 3:8-10). That's a prophecy for now.

And what a blessing that *will* be. None of the financial burdens that curse most peoples today.

God says financial blessings are to become the order of the day.

Take away thievery, robbery, accidents, weather damage, rust, rot and decay, from plants, stores, manufacturing concerns. How much less could merchandise then sell for—and at how much greater profits?

The Weather Patterns

Take away weather problems, insect damage, blight and fungus from farmers—losses through government price controls and overflooding of markets—and what would be their lot in life?

God will accomplish these things.

Our God is a multibillionaire heavenly Father. "The gold is mine," he says (Hag. 2:8).

And God wants every child of his to truly prosper. "Beloved, I wish above all things that thou mayest prosper and be in health . . ." (III John 2). Christ said, "I am come that they might have life, and that they might have it more abundantly" (John 10:10).

God wants fullness, abundance in every life.

But look at the material "successes" you've known. How truly happy are they? As J. Paul Getty, one of the world's richest men, is reputed to have said, "I'd give all my millions for just one happy marriage!"

In God's kingdom, commands of his will be obeyed. They'll become the standard for regulating commerce, business, finance, and the entire economic structure of the world.

And all will be on the giving basis. Christ said: "Give, and it shall be given unto you; good measure, pressed down, and shaken together, and running over, shall men give into your bosom. For with the same measure that ye mete withal it shall be measured to you again" (Luke 6:38).

The giving standard will be followed in God's rule on this earth—not the grasping, conniving, striving, deceitful, clandestine, furtive, scurrilous, devious, cheating and lying chicanery that is commonplace in today's business world.

But when God converts rebellious mankind by the display of his mighty power—when he brings to pass his promise: "As I live, saith the Lord, every knee shall bow to me, and every tongue shall confess to God" (Rom. 14:11), when he humbles the vain, proud spirit of man—then man will be made willing to give.

And until God breaks the haughty spirit of man (Isa. 2:10-12, 17)—the peoples of earth will not be ready to accept such a wonderful, loving, generous, honest, giving standard for the whole economy.

It would require a thick book to begin to describe the wonderful conditions that could prevail on this earth—and that *will* finally prevail, when the human heart is humbled, converted—given the very nature of God (II Pet. 1:4).

Never again will anyone build a building he can't afford, and doesn't need, to lease and rent to tenants who help him pay for it. No more interest. God says it is sin to lend money at "usury" or interest.

Once each fifty years, all debts, public and private, will be canceled, completely.

Economy of the World Healed

Since governments will be in the hands of the spiritual family of God, and partially administered by those human leaders directly under that great ruling family—and since there will be no huge bureaus watching other huge bureaus, which are suspiciously watching other bureaus; no military establishment; no "intelligence" (spy) agencies or members of Interpol; no huge cartels, monopolies, unions, or giant government spending—the economy of the world will be healed.

Think of it. No more foreign aid—none of the wasted billions to buy "lovers" (allies) (Ezek. 23:9, 22; Lam. 1:2, 19; Ezekiel, 16th chapter) who turn and rend you later. No more strings-attached government grants to industry, to science and space technology, to schools and institutions for research.

Instead, every necessary industry, educational institution, and business will be in sound financial condition.

What a world that will be!

Tomorrow's World Governmental Structure

Now notice just how the new world government will function during the next thousand years. It will not be so-called democracy. It will not be socialism. It will not be communism or fascism. It will not be human monarchy, oligarchy or plutocracy. It will not be man's government over man. Man has proven his utter incapability of ruling himself.

It will be divine government—theocracy—the government of God ruling over humans. It will not be government from the bottom up. The people will have no votes. It will not be government of or by the people—but it will be government for the people. It will be government from the top (God Almighty) down. It will be hierarchy in form.

There will be no election campaigns. No campaign fund-raising dinners. No dirty political campaigns, where each candidate attempts to put himself forward in the most favorable light, defaming, denouncing, discrediting his opponents. No time will be wasted in mudslinging campaigns in the lust for power.

No human will be given any government office. All in government service will then be divine Spirit beings, in the kingdom of God—the God family.

All officials will be appointed—and by the divine Christ, who reads and knows men's hearts, their inner character, and abilities or lack of ability. You'll find a description of Christ's supernatural insight into the very character of others in Isaiah 11:2-5.

Notice it: "And the spirit of the Lord shall rest upon him, the spirit of wisdom and understanding, the spirit of counsel and might, the spirit of knowledge and of the fear of the Lord; and shall make him of quick understanding ... and he shall not judge after the sight of his eyes, neither reprove after the hearing of his ears [hearsay]: but with righteousness shall he judge the poor, and reprove with equity for the meek of the earth ..." (Isa. 11:2-4).

Remember, God is the Supreme One who is love—who

gives—who rules with outgoing concern for the ruled. He will rule for the highest good of the people. The most able, the most righteous, those best fitted for office will be placed in all offices of responsibility and power.

There will then be two kinds of beings on earth—humans, being ruled by those made divine.

Some resurrected saints will rule over ten cities, some over five (Luke 19:17-19).

Think of it—no money wasted on political campaigns. No splits in political parties with quarreling and hatreds. No political parties!

What Is the New Covenant?

In short, under the New Covenant, which Christ is coming to usher in, what we shall see on earth is happiness, peace, abundance and justice for all. Did you ever read just what this New Covenant will consist of? Did you suppose it will do away with God's law? Exactly the opposite. "For this is the covenant [that Christ is coming to establish, you'll read in Hebrews 8:10] . . . I will put my laws into their mind, and write them in their hearts. . . ."

When God's laws are in our hearts—when we love God's ways, and in our hearts want to live by them, human nature will be put under subjection—people will want to live the way that causes peace, happiness, abundance, joyful well-being!

But remember, the humans remaining on the earth after Christ's return—ruled then by Christ and those resurrected or changed to immortality—will themselves still have human nature. They will be still unconverted.

Two Courses of Action

But Christ and the governing kingdom of God, then set up as the governing family, will bring about the coming utopia by two basic courses of action.

1) All crime and organized rebellion will be put down by force—divine supernatural force.

2) Christ will then set his hand to reeducate and to save or spiritually convert the world.

Notice, first, how the social and religious customs will be changed by divine force.

God gave seven annual Festivals and Holy Days he commanded to be observed. They contained great and important meaning. They pictured God's master plan for working out his purpose for humanity. They were established forever. Jesus observed them, setting us an example. The apostles observed them (Acts 18:21; 20:6, 16; I Cor. 5:8; 16:8). The true, original Church—including gentile converts—kept them.

They were God's way—God's customs for his people. But people rejected God's ways and customs, and turned, instead, to the ways and customs of the pagan religions. People did what seemed right to themselves. And since human minds in this world have been hostile against God (Rom. 8:7), attitudes of hostility against God's way of life have prevailed. The ways that seem right to a man have been ways contrary to the ways that produce peace, happiness and abundant living. These same wrong ways seem right to most people today! We realize they seem right—not wrong—to most who will be reading these words.

But can we realize that "there is a way which seemeth right unto a man, but the end thereof are the ways of death"? (Prov. 14:12). And if you turn to Proverbs 16:25 you will see the same thing repeated: "There is a way that seemeth right unto a man, but the end thereof are the ways of death."

God said through Moses: "Ye shall not do after all the things that we do here this day, every man whatsoever is right in his own eyes" (Deut. 12:8). And again: "Take heed to thyself that thou be not snared by following them [pagan religious customs] . . . and that thou inquire not after their gods, saying, How did these nations serve their gods? even so will I do likewise. Thou shalt not do so unto the Lord thy God: for every abomination to the Lord, which he hateth, have they done unto their gods . . ." (Deut. 12:30-31).

Today the professing Christian world rejects God's Holy Days; holy to him, but which a deceived "Christianity" hates. They observe instead the pagan days—Christmas, New Year's, Easter, and others—"which God hateth"! Many know and confess that these are pagan—but they argue, "We don't observe these in worshiping the pagan gods; we use their customs in worshiping Christ and the true God."

That is the way that "seemeth right" to people. They may not mean any wrong. They are deceived. A deceived man doesn't know he is wrong. He thinks he is right. He may be as sincere as those who have found God's way and obey it. Yet God says he will not accept that kind of observance or worship. It is an abomination to him—"which he hateth."

But it is those who have been deceived, whose eyes God will open to his truth when Christ returns to rule all nations of mortals still left alive.

All Will Keep God's Festivals

People will no longer be blinded and deceived in regard to God's commands and ways. Then he will enforce obedience to his customs.

Go back to the 14th chapter of Zechariah:

"And it shall come to pass, that every one that is left of all the nations which came against Jerusalem [that is, those who were not in the armies supernaturally destroyed] shall even go up from year to year to worship the King, the Lord of hosts, and to keep the feast of tabernacles" (verse 16).

This Feast of Tabernacles is one of the seven annual Festivals God commanded his people to observe. But ancient Israel rebelled. They rejected God's Festivals, and turned to pagan festivals. The Jewish people, after Ezra and Nehemiah, observed them. But false "Christian" ministers taught that God's Festivals were "part of the old Mosaic system—not for us today." The clergy deceived and prejudiced the people. The people were deceived into believing that Christmas, New Year's, Easter, etc., were days Christ ordained.

But now Christ is returning to earth to restore God's ways—including God's Festivals. Those who rebelliously won't keep God's Holy Days now—who sneer at them in scathing contempt—will observe them when Christ returns. Notice what this scripture says:

"And it shall be, that whoso will not come up of all the families of the earth [including gentile nations] unto Jerusalem to worship the King, the Lord of hosts, even upon them shall be no rain. And if the family of Egypt go not up, and come not, that have no rain; there shall be the plague, wherewith the Lord will smite the heathen that come not up to keep the feast of tabernacles. This shall be the punishment of Egypt, and the punishment of all nations that come not up to keep the feast of tabernacles" (Zech. 14:17-19).

These passages give us the method by which Christ will "rule with a rod of iron"—of how he will use supernatural force to bring people of all nations to his right ways—ways that are the cause of real blessings.

The Perfect Government

Yes, Jesus Christ very soon is going to return to this earth. He is coming in power and glory. He is coming to *rule* all nations!

But he is not going to do this ruling, supervising, all alone, by himself. He is coming to set up world government. It will be a highly organized government. There will be many positions of authority.

Right here, it is time we stop to explain the mechanics of this perfect form of government.

First, it is the government of God—not human government. Man won't acknowledge it yet, but man has demonstrated by 6,000 years of inefficient, bungling, wasteful efforts of human government that mortal man is utterly incapable of rightly governing himself.

As for man being qualified to rule and administer government, God says of government officials today: "None calleth for justice, nor any pleadeth for truth: they trust in vanity and speak lies; they conceive mischief, and bring forth iniquity. . . . Their feet run to evil, and they make haste to shed innocent blood: their thoughts are thoughts of iniquity; wasting and destruction are in their paths. The way of peace they know not; and there is no judgment in their goings: they have made them crooked paths: whosoever goeth therein shall not know peace."

Then the people, under this human *mis*-government, say: "Therefore is judgment far from us, neither doth justice overtake us: we wait for light [solution of civil, personal, national and world problems], but behold obscurity; for brightness, but we walk in darkness. We grope for the wall like the blind, and we grope as if we had no eyes: we stumble at noonday as in the night; we are in desolate places as dead men" (Isa. 59:4, 7-10).

Then, in this chapter foretelling our time, the final solution is given: "And the Redeemer shall come to Zion . . ." (verse 20). And, continuing: "Arise, shine; for thy light is come, and the glory of the Lord is risen upon thee" (Isa. 60:1).

The only hope of justice—of peace—of truth—of right solutions to all this world's problems—is the coming in power and glory of Christ to set up world government. Right government. The government of God!

In this, and many other passages, God shows in his Word to mankind how utterly helpless man is to govern himself and his fellows. Now 6,000 years of human experience have brought mankind to the very brink of world suicide.

So, in other words, the first 6,000 years of God's 7,000-year plan were allotted to allow Satan to labor at his work of deceiving the world, followed by 1,000 years (one millennial day) when Satan shall not be allowed to do any of his "work" of deception. Put another way, God marked out six millennial days to allow man to indulge in the spiritual labor of sin, followed by a millennium of spiritual rest, under the enforced government of God.

Government Planned from Beginning

And now comes a wonderful truth.

Now we come to a revealed insight into the wonderful planning, preparing and organizing of the perfect government of God.

There will be no incompetent and selfishly ambitious politicians seeking to get their covetous hands on the throttle of government power by the deceptive political methods of this world. Today people are asked to vote into office men they know little about—men whose qualifications are largely misrepresented. In the soon-coming government of God, every official placed in authority shall have been tried and tested, trained, experienced and qualified, by God's qualifications. The fact illustrates the purpose and necessity of the Church. The function of the Church is not merely to convert the "firstfruits"—not merely to bring about salvation to those specially called out of the world and into the Church, but to prepare and train them for these positions of leadership in the kingdom when salvation will be opened to all the living.

God has planned ahead, but not only for his government to rule the earth. He had said to Adam, in effect: "Go, plan your own human governments, create in your own imaginations your own gods and religions; develop your own knowledge and educational structure, plan your own social systems (in a word, organize your own human civilization)."

But in sentencing man to 6,000 years of being cut off from God, he reserved the prerogative of calling to special service and contact with God such as he should choose for his purpose. During this day of man, God has prepared for his own millennial civilization, in all its phases—governmental, educational, religious—his whole civilization.

It all began with Abraham.

In his day, there was only one man on earth who was at once a man of strong character and at the same time meekly and wholly submissive and obedient to God—to God's laws and his direction and rule. That man was Abraham.

God began training men for top positions of authority in his coming world, with Abraham. Abraham lived in the most "advanced" civilization—the most developed and, as people thought, most desirable locality.

God said to Abraham (then named Abram), "Get thee out of thy country, and from thy kindred, and from thy father's house, unto a land that I will shew thee" (Gen. 12:1).

There was no argument. Abraham didn't say, "But why? Why must I give up all the pleasures of this civilization—give up even my relatives and friends?" Abraham didn't argue or delay.

It is written, simply, "So Abram departed . . ." (verse 4).

Abraham was put to severe tests. But, after he died, God said, "Abraham obeyed my voice, and kept my charge, my commandments, my statutes [of government], and my laws" (Gen. 26:5).

Abraham was being trained for high position in the government of God, now soon to rule the world. He believed in, was obedient and loyal to, God's government—its statutes and laws.

Abraham was given the promises on which the salvation of every person, through Christ, is based. He is called the father (humanly) of the faithful (Gal. 3:7). To the gentiles of Galatia, the apostle Paul wrote: "And if ye be Christ's, then are ye [gentiles] Abraham's seed, and heirs according to the promise" (Gal. 3:29). In the 16th verse, he had said: "Now to Abraham and his seed [descendant—Christ] were the promises made. . . ."

God was starting to prepare for his kingdom—to train topflight personnel for positions in God's civilization—with Abraham. When Abraham proved obedient, God blessed his labors and allowed him to become wealthy. God gave him experience in the wise handling of wealth and in directing a great force of men.

Isaac was reared by God-fearing, God-obeying Abraham, in God's ways, obedient to God's government. He became heir along with his father Abraham. He too, was trained in obedience, and also in directing and ruling over others.

Then Jacob, born with this rich heredity, was educated to follow through on the same pattern Abraham and Isaac had learned. Even though his father-in-law deceived him, and held him down, Jacob also became wealthy. He was human—as were Abraham and Isaac and all humans. He made mistakes. But he overcame. He repented. He prevailed with God. He never quit! He developed the qualities and character of leadership. He became the father of the twelve greatest nations-to-be in the soon-coming world tomorrow.

The Pattern of Government Organization

God has not told us, in so many words, precisely how his coming world super government will be organized. Yet he has given us the general pattern. He has told us specifically where 14 high executives (including Christ) will fit in. And from them we may deduce a great deal of the remaining governmental structure. Much of the coming structure of government is at least strongly indicated by what is plainly revealed.

We know it will be the government of God. God Almighty—the Father of Jesus Christ—is Supreme Lawgiver, and Head over Christ, and over all that is. We know that Jesus Christ is to be King of kings, and Lord of lords—over both state and church, united through him.

We know that King David of ancient Israel (details later) will be king over the twelve great nations composed of literal descendants of the twelve tribes of Israel. We know the twelve apostles will each be a king, sitting on a throne, over one of those great nations descended from the tribes of Israel.

We know it will be government from the top down. There is to be a definite chain of authority. No one will be elected by the people. Mortal humans have proved they do not know how to judge qualifications, and do not know the inner minds, hearts, intents and abilities of men. All will be divinely appointed from above. All, in positions of governmental authority, will be resurrected immortals, born of God—no longer flesh-and-blood humans.

With this in mind—with the knowledge that Abraham is (humanly) the father of all who are Christ's and heirs of salvation—it becomes plain that Abraham will be given a greater position of authority in God's kingdom than David— and that he will be over both Israelites and gentiles. He is "father" of gentile converts as well as Israelites.

Then again, repeatedly the Bible uses the phrase, "Abraham, Isaac and Jacob," grouping them together as a team, and calling them, together, "the fathers." For the promises were repromised, also, to Isaac and Jacob, whose name was changed to Israel.

What is plainly revealed indicates, then, that Abraham, Isaac and Jacob will function as a topflight team, with Abraham as chairman of the team, next under Christ in the coming world government of God.

Jesus himself said, definitely, that Abraham, Isaac and Jacob shall be in that glorious and glorified kingdom (Luke 13:28).

Joseph qualified in a very special way, but we shall come back to him a little later.

Both Church and State

Another principle is made clear in God's Word: church and state will be united under Christ. There will be one government, over all nations. There will be one Church—one God—one religion—one educational system—one social order. And, as in God's original pattern in ancient Israel, they will be united.

Three men—Peter, James and John, among the original twelve disciples—were privileged to see the kingdom of God in a vision (Matt. 17:9). In this vision, Jesus, who was actually with them in person, became transfigured—appearing as the glorified Christ. His face became bright, shining as the sun, his clothing white as light. Two others appeared with him in this vision—this glimpse into the coming kingdom—and they were Moses and Elijah. These two, in the vision, represented the offices of church and state, with and under Christ, as they will be in God's kingdom. Both Moses and Elijah qualified in their human lifetime for very high positions in the kingdom of God.

Moses was the one through whom Christ (yes, he was the God of the Old Testament, as many, many scriptures prove) gave the laws and the statutes of government for the nation Israel. Moses was trained as a son of a pharaoh (king of Egypt). His training and experience were among gentiles, as well as the children of Israel.

Elijah, above all others, is represented in Scripture as the prophet who restored the worship of the true God—and obedience to his commandments. When Elijah ordered King Ahab to gather on Mount Carmel "all Israel" (I Kings 18:19-21) and the prophets of Baal and of Asherah (Easter), he said: "How long halt ye between two opinions? if the Lord be God, follow him: but if Baal, then follow him. . . ." (verse 21). And when, at Elijah's 18-second prayer (verses 36-37), the fire fell miraculously from heaven consuming Elijah's sacrifice, the people fell on their faces, and said, "The Lord, he is the God; the Lord, he is the God" (verse 39).

The vision of the Transfiguration (Matt. 16:27 through 17:9) gave the apostles Peter, James and John a preview of Christ coming in his kingdom—as he shall come. The indication is thus given that Moses and Elijah represented the heads, under Christ, of state or national world government (under Moses), and church or religious activity (under Elijah).

These two men, like the "fathers," Abraham, Isaac and Israel, will then be resurrected immortal, in power and glory. Certainly the indication is given us that, under Christ as King of kings, and under Christ's top team—the "fathers"—will be Moses over all organized national and international government; and Elijah, over all organized church, religious and educational activity.

Actually, the gospel and religious development is merely spiritual education. And it is significant that Elijah had organized and headed three schools or colleges (II Kings 2:3, 5; 4:38—at Bethel, Jericho and Gilgal) teaching God's truth in a world corrupted by false pagan education.

On the National Level

Now we gain further insight into God's coming world government organization.

On the purely national level, the nations descended from the two tribes of Ephraim and Manasseh (descended from Joseph), will become the two leading nations of the world (Jer. 30:16-18; 31:4-11, 18-20; Isa. 14:1-2; Deut. 28:13).

But, next to them will be the nations descended from the other tribes of Israel. And, after them, but still prosperous and full of abundant blessings, the gentile nations.

King David, resurrected, immortal, in power and glory, will be king, under Moses, over all twelve nations of Israel (Jer. 30:9; Ezek. 34:23-24; 37:24-25). Each of the twelve apostles will be king, under David, over one of these then super-prosperous nations (Matt. 19:28).

Under the apostles, each now king over a great nation, will be the rulers over districts, states, shires, counties or provinces, and over cities.

But, in every case, these kings and rulers will be resurrected immortals, born into the kingdom (family) of God as Spirit beings—not flesh-and-blood mortals. And, in every case, they will be those who qualified not only by conversion, but by overcoming, spiritual character development, growth in Christ's knowledge—training in being ruled by God's law and government, as well as learning to rule.

The parables of the pounds (Luke 19:11-27) and talents (Matt. 25:14-30) make this very clear. The one who multiplied his spiritual abilities ten times over is pictured as ruling over ten cities. The one who developed only half as much in God's character and abilities is pictured as being given rule over five cities. The parable of the talents shows the same thing, but also we are to be judged by how well we do with what we have to do *with*. That is, one of lesser ability will be judged according to motivation, application, diligence and persistence according to ability. To whom much—in natural ability, and spiritual gifts—is inherited and given, much will be required. The one of lesser ability stands just as good a chance for reward in God's kingdom as the one of great ability—if he tries as hard.

But what of all the gentile nations? Who will be given top positions of rule over them?

There is strong indication—not a definite, specific statement—but indication, according to principles and specific assignments that are revealed, that the prophet Daniel will be made king over them all, directly under Moses. What prophet—what man of God—did God send to be trained at top-level government authority, in the world's very first world empire? And what man refused to follow pagan ways and customs, even while serving next in authority to the king himself? What man proved loyal to God, and the worship of God, and obedient to the laws of God—even while serving at the top in the first world empire?

Why, of course, it was the prophet Daniel.

At first thought, one might suppose Christ will put the apostle Paul at the head—under Moses and under Christ—of all gentile nations. And indeed Paul qualified for high position over gentiles.

But Daniel was thrown into almost daily contact with the king in the world's first world government. And though that was human government, Daniel proved completely loyal and obedient to God and God's rule. He was used, to reveal to King Nebuchadnezzar, and immediate successors, that it is God who rules over all kingdoms. Daniel refused the king's rich food and delicacies—including what was unclean according to God's health laws. He prayed three times a day to God, even though it meant being thrown into the den of lions. He trusted God to protect and deliver him from the lions. He gained knowledge and wisdom in the affairs and administration of government over nations.

When God, through the prophet Ezekiel, named three of the most righteous men who ever lived, he named Daniel as one of them. The other two were Noah and Job (Ezek. 14:14, 20). And it is evident that God will assign Noah and Job to offices of very great magnitude. More of that, later.

God in his Word gave Daniel the assurance that he shall be in the kingdom of God, at the time of resurrection (Dan. 12:13).

It is an interesting possibility, in passing, to consider that Daniel's three colleagues in this Chaldean Empire service—Shadrach, Meshach and Abed-nego—might serve as a team directly with and under Daniel, even as the three "fathers" very possibly may serve as a team directly with and under Christ himself. In fact, there are a number of such teams that appear to be possibilities.

But what about Paul? As the twelve original apostles were sent to the lost house of Israel, Paul was the apostle to the gentiles. That is the key. Christ himself said specifically that each of the twelve shall be a king over one of the nations of Israel. It is inconceivable that Paul would be over no more than one gentile nation. It might even be inferred that Paul rated a little higher in ability and accomplishment than any one of the twelve apostles. And, again, no gentile nation will be as great as one of the Israelite nations.

The indication, then, seems to be that Paul will be given position over all gentile nations, but under Daniel.

Of course there will be kings appointed by Christ over every gentile nation. And district rulers under them, and rulers over cities. There is no indication as to the identity of any of these, except that those apostles and evangelists who worked with and directly under Paul—Barnabas, Silas, Timothy, Titus, Luke, Mark, Philemon, etc.—undoubtedly will be given offices of importance. And what of other saints of that same time, in the first flush years of the Church, when its membership at first multiplied in number of converts? And what of many converted since, and down to our present day?

We can mention, here, only what seems to be rather clearly indicated from what God has already revealed.

The International Level

Besides these revealed and indicated assignments of government over nations and groups of nations on the national level, there will be positions of great magnitude on the international level in the areas of scientific and social functions. And there are a few indications of what some of those operations will be, and the possible—if not probable—personnel.

Since Noah lived first, we now take a look at Noah. In Noah's day, the chief cause of the violence and chaos of world conditions was racial hatreds, and racial violence caused by man's efforts toward amalgamation of races, contrary to God's plan. God had set the boundary lines for the nations and the races at the beginning (Deut. 32:8-9; Acts 17:26). But men had refused to remain in the lands to which God had assigned them. That was the cause of the corruption and violence that ended that world. For more than 100 years Noah had preached God's ways to the people—but they didn't heed.

At that time, even as today, that world faced a population explosion. It was when "men began to multiply on the face of the earth" (Gen. 6:1). Jesus said, of our time, right now, "But as the days of Noe [Noah] were, so shall also the coming of the Son of man be" (Matt. 24:37)—or, as in Luke 17:26, "And as it was in the days of Noe, so shall it be also in the days of the Son of man." That is, the days just before Christ returns. Today civil wars, hatreds, riots and problems involving discrimination are among the world's greatest social troubles.

Noah merely preached to people in his human lifetime. But Noah, in the resurrection, immortal, in power and glory, will be given the power to enforce God's ways in regard to race.

It seems evident that the resurrected Noah will head a vast project of the relocation of national groups within the boundaries God has set, for their own best good, happiness and richest blessings. This will be a tremendous operation. It will require great and vast organization, reinforced with power to move whole nations and tribes. This time, peoples and nations will move where God has planned for them, and no defiance will be tolerated.

What a paradox. People are going to be forced to be happy, to have peace, to find abundant and joyful living!

Above, we said we would come back, later, to Joseph, son of Israel and great-grandson of Abraham.

Joseph became food administrator of the greatest nation on earth of that time—Egypt. Joseph was synonymous with "prosperity." "And the Lord was with Joseph, and he was a prosperous man; and ... the Lord made all that he did to prosper in his hand" (Gen. 39:2-3). He was made actual ruler for the pharaoh of the world's greatest nation. But his specialty was dealing with the economy—with prosperity. And what he did, he did God's way.

It seems evident, therefore, that Joseph will be made director of the world's economy—its agriculture, its industry, its technology, and its commerce—as well as its money and monetary system. These systems will be on the international level, the same in every nation.

Undoubtedly Joseph will develop a large and perfectly efficient organization of immortals made perfect, with and under him in this vast administration. This will be an administration that will eliminate famine, starvation, poverty. There will be no poverty-stricken slums. There will be universal prosperity!

Another tremendous project on the worldwide international level will be that of rebuilding the waste places, and the construction of whatever really great and large buildings or structures Christ will require for the world he will create. "And they shall build the old wastes, they shall raise up the former desolations, and they shall repair the waste cities, the desolations of many generations" (Isa. 61:4).

Job was the wealthiest and greatest man of the east (Job 1:3) and a noted builder. (Compare Job 3:13-14 with God's challenge in Job 38:4-6.) He was so upright and perfect, God even dared Satan to find a flaw in his character. Actually, there was a terrible sin in his life—self-righteousness. But God brought him to repentance. (See Job, chapters 38-42.) Once this man, of such strength of self-mastery that he could be so righteous in his own strength, was humbled, brought to reliance on God, filled with God's Spirit—well, surely no man who ever lived could equal him as an engineer over vast stupendous world projects.

Indication is strong, therefore, that Job will be director of worldwide urban renewal, rebuilding the waste places and the destroyed cities, not as they are now, but according to God's pattern; vast engineering projects, such as dams and power plants—or whatever the ruling Christ shall decree.

At least one other man seems indicated as a top assistant in this vast administration. That is Zerubbabel (Haggai, and Zech. 4).

So much for the new world super-civilization on the national and international level.

Now we come to the world tomorrow on the individual level—the Church—the religion—the educational system.

Education and Religion Tomorrow

When Jesus Christ returns to earth in the full supreme power and glory of the Creator God, he is coming, this time, to save the world, spiritually.

When he sits on the throne of his glory, in Jerusalem, all nations composed of flesh-and-blood mortal humans will be there before him. He shall begin dividing the "sheep from the goats." To the sheep, on his right hand, "Then shall the King say unto them on his right hand, Come, ye blessed of my Father, inherit the kingdom prepared for you from the foundation of the world" (Matt. 25:34).

Those converted, now, are heirs. We shall inherit the kingdom at Christ's coming. The dead in Christ shall be resurrected, rising first—changed to Spirit immortality. We that are then alive, in Christ, shall be instantaneously changed to Spirit immortality, and caught up with the resurrected ones, to meet the descending Christ in the air.

We shall then be separated by immortality from the mortal humans on earth.

Wherever Jesus is, from there, we shall be ever with him. Where, then, will he be? His feet shall stand that same day on the Mount of Olives (Zech. 14:4).

It is after this that he separates the sheep (those who repent, believe, and receive his Holy Spirit) from the goats (those who rebel). This separation—this educating of converts for God's kingdom—will continue throughout the entire thousand years of Christ's reign on earth.

Christ will give to all nations a new and pure language: "For then will I turn to the people a pure language, that they may all call upon the name of the Lord, to serve him with one consent" (Zeph. 3:9).

The pure truth of God will be proclaimed to all people. No one will be deceived any longer. But "the earth shall be full of the knowledge of the Lord, as the waters cover the sea" (Isa. 11:9).

Christ is the "root of Jesse," father of David. To Christ, then, will the gentiles seek (Isa. 11:10). Christ will set his hand to save all Israel (verse 11). (See also Romans 11:25-26.)

But all this work of world evangelism—of spiritually saving the world (as a whole, not necessarily every individual but surely a majority)—will require, simultaneously, reeducating the world.

One of the great problems facing the returned glorified Christ, will be that of reeducating the supposedly educated. These minds—and they are, indeed, the world's finest and best minds—have become so perverted with false education that they will be unable to accept truth until they first *un*learn error. And it is at least ten times more difficult to unlearn error, firmly imbedded in the mind, than it is to start from "scratch" and learn new truth.

It may actually take them longer to come to a knowledge of truth—to become truly educated—than the illiterate of this world.

God's inspired Word, the Holy Bible, is the foundation of knowledge. But they have been trained to hold this true foundation in prejudiced contempt.

Yes, indeed, the educating and reeducating of the world will be one of the most important tasks the kingdom of God will face, after Christ returns to rule. Today people follow the false and deceptive values. Their entire thinking will require a reorientation—a change of direction.

A Headquarters Church

We have seen that the earth, after this thousand-year period begins, will be as full of the true knowledge of God as the oceans are full of water (Isa. 11:9). How will this be brought about?

The prophet Micah gives part of the answer: "But in the last days it shall come to pass, that the mountain of the house of the Lord shall be established in the top of the mountains, and it shall be exalted above the hills; and people shall flow unto it" (Mic. 4:1).

Prophecy uses "mountain" as a symbol of a major nation, and "hills" as a symbol of smaller nations. In other words, the kingdom of God, the kingdom of resurrected immortals—the ruling kingdom—will be established in complete authority over the major nations (of mortals) and exalted above the small nations—and people will flow to God's kingdom. Now continue:

"And many nations shall come, and say, Come, and let us go up to the mountain of the Lord, and to the house of the God of Jacob; and he will teach us of his ways, and we will walk in his paths: for the law shall go forth of Zion [the Church], and the word of the Lord from Jerusalem. And he [Christ] shall judge among many people, and rebuke strong nations afar off; and they shall beat their swords into plowshares, and their spears into pruninghooks: nation shall not lift up a sword against nation, neither shall they learn war any more" (verses 2-3).

This knowledge—this teaching—and even knowledge of God's law—shall go forth from the Church—and from Jerusalem, the new world capital.

Christ, himself, will be ruling from Jerusalem. Stationed there with Christ, under immediate direction of Elijah, it is indicated, will be those immortals chosen by Christ to constitute the Headquarters Church. Revelation 3:12 indicates those of the "Philadelphia era" will be pillars in that Headquarters Church.

Next, in this all-important Headquarters Church organization, working with and directly under Elijah, it appears, will be the resurrected John the Baptist. He came "in the spirit and power of [Elijah]" (Luke 1:17). Of him, Jesus said, "Verily I say unto you, Among them that are born of women there hath not risen a greater than John the Baptist..." (Matt.

11:11). He was the Elijah prophesied to come (Matt. 11:7-11).

Jesus said that no man who ever lived was greater than John the Baptist. Yet, even the least in the resurrected kingdom will be greater (Matt. 11:11). It is evident that John the Baptist will be placed in very high office. It seems logical that he should be placed with, or immediately under, Elijah.

Elijah to Come in Our Day

Remember, once again, God's principle of duality. As Jesus said in Matthew, the prophecy of Malachi 3:1 applied to John the Baptist in type; but if you will continue reading through verse 5, it becomes very clear that the prophecy is speaking of one to prepare the way before the Second Coming of Christ. John the Baptist was a voice crying out in the physical wilderness of the Jordan River, preparing the way for the First Coming of Christ, as a physical human being, to his physical Temple at Jerusalem and to the physical people of Judah, announcing the advance good news that the kingdom of God would in the future be established. But also preparing the way before his Second Coming was a messenger of whom Elijah was a type. A voice crying out in the worldwide spiritual wilderness of religious confusion, preparing the way for the spiritual glorified King of kings and Lord of lords to come in the supreme power and glory of God to his spiritual temple, the Church (Eph. 2:21), to actually establish the kingdom of God.

Further, in Matthew 17:1-8, Peter, James and John saw the vision of Moses, Elijah and Christ glorified in the kingdom of God. Then in verse 10 the disciples asked Jesus, "Why then say the scribes that Elias [Elijah] must first come?" Remember John the Baptist had finished his ministry and had been imprisoned before Jesus even began his ministry. At the time the disciples asked this question, John the Baptist had come and been put to death. Yet Jesus answered, speaking of the yet future, "[Elijah] truly shall first come, and restore all things" (verse 11).

This could not possibly refer to John the Baptist. John the Baptist restored nothing, but called on people to repent in preparation for the First Coming of Jesus as a physical human.

In the first few years of the New Testament Church, Jesus' true gospel had been suppressed and supplanted with a false gospel—not the gospel of Christ (the kingdom of God) but man's false gospel about a Christ who did away with his Father's commandments.

Also Malachi 4:5-6 pictures the Elijah to come at the very end of the Church age—at a time when, if this end-time message were not proclaimed, the glorified Christ would come and smite the world with total destruction. (The word *curse* in this verse is translated from the Hebrew, which in Moffatt's translation is given the meaning *total destruction*.)

Education in the World Tomorrow

This Headquarters Church, at Christ's own world capital of Jerusalem, then, undoubtedly will be given the administration of the world's new system of education.

Also the indication is that the teaching of spiritual truth—of the true gospel, the spiritual conversion of the world—will be directed, worldwide, from this Headquarters Church, under Elijah and the overall direct supervision of Jesus Christ.

The principal purpose for which Christ is returning to earth is to spiritually develop in humanity godly character, and to save the world. Most religious people, ministers, and evangelists (fundamentalist) have supposed that this time, now, is the only day of salvation. The verse of Scripture they rely on is a mistranslation (II Cor. 6:2). It should read *"a* day of salvation," not *"the"* (quoted from Isaiah 49:8, where it is *a*, not *the*). If Christ had been trying to "save" the world, he would have saved the world. It hasn't been "saved." God doesn't use a babylon of confused, disagreeing religious organizations, divided into hundreds of different concepts of theological doctrine, as his instruments.

But the real world evangelism will be administered by this Headquarters Church, composed of resurrected immortals, under direct personal supervision of Christ himself.

One thing there will not be in the millennial Headquarters Church is a doctrinal committee of intellectual "scholars" to decide whether Christ's teachings are true doctrines.

There was no such doctrinal committee in the first century Headquarters Church at Jerusalem. All teaching came from Christ through the apostles—and a few times Christ communicated to apostles via the prophets (of which there are none in God's Church today since the Bible for our time is complete). God's Church today, as in the first century, receives its teachings from the living Christ, through an apostle, just as in A.D. 31.

One other tremendous organizational function will be directed from this Headquarters Church—that of direction of all the local churches over the world. These churches will be composed of those who become converted—begotten of God by receiving his Holy Spirit—though still mortal.

Millennial Growth in Knowledge, Overcoming

Just as the converted Christian in this present age must continue to live a life of overcoming, and of spiritual growth and development (II Pet. 3:18), so will they in the millennium. Happily they then will not have to overcome Satan. But they shall have to overcome all evil impulses, habits or temptations, innate within themselves.

With only one Church—one religion—one faith—there will be many church congregations in every city, others scattered through rural areas. There will be district superintendents over areas, and pastors, elders, deacons and deaconesses in every local church.

This, then, gives an insight into how the world will be organized.

This shows how a super world government can, and will, be established on earth.

The very purpose of the Church of this present time is to provide God's training school or teachers' college to train in spiritual knowledge, education and godly character, to supply all the positions at the beginning of this wonderful 1,000-year reign of Christ on earth.

After the end of this coming millennial rule of Christ on earth, will come the final judgment.

I have mentioned in this book that at the time of the first

Adam's sin, God closed off from humanity as a whole the "tree of life" symbolizing God's gift of his Holy Spirit and begettal of immortal God-life, until Christ the second Adam shall have replaced Satan on earth's throne and come to reign over all nations on earth.

Meanwhile, we have covered how the prophets were a pre-foundation of the Church of God. And the apostle Peter mentioned (I Pet. 4:17) that the JUDGMENT had begun with the Church. Those God has called to come to him through Jesus Christ during this Church age have been here and now judged, during this life. But judgment has not yet come to the world.

Does that mean the world is freed to commit sin? Not at all. God allows people to sin, but they are not now as yet judged for their sins.

After the Millennium

Following the millennial reign of Christ and the Church on earth, however, shall come the time of God's JUDGMENT on this world. A criminal may have committed a great crime—even murder. But until caught, and brought to trial before a judge, he has not yet been judged or condemned.

In the final judgment, with Christ on the judgment seat, every human who has lived in this world shall be brought back to life (Rev. 20:11-12). They shall then give account for their sins committed in their first life.

The dead IN Christ at the time of Jesus' Second Coming shall be resurrected to immortal God-life if they shall have died, and those still living who are IN Christ at his coming and led by his Holy Spirit shall be changed instantly into immortal God-life. They shall rule and teach with and under Christ during the thousand years. But all others who have died shall not live again until the end of the millennium (Rev. 20:5).

The 37th chapter of Ezekiel also shows the resurrection at the time of the judgment. This 37th chapter is the prophecy of the "dry bones." The Bible itself interprets these dry bones in verse 11 where it says these dry bones are the House of Israel: ". . . behold, they say, Our bones are dried, and our hope is lost. . . ." Like the prophecy says: "Again he said unto me, Prophesy upon these bones, and say unto them, O ye dry bones, hear the word of the Lord. Thus saith the Lord God unto these bones; Behold, I will cause breath to enter into you, and ye shall live: and I will lay sinews upon you, and will bring up flesh upon you, and cover you with skin, and put breath in you, and ye shall live; and ye shall know that I am the Lord" (verses 4-6).

Next this prophecy tells of the Great White Throne Judgment when this whole house of Israel, who sinned so greatly against God, shall be resurrected.

The prophecy continues: "So I prophesied as I was commanded: and as I prophesied, there was a noise, and behold a shaking, and the bones came together, bone to his bone. And when I beheld, lo, the sinews and the flesh came up upon them, and the skin covered them above: but there was no breath in them. Then said he unto me, Prophesy unto the wind, prophesy, son of man, and say to the wind, Thus saith the Lord God; Come from the four winds, O breath, and breathe upon these slain, that they may live.

"So I prophesied as he commanded me, and the breath came into them, and they lived, and stood up upon their feet, an exceeding great army" (verses 7-10). This shows being brought back to mortal life, sustained by breathing of air, just as in their original life. That is, mortal life—still unconverted. Then God says, "Behold, O my people, I will open your graves, and cause you to come up out of your graves, and bring you into the land of Israel." This is the resurrection in the Great White Throne Judgment. All the ancient Israelites are resurrected mortal, precisely as in their first life. Then what? "And ye shall know that I am the Lord, when I have opened your graves, O my people, and brought you up out of your graves, and shall put my spirit in you, and ye shall live, and I shall place you in your own land: then shall ye know that I the Lord have spoken it, and performed it, saith the Lord" (verses 13, 14).

In other words, in the Great White Throne Judgment after the millennium, Old Testament Israel will be resurrected; then they shall come to "know the Lord." God's knowledge will come to them. The resurrected then will read this: "And there shall ye remember your ways, and all your doings, wherein ye have been defiled; and ye shall lothe yourselves in your own sight for all your evils that ye have committed. And ye shall know that I am the Lord, when I have wrought with you for my name's sake, not according to your wicked ways, nor according to your corrupt doings, O ye house of Israel, saith the Lord God" (Ezek. 20:43-44).

Then upon this repentance, notice again in Ezek. 37:14: "And shall put my spirit in you, and ye shall live, and I shall place you in your own land: then shall ye know that I the Lord have spoken it, and performed it, saith the Lord."

Thus, in the Great White Throne Judgment, they will come to know that Christ the Savior had come and died for them. And upon their repentance they shall receive the Holy Spirit and with it salvation and eternal life.

All who had lived, previously unjudged, not only Israel, but of all nations, will be resurrected MORTAL, physical, as they were in their first life up to the time of death. Those in this judgment will be mortals. They will then give account and be judged. Concerning this Great White Throne Judgment Jesus said: "The men of Nineveh shall rise in judgment with this generation, and shall condemn it: because they repented at the preaching of Jonas; and, behold, a greater than Jonas is here. The queen of the south shall rise up in the judgment with this generation, and shall condemn it: for she came from the uttermost parts of the earth to hear the wisdom of Solomon; and, behold, a greater than Solomon is here" (Matt. 12:41-42; also in Luke 11:31-32). Also: "But I say unto you, that it shall be more tolerable in that day for Sodom, than for that city. . . . But it shall be more tolerable for Tyre and Sidon at the judgment, than for you" (Luke 10:12, 14). There will be punishments. Those who have sinned little will be beaten with few stripes, but those who have sinned greatly, knowing God's will, with many stripes (Luke 12:47-48).

But the penalty for sin is DEATH in the final last judgment. Since all have sinned, all shall be judged guilty and sentenced. But they shall learn that Jesus Christ paid their penalty in their stead. And in repentance, demonstrated by performance, they will be given an opportunity yet at that time to choose LIFE, and be made immortal.

What a merciful God is the Creator, whose mercy is as

great toward us as the heavens are high above the earth. And he is able to remove our transgressions from us as far as the east is from the west (Ps. 103:12).

BUT THERE IS MORE! MUCH MORE!

Incredible Human Potential Revealed

In the book of Hebrews we read: "For unto the angels hath he [God] not put in subjection the world to come, whereof we speak" (Heb. 2:5). The theme of the context here is "the world to come."

There is but one earth, but the Bible speaks of three worlds, ages or civilizations on the earth—the "world that then was" (the antediluvian world from Adam to Noah); this "present evil world" (from the Flood until Christ's return, yet future); and "the world to come" (which will start when Christ comes and sets up the kingdom of God).

This verse speaks of angels as if the world had been put in subjection to angels; in fact, in the very beginning of this book of Hebrews, the first chapter, it is speaking of Christ and angels and the relation of angels to humans. This was explained in chapter two of this book.

But bear in mind the general theme here, or context, is "the world to come, whereof we speak"—not this present age, now coming rapidly to its *end!* Continue on in verse 6: "But one in a certain place testified, saying. . . ." Then follows a quotation from the first six verses *only* of the eighth Psalm.

In this psalm, David continued showing specifically that God has now placed in subjection under man the solid earth, the earth's atmosphere or air, and the sea. But now the writer of the book of Hebrews is inspired to expand David's prophecy to add something radically *different*—something to happen in the world to come!

This revealed knowledge of God's purpose for mankind—of man's incredible awesome potential—staggers the imagination. Science knows nothing of it—no religion reveals it, so far as I know—and certainly higher education is in utter ignorance of it.

Nevertheless, it is what God says he has prepared for them that love him (I Cor. 2:9-10).

I have said before that God revealed necessary knowledge

to our first parents, but *they didn't believe what he said!* Some 4,000 years later, Jesus Christ the second Adam appeared on earth with a message direct from God the Father in heaven, revealing the same necessary knowledge—but only a handful—a hundred and twenty—believed what he said, though many professed to "believe on him" (as in John 8:30-31, 37-38, 40, 45-46).

Today science, religion and education still do not believe WHAT HE SAID.

But now let's see what is said in this passage in Hebrews, beginning where Hebrews leaves off quoting the eighth Psalm: "Thou hast put all things in subjection under his [man's] feet. For in that he [God] put all in subjection under him [man], he [God] left NOTHING that is not put under him" (Heb. 2:8).

Is it possible God could mean what he says ("all things")? *Nothing* excluded?

In the first chapter, the Moffatt translation of the Bible renders the Greek word translated "all things" as "the universe" (verse 8).

In other words, for those willing to believe what God says, he says that he has decreed the entire universe—with all its galaxies, its countless suns and planets—*everything*—will be put under man's subjection.

But *wait a moment!* Before you disbelieve, read the next words in the same eighth verse: "But now we see *not yet* all things [the endless universe] put under him [man]." Remember (verse 5), this is speaking of the "world to come"—not today's world. But what do we see now, today? "But we see Jesus, who was made a little lower than the angels [or, "for a little while lower"] for the suffering of death, crowned with glory and honour." Man, other than Christ, is NOT YET "crowned with glory and honour."

But see how Christ is already crowned with glory and honor. Continue: "For it became him, for whom are *all things* [the entire universe] and by whom are all things, in bringing many sons unto glory, to make the captain of their salvation perfect through sufferings. . . . for which cause he [Christ] is not ashamed to call them brethren" (verses 10-11).

In other words, Christians having God's Spirit are joint heirs with Christ to INHERIT all that Christ already has inherited. He is now in glory! He has already inherited the entire universe. He *sustains* it by his power. Man, if he is converted, having God's Holy Spirit (Rom. 8:9), is now only an HEIR—*not yet* a possessor.

But see now how Christ already *has been* crowned with glory and honor—and is already in possession—has already inherited. Begin with Hebrews, chapter 1:

"God . . . hath in these last days spoken unto us by his Son, whom he hath appointed heir of all things [the entire universe], by whom also he made the worlds; who being the brightness of his glory, and the express image of his person, and upholding [sustaining] all things [the entire universe] by the word of his power . . ." (Heb. 1:1-3).

The living Christ already sustains the entire universe by his limitless divine power. The passage continues to show his superiority over the angels—he is the begotten and born Son of God—angels are merely individually created beings. Angels are now administering spirits (invisible to us), ministering to us—to us who are now in lower status than angels—but who are *heirs* of salvation, when we, like Christ, shall become *born* sons of God (Heb. 1:4-14).

Outer Space—Planets Now Dead

Now put this together with what is revealed in the eighth chapter of Romans.

Here it speaks of Christ as God's Son: ". . . that he might be the *firstborn* among many brethren" (Rom. 8:29). Humans, having God's Holy Spirit, are *heirs* of God and joint heirs with Christ—who, alone of all humans, has already been born as God's Son by a resurrection from the dead (Rom. 1:4). He is the FIRST of the human family to be born into the family of God—the kingdom of God. He is our pioneer who has gone on before. We shall follow at the resurrection of the just at Christ's return to earth in supreme power and glory.

This eighth chapter of Romans, verse 9, says if we have within us the Holy Spirit of God we are his begotten sons, but if we do not have his Spirit we are none of his—not Christians at all. But verse 11 says that if we have God's Holy Spirit growing within and leading us we shall be raised from the dead by his Spirit—(or if living when Christ comes we shall be changed from mortal to immortal).

Now continue: "For as many as are led by the Spirit of God, they are the sons of God.... The Spirit itself beareth witness with our spirit, that we are the children of God: and if children, then heirs; heirs of God, and joint-heirs with Christ ... also glorified together. For I reckon that the sufferings of this present time are not worthy to be compared with the glory which shall be revealed in us ..." (Rom. 8:14-18).

Continue, Revised Standard Version: "For the creation waits with eager longing for the revealing of the sons of God; for the creation [all the suns, planets, stars, moons] was subjected to futility, not of its own will but by the will of him who subjected it in hope; because the creation itself will be set free from its bondage to decay and obtain the glorious liberty of the children of God. We know that the whole creation [stars, suns and moons now in decay and futility] has been groaning in travail together until now; and not only the creation, but we ourselves [we Spirit-begotten humans], who have the first fruits of the Spirit [the very FEW now being called to salvation—the "firstfruits"], groan inwardly as we wait for the [birth] as sons" (verses 19-23).

What an amazing marvelous revelation of knowledge!

No more amazing, awesome, eye-opening passage could be written!

It is so astonishingly revealing, one doesn't fully grasp it just reading quickly through.

First I quoted from verse 29 of Romans 8 stating Christ WAS the firstborn of MANY BRETHREN.

In Hebrews 1, we see that Christ, the first human to be born by a resurrection from the dead, has been glorified and now sustains the entire universe. He is our Pioneer who has gone on ahead. At his return to earth in power and glory, those who have been converted and received God's Holy Spirit shall be born into the God family by a resurrection. Then the *entire universe* will be put into subjection UNDER them!

Then, from Romans 8, *if* we have and are led by the Holy Spirit of God, we shall be raised to Spirit composition and immortality in the God family even as Christ was in A.D. 31 upon his resurrection.

Now once again from verse 19: "For the creation waits with eager longing for the revealing of the sons of God" (RSV). This shall happen after the time of the resurrection, when those who are human actually become—by a resurrection or instantaneous *change* from mortal flesh to Spirit immortality—sons of God.

Astonishing?—Entire Universe to Be Renewed

Now understand please. *Why* should the whole universe—the creation—be waiting with *eager longing* for the actual birth and appearing of all these sons of God, to be born into the family of God? The following verses portray a universe filled with planets in decay and futility—yet as if subjected *now* to this dead state in hope! "Because the creation itself [the universe not now capable of sustaining life] will be set free from its bondage to decay and obtain the glorious liberty of the children of God."

How did all the planets fall into the bondage of decay? Surely God did not so create them!

Decay signifies a state or condition caused by degeneration and decomposition from a previous undecayed state. God, then, created these planets in a state of NONdecay.

But something *caused* deterioration to set in.

What could have caused all this "bondage to decay"?

It cannot be the state in which God created them! Everything we read in God's revealed Word about God's creation shows it to have been a perfect creation. The earth was first created a perfect creation of glorious beauty.

We see that angels inhabited the earth prior to the creation of man. Angels, who were perfect from the creation until iniquity or lawlessness was found in them, caused the whole surface of the earth to turn into a state of decay, confusion and emptiness, as shown in chapter two.

Could the whole universe with its myriad of other planets have been created for the eventual purpose of sustaining life? We are not told specifically by revelation in God's Word whether it was or not, but what we are told throws additional light on why God decided to create man!

Continue this passage in Romans 8:22: "We know that the whole creation [universe] has been groaning in travail together until now." Consider that the creation is compared to a mother about to be delivered of her child. The creation is pictured as groaning in travail in hope (verse 20), awaiting the birth by resurrection to immortality, of the children of God. It is as if the creation [universe] is the mother and God is the father.

Anyway the whole thrust of the passage is that when we (converted humans) are born of God—then having the power and glory of God—we are going to do as God did when this earth had been laid "waste and empty"—Hebrew, *tohu* and *bohu* (Gen. 1:2). Christ, who renewed "the face of the earth" (Ps. 104:30), was renewing what had been destroyed by the rebellion of the sinning angels.

What these wonderful passages imply and indicate goes far beyond the amount specifically revealed.

This passage indicates precisely what all astronomers and scientific evidence indicate—the suns are as balls of fire, giving out light and heat; but the planets, except for this earth, are in a state of death, decay and futility—but not forever—*waiting* until converted humans are BORN the children of God; born into the very divine family of God, forming the kingdom of God.

Jesus' gospel was the kingdom of God. What I am showing you here is that Christ's gospel of the kingdom actually includes all this knowledge here revealed—even the whole universe is to be ruled by us, who, with God the Father and Christ, become the kingdom of God.

God is first of all Creator, but God is also Ruler. And he is Educator, who reveals knowledge beyond and outside the scope of human mind of itself to comprehend!

Put together all these scriptures I have used in this chapter, and you begin to grasp the incredible human potential. Our potential is to be born into the God family, receiving total power! We are to be given jurisdiction over the entire universe!

What are we going to do then? These scriptures indicate we shall impart life to billions and billions of dead planets, as life has been imparted to this earth. We shall create, as God directs and instructs. We shall rule through all eternity! Revelation 21 and 22 show there will then be no pain, no suffering, no evil, because we shall have learned to choose God's way of good. It will be an eternal life of accomplishment, constantly looking forward in super-joyous anticipation to new creative projects, and still looking back also on accomplishments with happiness and joy over what shall have been already accomplished.

We shall never grow tired and weary. Always alive—full of joyous energy, vitality, exuberant life and strength and power!

Earth To Become UNIVERSE Headquarters

Finally, even God the Father will come to this earth. His throne over the whole universe will be established on this earth.

Notice in I Corinthians 15:24, after speaking of the various resurrections, it is recorded: "Then cometh the end, when he shall have delivered up the kingdom to God, even the Father; when he shall have put down all rule and all authority and power."

In Revelation 21:3: "And I heard a great voice out of heaven saying, Behold, the tabernacle of God is with men, and he will dwell with them, and they shall be his people, and God himself shall be with them, and be their God."

And further in Revelation 22:3: "And there shall be no more curse: but the throne of God and of the Lamb shall be in it; and his servants shall serve him."

When it speaks of God and the LAMB, the LAMB represents Christ and God refers to the FATHER. .

Finally the at-one-ment shall be completed. Both God the Father and the Son Jesus Christ in us and we united with them as the one great supreme God family.

How wonderful beyond the ability of words to express is the glory of God and his wonderful purpose actually now in progress. Praise, honor and glory be to God and to Jesus Christ forever and forever.

With God's great master plan of 7,000 years finally completed—the mystery of the ages finally revealed, and with the re-creating of the vast universe and eternity lying ahead, we come finally to

THE BEGINNING.

Scripture Index

CHAPTER VII:
MYSTERY OF THE KINGDOM OF GOD

Subject Index

SUGGESTED READING

from the published works of Herbert W. Armstrong

*The Autobiography of Herbert W. Armstrong—
The Early Years*

Did God Create a Devil?

Does God Exist?

Human Nature—Did God Create It?

The Incredible Human Potential

Just What Do You Mean—Born Again?

Just What Do You Mean—Conversion?

Just What Do You Mean—Kingdom of God?

The Missing Dimension in Sex

*Never Before Understood—Why Humanity Cannot
Solve Its Evils*

Predestination—Does the Bible Teach It?

The United States and Britain in Prophecy

What Do You Mean—Salvation?

What Is the Reward of the Saved?

What Is the True Gospel?

*What Science Can't Discover About the
Human Mind*

Where Is the True Church?

Why Were You Born?

*The Wonderful World Tomorrow—What It Will
Be Like*

A World Held Captive

World Peace—How It Will Come

Your Awesome Future—How Religion Deceives You

These publications are provided free of charge by the Worldwide Church of God in the public interest.

A Unique Cours Understanding

Have you found it difficult—even impossible—to understand what the Bible says? The Ambassador College Bible Correspondence Course can help you begin to comprehend the bible as never before. More than 2,000,000 people have enrolled in this unique course!

These informative, eye-opening lessons make plain the answers to the "unanswerable" problems facing millions today. They explain the very purpose of human life. You will study the plain truths of your Bible!

You will learn the truth about the purpose of life, about what Bible prophecy says concerning world events today, about the God-inspired way to true happiness. All these topics and more are presented in step-by-step detail. A different major subject is explored in each monthly

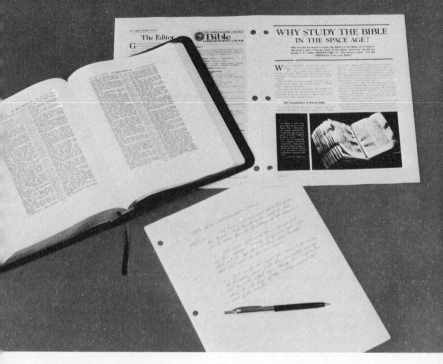

n Bible

lesson. And the Bible itself is the only textbook you will need.
You will find each lesson richly rewarding, and periodic
quizzes will help you evaluate your
progress. And there is no tuition fee
or obligation—these lessons are
absolutely free! Why not enroll now?
Send your request in the reply
envelope or write to our address
nearest you.

Enroll Today
*Just mail the reply envelope
stitched into this booklet.*

MAILING ADDRESSES WORLDWIDE

United States: Worldwide Church of God, Pasadena, California 91123

United Kingdom, rest of Europe and Middle East: The Plain Truth, P.O. Box 111, Borehamwood, Herts, England WD6 1LU.

Canada: Worldwide Church of God, P.O. Box 44, Station A, Vancouver, B.C. V6C 2M2

Canada (French language): Le Monde à Venir, B.P. 121, Succ. A, Montréal, P.Q. H3C 1C5

Mexico: Institución Ambassador, Apartado Postal 5-595, 06500 Mexico D.F.

South America: Institución Ambassador, Apartado Aéreo 11430, Bogotá 1, D.E., Colombia

Caribbean: Worldwide Church of God, G.P.O. Box 6063, San Juan, Puerto Rico 00936

France: Le Monde à Venir, B.P. 64, 75662 Paris Cédex 14

Switzerland: Le Monde à Venir, Case Postale 10, 91 rue de la Servette, CH-1211 Genève 7, Suisse

Germany: Ambassador College, Postfach 1129, D-5300 Bonn 1, West Germany

Holland and Belgium: Ambassador College, Postbus 444, 3430 AK Nieuwegein, Nederland

Belgium: Le Monde à Venir, B. P. 31, 6000 Charleroi 1, Belgique

Denmark: The Plain Truth, Box 211, DK-8100 Arhus C

Norway: The Plain Truth, Postboks 2513 Solli, N-0203 Oslo 2

Sweden: The Plain Truth, Box 5380, S-102 46, Stockholm

Australia: Worldwide Church of God, G.P.O. Box 345, Sydney, NSW, 2001

India: Worldwide Church of God, P.O. Box 6727, Bombay 400 052, India

Sri Lanka: Worldwide Church of God, P.O. Box 1824, Colombo, Sri Lanka

Malaysia: Worldwide Church of God, P.O. Box 430, Jalan Sultan, Petaling Jaya, Selangor, Malaysia

Singapore: Worldwide Church of God, P.O. Box 111, Farrer Road Post Office, Singapore 9128

New Zealand and the Pacific Isles: Ambassador College, P.O. Box 2709, Auckland 1, New Zealand

The Philippines: Worldwide Church of God, P.O. Box 1111, Makati, Metro Manila, Philippines 3117

Israel: Ambassador College, P.O. Box 19111, Jerusalem

South Africa: Ambassador College, P.O. Box 5644, Cape Town 8000

Zimbabwe: Ambassador College, Box UA30, Union Avenue, Harare, Zimbabwe

Nigeria: Worldwide Church of God, PMB 21006, Ikeja, Lagos State, Nigeria

Ghana: Worldwide Church of God, P.O. Box 9617, Kotoka International Airport, Accra

Kenya: Worldwide Church of God, P.O. Box 47135, Nairobi

Mauritius and Seychelles: Ambassador College, P.O. Box 888, Port Louis, Mauritius